Story of the Sess

The California Legisla

Franklin Hichborn

Alpha Editions

This edition published in 2024

ISBN : 9789362995216

Design and Setting By
Alpha Editions
www.alphaedis.com
Email - info@alphaedis.com

CONTENTS

PREFACE.

In writing the Story of the Session of the California Legislature of 1909, the purpose has been, not only to show what was done at Sacramento last Winter, but, what is by far more important, how it was done. To this end, the several measures are divided under three heads, namely, those dealing with moral, with political and with industrial issues. Instead of scattering on all the measures introduced, or even a considerable part of them, the principal issue of each group, that which meant the most to The People, and upon which the machine centered its efforts, has been selected for detailed consideration. On the score of the moral issues, the Anti-Racetrack Gambling bill has been taken as the most important; while the Direct Primary bill is dealt with as the chief political issue, and the railroad regulation measures as involving the chief industrial issue. The story of the fight over these bills is the story of the session of 1909. The events attending the passage of the Anti-Racetrack Gambling bill, the amendment of the Direct Primary bill, and the defeat of the Stetson Railroad Regulation bill, with the attending incident of the passage of the Wright Railroad bill, show, as nothing else can, how the machine controls and manipulates a Legislature - and such is the purpose of this little volume.

The efforts of justice-loving men to simplify the criminal codes, to the end that rich and poor alike may have equal opportunity in the trial courts - not in theory alone but in fact - and the successful efforts of the machine to block this reform, have made detailed consideration of the defeat of the Commonwealth Club bills and the passage of the Wheelan bills, and the so-called Change of Venue bill timely. And the story of these measures illustrates again how the machine element defeats the purpose of The People, and overrides what are the constitutional rights - and should be rights in fact - of every American citizen.

Measures which involved no particular contest between the good government and the machine forces - measures patched up by interested parties and slipped through the Legislature without opposition and generally without comment - although many of them of great importance, are not touched upon. The histories of those selected for consideration show the machine, or if you like, the system, at its work of passing undesirable measures, and of blocking the passage of good measures. If the Story of the Session of the California Legislature of 1909 assist the citizens of California to understand how this is done; if it give them that knowledge of the weakness, the strength, the purposes, and the affiliations of the Senators and Assemblymen who sat in the Legislature of 1909, a knowledge of which the machine managers have had heretofore a monopoly; if it point the way for a new method of publicity to crush corruption and to promote reform - a way which others better prepared for the work than I, may, in California and even in other States, follow - the labor of preparing this volume for the press will have been justified.

Franklin Hichborn.

Santa Clara, Cal., July 4, 1909.

CHAPTER I.

Breaking Ground.

Although the Reform Element had a Majority in Both Senate and Assembly,
Good Bills Were Defeated, and Vicious Measures Passed - Three Reasons for
This: (1) Reform Element Was Without Plan of Action, (2) Was Without Organization; (3) The Machine Was Permitted to Organize Both Senate and Assembly.

The personnel of the California Legislature of 1909, was, all things considered, better than that of any other Legislature that has assembled in California in a decade or more. There were, to be sure, in both Senate and Assembly men who were constantly on the wrong side of every question affecting the moral, political or industrial well-being of the State, but a majority of each House labored for the passage of good laws, laws which would not only silence and satisfy constituents, but prove effective and accomplish the purpose for which they had been drawn. Just as earnestly as they worked for the passage of good laws, a majority of the members of the Senate as well as a majority of the members of the Assembly opposed the passage of vicious measures, and of measures ostensibly introduced to work needed reform but drawn in such a manner as to be, from a practical standpoint, ineffective.

And yet, regardless of the purpose of this majority, the so-called "Change of Venue" [1] bill was passed, and the "Judicial Column" bill, intended to take the Judiciary out of politics, was denied passage. The infamous "Wheelan bills," aimed at the complication of the Grand jury system, went through both Houses, while the Commonwealth Club bills, drawn to simplify the methods of criminal procedure, were held up and eventually defeated. The ineffective Wright Railroad Regulation bill became a law, while the Stetson Railroad measure effective as finally amended - was rejected. The provision in the Direct Primary bill for the selection of United States Senators by State-wide vote was stricken out, and the meaningless advisory, district vote plan substituted.

Certainly, the accomplishment of the Legislature does not line with the purpose of a majority of its members. The voter is naturally asking why the majority in both Houses standing for good legislation and opposing bad, accomplished so little; how it was that a minority, at practically every turn, defeated a majority.

There were three principal reasons for this outcome.

(1) The machine, as its name indicates, is a definite organization, with recognized leaders. The anti-machine element was without organization or recognized leaders.

(2) The reform-advocating majority, except in the anti-racetrack gambling fight, was without definite plan of action. The majority was, for example, for the passage of a direct primary law that would, first, take the control of politics out of the hands of political bosses big and little, and, second, give the people of California the privilege of naming their United States Senators, a privilege already enjoyed by the people of the more progressive States of the Union. But the reform element knew little or nothing of the details of direct primary legislation.

They were equally unprepared on other reform issues. They recognized the necessity of passing an effective railroad regulation law, for example, but had little or no conception of what the provisions of the measure should be. They recognized that the criminal laws cannot be impartially enforced against rich and poor alike until the methods of criminal procedure be simplified, put on a common sense basis. But even here they had no definite policy and when told by machine claquers that the proposed reforms were revolutionary, even the most insistent of the reform element were content to let the simplifying amendments to the codes die in committees or on the files.

On the other hand, the machine element, even before a member had reached Sacramento, had their work for the session carefully outlined. This session the bulk of the machine's work was negative; that is to say, with a majority in both houses opposed to machine policies, the machine recognized the difficulties of passing bad laws except by trick - and spent the session in amending good measures into ineffectiveness, or, where they could, in preventing their passage. Down to a comma the machine leaders knew what they wanted for a direct primary law, for an anti-racetrack gambling law, for a railroad regulation law. From the hour the Legislature opened until the gavels fell at the moment of adjournment the machine element labored intelligently and constantly, and as an organized working unit, to carry its ends. There were no false plays; no waste of time or energy; every move was calculated. By persistent hammering the organized machine minority was able to wear its unorganized opponents out.[2]

(3) The third reason for the failure of the reform majority is found in the fact that the minority was permitted to organize both Senate and Assembly. In the Assembly the machine element named the Speaker without serious opposition. The Speaker named the Assembly committees. It developed at

the test that the important committees of the Assembly were, generally speaking, controlled by the machine.

The Lieutenant-Governor is, under the State Constitution, presiding officer of the Senate, under the title of President of the Senate. But the Senators elect the President pro tem., who, in the absence of the President, has the same power as the President. The reform element, although in the majority, permitted the election of Senator Edward I. Wolfe as President pro tem. Wolfe was admittedly leader of the machine element in the Senate. At critical times during the session, the fact that both the President and President pro tem. of the Senate were friendly to machine interests gave the machine great advantage over its anti-machine opponents.[3]

The reform majority in the Senate made the further mistake of leaving the appointment of the Senate committees in the hands of Lieutenant-Governor Warren Porter. Governor Porter flaunts his machine affiliations; is evidently proud of his political connections; indeed, in an address delivered before the students of the University of California, Porter advised his hearers to be "performers" in politics rather than "reformers." It was not at all surprising, then, that the Senate committees were appointed, not in the interest of the reform element, but of the machine. And yet, the reform element, being in the majority, could have taken the appointment of the committees out of Porter's hands. In the concluding chapter it will be shown there is ample precedent for such a course. But the reform element let the opportunity pass, and Warren Porter named the committees. Thus in both Senate and Assembly the strategic committee positions were permitted to fall into machine hands.

The importance of this on legislation can scarcely be over-estimated. Under the system in vogue in California, the real work of a legislative session is done in committee. When a bill is introduced in either House, it is at once referred to a committee. Until the committee reports on the measure no further action can be taken. Thus a committee can prevent the passage of a bill by deliberately neglecting to report it back to the main body.

When a measure passes either Senate or Assembly, it goes to the other House, and is once again referred to a committee. Again does the fate of the bill hang on committee action. Thus, every measure before it can pass the Legislature must, in the ordinary course of legislation, pass the scrutiny of two legislative committees, either one of which may delay its passage or even deny Senate or Assembly, or both, opportunity to act upon it.

To be sure, one of the rules of the Assembly of 1909 required that all bills referred to committees should be reported back within ten days, while the Senate rules provided that committees must act on bills referred to them as soon as "practicable," with the further provision that a majority vote of the

Senate could compel a report on a bill at any time. But these rules were employed to little advantage. In the Assembly, for example, the Commonwealth Club bills, referred to the Judiciary Committee on January 15, were not acted upon by the committee at all. These bills, in spite of the ten days' rule, remained in the committee sixty-seven days. The Direct primary bill was held up in the Senate Committee on Election Laws from January 8 until February 16, and at that late day came out of the committee with practically unfavorable recommendation. It was noticeable that few, if any, important reform measures were given favorable recommendation by a Senate committee. Thus the Anti-Racetrack Gambling bill, the Direct Primary bill, the Local Option bill, received the stamp of Senate committee disapproval. They were returned to the Senate with the recommendation that they do not pass. The same is largely true of the action of the Assembly Committees.[4]

If machine-controlled committees could delay action on reform measures, they could at the same time expedite the passage of bills which the machine element favored, or which had been amended to the machine's liking. Thus the Change of Venue bill, which reached the Senate on March 15, was returned from the Senate Judiciary Committee the day following, March 16, with the recommendation that it "do pass." The Wheelan bills reached the Senate on March 17, and were at once referred to the Judiciary Committee. The Judiciary Committee that very day reported them back with favorable recommendation. Had they been delayed in the committee even 48 hours, their final passage would have been improbable.

Curiously enough, the Judiciary Committee was the one Senate committee whose members President Porter did not name. Following a time-honored custom, every attorney at law in the Senate was made a member of the committee. It so happened that ten of the nineteen lawyers in the Senate were on the side of reform as against machine policies, eight generally voted with the machine, while the nineteenth gave evidence of being in a state of chronic doubt. This gave the reform element a majority of the Senate Judiciary Committee. But President Porter had the naming of the chairman of the committee, and the order of the rank of its members. The Lieutenant-Governor's fine discrimination is shown by the fact that the Chairman of the Committee and the four ranking members were counted on the side of the machine.

The Assembly committees acted quite as expeditiously on measures which had passed the Senate in a form satisfactory to machine interests. Thus, the Wright Railroad Regulation bill, which reached the Assembly on March 12, was reported back to the Assembly by the Assembly Committee on Common Carriers the day following, March 13.

It will be seen that the reform majority unquestionably weakened its position by permitting the machine minority to organize the Legislature.

This phase of the problem which confronts the State will be dealt with in the concluding chapter.

[1] One of the best witnesses to the viciousness of this measure is Governor Gillett, surely an unprejudiced observer. In giving his reasons for vetoing the bill, Governor Gillett said:

"I have several reasons for saying that I will veto the bill. One reason is that I have always been opposed to it. When I was in the Senate in 1897 I was against it and again in 1899 I fought it in the Judiciary Committee. Two years ago I ignored another such measure that had passed through the Legislature, so that I would not be living up to my policy of the past if I should sign this bill."

"But even if I had never had the opportunity to record my opposition on these different occasions, I should have vetoed the bill anyway, because it is a vicious bill. The bill is not a change of venue bill in the strict sense of the word. It simply gives the man on trial the right to disqualify the Judge on the ground of bias on the slightest pretext."

"The worst feature about the bill is that it grants this right to the accused after the jury has been secured. Why, if the defendant didn't like the adverse rulings of the Judge he could easily claim bias and the law would upheld his demand for another Judge. Think of how that would operate in the Calhoun trial in San Francisco. Such a law would cost the State thousands of dollars. It's vicious and I will not sign it."

[2] Most suggestively shown in the amendment of the Direct Primary bill.

[3] The seriousness of the mistake made by the reform element in acquiescing in Wolfe's election, was emphasized at the time of the deadlock in the Senate over the Direct Primary bill. The President of the Senate, Lieutenant-Governor Porter - and in his absence the President pro tem., Wolfe, - was charged with the duty of calling the Senate to order. Inasmuch as it did not suit the machine's interests that the Senate should be called to order, the Senators were obliged to sit in idleness for hours at a time, while the machine leaders and lobbyists were working openly on the floor of the Senate to force certain of the pro-primary Senators to join the machine forces. Had the President pro tem. been one of the group of Senators who were opposing the machine he would have called the Senate to order, thus permitting the regular work of the session to proceed. See Chapter 10, "Fight on Assembly Amendments."

[4] The action of the Assembly Committee on Public Morals on the Anti-Racetrack Gambling bill was a notable exception to this. See chapters 6 and 7.

CHAPTER II.

Organization of the Senate.

Anti-Machine Republicans, Led Into a Caucus Trap, Surrendered the Appointment of President Pro Tem., Secretary and Sergeant-at-Arms to the Machine - Machine Given the Selection of the Standing Committees.

In the light of the events of the session, the division between the machine or "organization" and anti-machine forces in the Senate for purposes of organization may be regarded as follows:

Anti-machine - Anthony[5], Bell, Birdsall, Black, Boynton, Burnett[5], Cutten, Estudillo, Hurd[5], Roseberry, Rush, Stetson, Strobridge, Thompson, Walker (labeled Republicans), Caminetti, Campbell, Cartwright, Holohan, Miller, Sanford (labeled Democrats) - 21.

Machine - Hare, Kennedy (labeled -Democrats), Bates, Bills, Finn, Hartman, Leavitt, Lewis, Martinelli, McCartney, Reily, Savage, Weed, Willis, Wolfe, Wright (labeled Republicans) - 16.

Doubtful - Curtin (Democrat).

Seekers of the winning side - Price and Welch (labeled Republicans).

Curtin is put down as doubtful because, justly or unjustly, he was at the opening of the session so regarded. But Curtin's record shows that generally speaking from the beginning to the end of the session he voted with the anti-machine element. Had the anti-machine forces made a determined effort to organize the Senate and demonstrated a strength of twenty-one votes, which would have been enough to organize,. Curtin would certainly have been with them. The same is true of Welch, and it is probably true of Price. This would have given the anti-machine forces from twenty-two to twenty-four votes, a safe margin to have permitted them to organize the Senate to carry out anti-machine policies.

The machine claquers will no doubt point gleefully to the fact that when the test on the Railroad Regulation bills came, Anthony, Burnett, Estudillo, Hurd and Walker strayed from the anti-machine fold. This objection would have more weight had there ever been an anti-machine fold. As a matter of fact, the anti-machine element in the Senate from the day the session opened until it closed was unorganized, and without leaders or detailed plan of action.

Admittedly Estudillo and Burnett strayed on the railroad regulation question, but they did so believing the absolute rate provided in the Stetson bill to be unconstitutional. All this will be brought out in the chapters on railroad regulation measures, but in passing, it may be said that Burnett, in the closing hours of the session, stated on the floor of the Senate that he had voted against the Stetson bill and for the Wright bill on the understanding that a constitutional amendment would be passed setting at rest all question of the constitutionality of the absolute rate. The machine leaders misled Senator Burnett. Machine votes defeated the amendment.

Anthony, Estudillo and Walker stood out against the machine in the direct primary fight which followed the defeat of the Stetson bill, and before the fight was over, Burnett had returned to the anti-machine forces.

The case of Senator Hurd is not at all creditable to the machine. But Hurd's instincts and sympathies are not those of Gus Hartman, Hare, Wolfe and Leavitt. Had the anti-machine forces had even semblance of organization there would have been no straying, and the accomplishment of the legislative session of 1909 would have been more satisfactory to the best citizenship of the State.

The fact that the anti-machine forces, without leaders and without organization, stuck together so well as they did is one of the most extraordinary and at the same time encouraging features of the session.

Although the anti-machine forces numbered a majority of the Senate, nevertheless a bare majority of the regular Republican Senators - those who were eligible to admittance to the Republican caucus - were with the machine. The division in the Republican caucus, counting Welch and Price with the machine element, was on machine and anti-machine lines as follows:

Anti-machine - Anthony, Birdsall, Black, Boynton, Burnett, Cutten, Estudillo, Hurd, Roseberry, Rush, Stetson, Strobridge, Thompson, Walker - 14.

Machine - Bates, Pills, Finn, Hartman, Leavitt, Lewis, Martinelli, McCartney, Price, Reily, Savage, Weed, Welch, Willis, Wolfe, Wright - 16.

By time-honored custom it has become a rule for the majority[5a] in the Senate - and the same holds in the Assembly - to meet in caucus to decide upon the details of organization. This is done on the theory that the House should be so organized as to permit the majority to carry out its policies as expeditiously and with as little friction as possible. By the unwritten rule of the caucus, the majority governs and each member who attends the caucus is bound in honor to vote - regardless of his individual views or wishes - on the floor of the Senate or Assembly, as the majority of the caucus decides. Thus, by going into caucus with the sixteen machine Senators, the fourteen anti-machine Senators were placed in a position where they were, under caucus rule, compelled to vote on the floor of the Senate as the sixteen machine Senators dictated. This gave the machine on the floor of the Senate thirty votes out of forty on questions affecting organization, and permitted it to name the President pro tem., the Secretary of the Senate, the Sergeant-at-Arms, and gave it filial voice in the appointment of the various attaches.

Had the line of division in the Senate been Republican and Democratic, the Republicans in the Senate might very properly have caucused. But inasmuch as the machine Republicans stood during the entire session for one set of policies, and the anti-machine Republicans for another, the caucus was at best an incongruous affair. Especially is this true when it is considered that the anti-machine Republicans immediately after they had left the caucus united with the anti-machine Democrats in a three-months contest with the united machine Democrats and machine Republicans. But having surrendered the organization of the Senate to the machine, the anti-machine Senators, although in the majority, fought under a handicap, finally lost the weaker of their supporters[6], and in the end went down in defeat. Had the real majority, rather than the artificial majority, of the Senate caucused on organization, that is to say, had the anti-machine Republicans and the anti-machine Democrats caucused, and organized to carry out the policies for which they stood and for which they fought together during the entire session, the Republican-Democratic-machine element would have been defeated at every turn. But no such policy governed, and the anti-machine Republicans waddled after precedent into the caucus trap that had been set for them. Later on in the session the anti-machine Republicans and anti-machine Democrats did go into caucus together, and by doing so won the hardest fought fight of the session.[7]

In the Republican Senate caucus on organization, the machine Senators, under the crafty leadership of Wolfe and Leavitt, worked their unhappy anti-machine associates much as a playful cat, with a sense of humor, toys with a mouse. As the cat lets the mouse think that it has escaped, the machine let the anti-machine forces think they were organizing the caucus. Leavitt had been leader of the Republican caucus at previous sessions but he suffered "overwhelming defeat" at the hands of a "reformer." The "reformer" in question was Senator Wright, who had been well advertised as the father of the reform Direct Primary law. Before the session closed, the anti-machine element was to learn just the sort of "reformer" Wright is. Wright, however, in the interest of "harmony," was nominated for caucus leadership by Senator Wolfe. Leavitt's name was not even mentioned. The unanimous vote went to Senator Wright, who was duly declared elected Chairman of the Senate Republican caucus for the Thirty-eighth Session of the California Legislature.

The reformers were also permitted to name the Secretary of the caucus. This time a genuine anti-machine Senator was selected, A. E. Boynton.

And then came a question which brought out the gleam of the machine's teeth. Senator Boynton moved that Senator Bell, of Pasadena, be admitted to the caucus. Somewhat to the discomfiture of the reformers, Bell was not admitted.

Senator Bell's case is a suggestive one. He is a Republican, having been elected from one of the strongest Republican districts of the State, the Thirty-sixth Senatorial District, which takes in Pasadena. But Senator Bell was not named by the machine; in fact, he was elected as protest against machine methods. The Pasadena Republicans tolerated machine domination as long as they could. Then, in 1906, they induced Bell to run against the "regular" machine nominee for the State Senate. Bell ran as an independent Republican. He overwhelmingly defeated his machine opponent. Arrived at Sacramento at the session of 1907, he applied for admittance to the Republican caucus.

There was ample precedent for his admittance, but curiously enough no anti-machine Republican who had defeated a machine Republican had ever been admitted to caucus privileges. In 1902, however, Charles M. Shortridge, having failed to receive the nomination for the state Senate from Santa Clara County, ran as an independent candidate against the regular Republican nominee. The machine supported Shortridge's candidacy, and by most questionable methods succeeded in defeating the regular Republican. But Shortridge was admitted to the Senate caucus of 1903 without question. Senator Bell, however, was denied admittance to the Republican Senate caucus of 1907, on the grounds that he had defeated a regularly nominated Republican. Shortridge had defeated a regularly nominated Republican. But Shortridge stood for machine policies; Bell stands opposed to machine policies. The machine's policy is to keep the caucuses of the dominant party in the Legislature as much a close corporation as possible. So in 1907, Bell's application was rejected. Bell, throughout the session, opposed machine policies. Both for the session of 1907 and of 1909, Senator Bell's record is absolutely clean. The machine does not approve such men, nor want them to participate in party caucuses.

Senator Bell, who had, although refused admittance to his party caucus, done very well in 1907, did not propose to apply for admission to the caucus of 1909. But the reform element in the Senate insisted upon presenting his name. From machine sources it was intimated to Senator Bell that if he would make his peace with Walter Parker, the Southern Pacific lobbyist who acts as machine leader south of the Tehachepi, no opposition would be offered his admission to the caucus. Bell rejected the offer with characteristic promptness. So the anti-machine Senators, since they had "organized the caucus," proceeded to admit Bell in the face of machine opposition.

But the inexperienced political mouse discovered that it was not out of the reach of the claws of the experienced political cat. Boynton's motion to admit Bell to the caucus was lost by a vote of 16 to 14.

Had the reform element been organized, however, Bell would have been admitted to the caucus. Three Senators, Reily, Savage and Welch, who ordinarily voted with the machine, because of personal friendship voted to admit Bell to the caucus. But their votes were offset by those of Burnett, Estudillo and Hurd.[8] The vote was as follows:

To admit Bell to the caucus - Anthony, Birdsall, Black, Boynton, Cutten, Reily, Roseberry, Rush, Savage, Stetson, Strobridge, Thompson, Walker, Welch - 14.

Against admitting Bell to the caucus - Bates, Bills, Burnett, Estudillo, Finn, Hartman, Hurd, Leavitt, Lewis, Martinelli, McCartney, Price, Weed, Willis, Wolfe, Wright - 16.

The Bell matter out of the way, the real work of organizing the Senate was taken up. Curiously enough, the only contest came over the election of the Chaplain of the Senate; the naming of the President pro tem., of the Secretary of the Senate and of the Sergeant-at-Arms was not opposed. Senator Price moved that Lewis A. Hilborn be the caucus nominee for Secretary of the Senate, and J. Louis Martin for Sergeant-at-Arms. His motion carried unanimously. Price also nominated Senator Wolfe for President pro tem. Not an anti-machine Senator protested. Wolfe was accordingly declared the caucus nominee, with the thirty Senators present, machine and anti-machine, obligated to vote for him on the floor of the Senate.

The election of a Chaplain was then taken up and several candidates nominated for the office. Rev. Father H. H. Wyman being finally selected, which, of course, was equivalent to election.

The caucus was held at 9 o'clock of the morning of January 4. At noon of the same day a second caucus was held at which it was decided that the division of patronage[8a] should be on the following basis: That $18 a day should be set aside for the Secretary, Sergeant-at-Arms and Chaplain; that the Lieutenant-Governor should be allowed $22 a day, and each of the thirty caucus Senators $15 a day. This practically concluded Republican caucusing for the session. At previous sessions the Republicans caucused practically every day. But before the session of 1909 had advanced far, the real line that divided the Senators, the line that separated the machine from the anti-machine members, had become so pronounced that caucuses of machine and anti-machine Republicans became impracticable. Senator Wright, toward the end of the session, made frantic efforts to get the caucus together; but he failed. The caucus on organization was about all that the anti-machine Republicans could stand.

As they had left the election of the officers of the Senate to the machine, the anti-machine element left the appointing of the Senate committees to the machine Lieutenant-Governor.[9]

How well the machine, given the appointment of the committees, fortified itself is shown by consideration of practically any one of the committees. A few examples will suffice.

There were, for example, three great issues before the Legislature; namely, the Anti-Racetrack Gambling bill, a moral issue; the Direct Primary bill, a political issue; and the Railroad Regulation bills, a commercial issue.

The Anti-Gambling bill was to come before the Public Morals Committee, and the machine took good care that not an anti-machine Senator should be given a place on that committee. The committee consisted of Weed, Wolfe, Leavitt, Savage (labeled Republicans), Kennedy (labeled Democrat), all machine men. The committee reported back the Anti-Gambling bill under pressure, with the recommendation that it "do not pass." Public opinion was such at the time that Savage and Kennedy did not vote for the unfavorable recommendation. But Weed, Wolfe and Leavitt, a majority of the committee, stood out against the bill until the last.

The Direct Primary bill was to be considered by the Election Laws Committee and the machine took good care to keep hand upon that committee. The committee was made up of seven machine and two anti-machine Senators, as follows:

Machine Senators - Leavitt, Hartman, Wolfe, Savage, Wright (labeled Republicans), Kennedy and Hare (labeled Democrats).

Every one of the seven opposed the State-wide plan for the selection of United States Senators.

The anti-machine Senators on the committee were Estudillo and Stetson.

It is an open secret that the machine expected to control Estudillo through Walter Parker, the Southern Pacific political agent. Its failure brought some confusion upon machine circles. Thus, the machine really thought when it picked the Committee on Election Laws that it controlled eight of the nine members.

The Railroad Regulation measures were to be passed upon by the Committee on Corporations. The machine took care to be in control of that committee. It consisted of eleven members. Seven of the eleven, if Burnett who voted with the machine on this issue be counted with them, were machine, one was "band wagon[10], which is a trifle worse than machine, and three anti-machine, as follows:

Machine - Bates, Wright, McCartney, Burnett, Bills, Finn (labeled Republicans), Kennedy (labeled Democrat).

Band wagon - Welch.

Anti-machine - Walker, Roseberry (labeled Republicans), and Miller (labeled Democrat).

But here again the machine was more generous than it intended to be. It figured on controlling Walker. But in the committee Walker stood out manfully for the Stetson bill and against the Wright bill. On the floor of the Senate, however, Walker made his one slip of the session, by voting for the Wright bill and against the Stetson bill.

It is not necessary to continue consideration of the committees. Enough has been said to show how thoroughly the machine minority, given the appointment of the committees, strengthened itself in the Senate by seizing every strategic position. Indeed, the machine fortified itself with such far-seeing intelligence, that one marvels that the anti-machine majority was able to offer even temporarily effective opposition.

[5] Anthony's vote was in the majority of cases cast on the side of the machine. But the determined stand that he took on the Direct Primary bill issue, demonstrated that Anthony, had the anti-machine forces maintained any sort of organization, or had they had definite plan of action, would have been found consistently on the side of good government. Burnett was unquestionably misled by the machine leaders. Neither Burnett nor Anthony can be justly classed with Hartman, Wolfe, Leavitt, Bills, etc., etc. Hurd, who toward the end of the session voted constantly with the machine, and is considered hopeless by many observers, nevertheless took active part in the anti-machine caucus on the Direct Primary bill, and, had the organization of the Senate been in the hands of the anti-machine element, the writer firmly believes, would have continued with the reform forces. At any rate, he was available for any anti-machine movement that might have been started to organize the Senate. Hurd, like Burnett, will have his opportunity in 1911. Both Senators hold over.

[5a] In this instance, the Republican Senators. The Senate minority was made up of the Democratic Senators, if we make the division on party lines. But as a matter of fact, when it came to the real business of the session, the

Senate did not divide on party lines. The actual division was between the machine and the anti-machine Senators. Thus the real majority consisted of anti-machine Senators, and the minority of the Senators controlled by the machine.

[6] Hurd's case illustrates this very well.

[7] See chapter nine - Machine defeated in the Senate.

[8] Burnett of San Francisco, voted against Bell on partisan grounds, and inability to grasp the situation. Estudillo's vote was inconsistent with the majority which he cast during the session, while Hurd's was inconsistent with those which he cast up to the time of his vote with the machine forces against the Stetson bill.

[8a] Up to the session of 1909, the members of the Legislature fixed the amount of patronage. At the session of 1907, the payroll of the officers and attaches of the Assembly alone ran up to nearly $10,000 a week, or more than $1300 a day. But in 1908, the People adopted a constitutional amendment limiting the amount of patronage, the money to be expended for legislative officers and attaches, to $500 a day for each House. This cut the Patronage down something more than one-half, which gave the Senators and Assemblymen who divided it great concern.

The development of the patronage scandal during the last decade is interesting. At the session of 1901 the Assembly patronage ran about $580 a day the Senate patronage about $610. This was only $80 a day more in the Assembly, and $110 more in the Senate than the limit now fixed by the Constitution.

In 1903, the patronage in the Assembly totaled $6312.50 a week, more than $900 a day. In the Senate it was $5612.50, or $800 a day.

The increase continued in 1905. in that year Assembly Patronage totaled $7956.50 a week, or $1135 a day, while the Senate patronage was $6002.50 a week, or $857 a day.

The climax came in 1907, when the Assembly patronage went to $9660.50 a week, or $1350 a day, and the Senate patronage to to $6893.50 a week, or $985 a day. What it would have been in 1909 had there been no Constitutional restriction placed upon it, is a matter for speculation.

[9] See concluding chapter as to how this could have been avoided.

[10] The term "band wagon" was applied during the session to those members who were in the habit of joining the winning side at the last moment.

CHAPTER III.

Organization of the Assembly.

Independent Movement to Resist the Machine's Program Failed - Reform Element Rallied and Rejected Rules Prepared by Committee Appointed by Stanton, Which Would Have Placed Majority at Mercy of the Machine-Controlled Minority.

The machine-free members of the Lower House at least did better than the reformers in the Senate; they made an attempt to organize the Assembly independent of the machine. The effort was, however, as uncertain as that of a nestling taking its first lesson in flying. Nothing came of the venture; but it indicates what may be done in future.

The organization of the Assembly hinges on the election of the Speaker. The machine ordinarily picks the Speaker before the November elections, so his election need not stir up any particular enthusiasm. But there is always something of a contest started - for the sake of appearances, probably.

This year the machine had picked Phil Stanton, of Los Angeles, for the job, but Bob Beardslee, of Stockton, was permitted to give Stanton "a run."

The San Francisco newspapers along in November and December recorded the political ripple of the contest, but the fight was a dead affair, and nobody enthused. The play came to a tame ending when Beardslee nominated Stanton for the Speaker's job and got the Chairmanship of the important Committee on Ways and Means for being good, or taking program, however one may view it.

But at one time a real fight for the Speakership threatened. Assemblyman Drew, of Fresno, and other stanch anti-machine men, conceived the radical notion that it was idiotic for them to sit around like lambs waiting to have their throats cut, while the machine organized the House. They accordingly decided to take a hand in the organization of the Assembly themselves by refusing to vote for any man for Speaker who was known to be under the influence of the machine.

Forty-one votes are required to elect the Speaker. The reformers figured on the nineteen Democratic members as with them. The Lincoln-Roosevelt League had elected Assemblymen from several counties, including Alameda. These were naturally counted on. Other reputable Republican members were expected to join the movement in numbers sufficient to secure the necessary forty-one votes.

The purpose of the leaders of this departure from the regular rules of the political game should have commended itself to every good citizen. Their idea was to organize the Assembly, not for self-advancement, or the promotion of special privileges as the machine leaders do year after year, but that good bills might be passed and bad bills defeated; that the waste of the public funds might be stopped; that worthy citizenship might be placed above predatory partisanship. And yet, they were compelled to proceed with the utmost caution; were discouraged at every turn, and abused like pickpockets, even by those upon whom they depended for support. Gradually it dawned upon them that not a few of the Democratic members were not in sympathy with reform legislation. But more discouraging still was the fact that certain Republicans elected to the Assembly by the Lincoln-Roosevelt faction of the party were as little to be depended upon. By consulting the tables "B" and "C" of Assembly votes in the appendix, it will be seen that Democrats like Baxter, Collum, Hopkins, O'Neil and Wheelan, and Lincoln-Roosevelt Republicans like Mott, Pulcifer and Feeley, as a general thing voted with the machine Republicans. There were, to be sure, Democrats like Gillis, Johnson of Placer, Juilliard, Maher, Mendenhall, Polsley, Preston, Wilson, Odom and Stuckenbruck, who were against the machine on every issue, but the record shows the utter foolishness of regarding either party free of machine influences. Without being able to understand just how it was, Mr. Drew and his associates failed to secure the encouragement for their independent movement which they expected. The stealthy move upon the Speaker's chair was found in some unaccountable way to be blocked. Then some cautious soul suggested that if they should fail the machine would hold up the appropriation bills of those identified with the movement. That settled it. The attempt to elect as Speaker some member free of machine influence ended right there. The reformers skurried for cover.

The part which the appropriation bills play in the enactment of bad laws is one of the least understood of a legislative session. Each session money must be appropriated by legislative enactment for the maintenance and enlargement, where necessary, of the various State institutions, such as hospitals for the insane, reform schools, normal schools, and the like. These institutions are not local at all, but State. But the Senators and Assemblymen from the counties in which they are situated are, by custom, charged with the responsibility of securing the appropriations necessary for their support. The San Jose Normal School, for example, and the Agnew Asylum for the Insane, are situated in Santa Clara County. They are no more Santa Clara County institutions than they are Del Norte or San Diego institutions, but the Senators and Assemblymen from Santa Clara County are held responsible for the passage of the appropriation bills affecting them. Too often, the ability of the Assemblyman or Senator is measured, not by his real work in the Legislature, but by the size of the appropriations which he manages to secure for his district. Under the present system by which the machine organizes the Legislature, it is in a position to defeat or materially reduce practically any appropriation bill. The member of the Legislature who would oppose the machine thus finds himself between the constituents at home, who demand that he secure generous appropriations for his district, and the machine, which he understands very well requires support of its policies as one of the prices of the constituent-demanded appropriations. Thus those who would have opposed the machine in the organization of the Assembly realized that failure would probably mean a hammering of their appropriation bills, which would result in their political undoing at home. So the independent movement to organize the Assembly came to a sorry ending.

Stanton was elected Speaker without opposition. The "defeated" Beardslee placed him in nomination. Complete harmony prevailed. Stanton started proceedings by appointing the Committee on Rules. This committee was charged with drafting rules for the government of the Assembly during the session. It was made up of Assemblymen Johnston of Contra Costa, Transue, Johnson of Sacramento, Beardslee and Stanton.

Without the people knowing much about what is going on, the rules governing legislative bodies are being amended from time to time, so that the power of influencing legislation is being taken out of the hands of the duly elected representatives of the people and placed with presiding officers and important committees. The "system," or the machine, call it what you may, finds it easier to control presiding officers and committees appointed by presiding officers, than to control Legislatures. This stealthy advance upon the liberties of the people, seems to have reached its climax at Washington, where the independent members of both parties are in open revolt against "Cannonism." But "Cannonism" is not confined to the National Congress alone; in a small way it has its hold on the California Legislature. The rules prepared by Speaker Stanton's committee were well calculated to give "Cannonism" a stronger hold in California, which would have influenced not only the session of 1909 but, as a precedent, many sessions to come.[11] The proposed rules in saddling "Cannonism" upon the Assembly were well calculated to strengthen the machine's grip upon the Legislature.

The departure from the rules of 1907 was most radical. Under the rules that governed the Assembly in 1907, committees were required to report on each bill referred to them within ten days after the measure had been submitted.

The rules proposed by the committee provided that the report should be made as soon as "practicable."

The rules of 1907 provided that a mere majority could recall a bill from committee.

Under the proposed rules a two-thirds vote would have been necessary.

Under the rules of 1907 a measure could be advanced on the files at the request of its author.

Under the committee's rules unanimous consent of the Assembly was made necessary for such advancement.

The proposed rules would have enabled the machine forces to smother in committee any measure the machine wished to defeat. A two-thirds vote would have been necessary to suspend the rules to have a bill recalled from committee, that is to say, the votes of fifty-four Assemblymen. Twenty-seven Assemblymen could then have held the measure in committee until the session closed.

Had the committee-prepared rules been adopted, the probabilities are that the battleground of the session would have been transferred from the Senate Chamber to the Assembly.

But the proposed rules were not adopted. A fight against adopting the committee's report was started by Drew of Fresno. Mr. Drew introduced a resolution rejecting the rules submitted by the committee, and substituting the rules of 1907, to govern the session of 1909. Johnson of Sacramento led the defense that rallied to the committee's report. But Johnson's wit failed against the argument which Drew, Callan, Preston, Young and Cattell offered. The gentlemen denounced the rules which the committee had offered as "vicious, despotic and gagging." Drew's resolution was adopted by a vote of 41 to 32, the committee's report rejected and the rules of 1907 accepted for the session of 1909[12]. It was a decided victory for the anti-machine forces, and brought gloom to the scheming machine leaders. But it developed later that not a few who had voted for the Drew resolution were safely machine; while many who had voted against it were anti-machine, but had voted against the resolution under misapprehension of just what it stood for[13].

Although the reform majority in the Assembly could prevent the adoption of the "gag rules," it could not, after it had failed to elect the Speaker, govern the appointment of the committees. By and large, the Assembly committees were controlled as were the Senate committees by machine standbys. The Election Laws Committee, which was to pass upon the Direct Primary bill, was safely in machine hands. Grove L. Johnson, as

Chairman of the Judiciary Committee, herded the young lawyers thereon like so many sheep. Johnson was in effect the committee.

The Committee on Corporations and the Committee on Common Carriers, before which railroad regulation bills might come, were safely in majority for the machine.

One apparent exception to the rule was the Committee on Public Morals, which gave the Anti-Gambling bill its start toward passage. But this committee, which did so much to secure the passage of the Anti-Gambling bill, held up the Local Option bill at Speaker Stanton's request, until the last week of the session, thus making its passage in the Assembly impossible.

A curious mistake was made by the machine, when Telfer of San Jose was made Chairman of the Committee on Contingent Expenses. Telfer is not only anti-machine, but possessed of a non-political honesty which proved very distressing to the machine before the session was over.

Telfer as Chairman of the committee refused to "O. K." extravagant charges for the materials furnished the Assembly. As a result, bills for hire of typewriters had to be reduced, pencils counted and other astonishing reductions made.

Telfer saved the State several hundred dollars, but caused many a heartache. Telfer's appointment to a committee which he made important, shows that the machine element as well as the anti-machine sometimes makes mistakes. But in spite of its minor mistakes, in spite of the anti-machine majority, so admirably did the machine organize the Assembly for its purposes, that in the closing days of the session not only were vicious measures passed without much difficulty, but the Assembly was made the graveyard of good bills[14].

[11] If ever the People of California secure control of the State Legislature through machine-free representatives with the courage to dare and the ability to do, one of the most important pieces of work will be to sweep aside the mass of precedent which the machine has for years been gradually embodying into the rules of Senate and Assembly. What is needed is a set of rules that shall promote the expression of the wishes of the majority. The curse of technicality does not hamper the Judiciary alone; it hampers the legislative branch of government as well. Note Wolfe's ability to deadlock the Senate after the Assembly Amendments to the Direct Primary bill had been rejected. Chapter XI.

[12] The vote by which this was done was as follows:

For the Drew resolution and against the committee rules: Assemblymen Black, Bohnett, Callan, Cattell, Cogswell, Collum, Costar, Cronin, Drew,

Flint, Gibbons, Hammon, Hanlon, Hayes, Hewitt, Hinkle, Hopkins, Irwin, Johnson of Placer, Juilliard, Lightner, Maher, Melrose, Mendenhall, Odom, Otis, O'Neil, Polsley, Preston, Rech, Rutherford, Sackett, Silver, Stuckenbruck, Telfer, Wagner, Webber, Wheelan, Whitney, Wilson and Young. - 41.

Against the Drew resolution and for the committee rules: Assemblymen Barndollar, Beardslee, Beban, Coghlan, Collier, Cullen, Dean, Feeley, Flavelle, Fleisher, Gerdes, Greer, Griffiths, Hans, Hawk, Holmquist, Johnson of Sacramento, Johnson of San Diego, Johnston, Leeds, Macauley, McClelland, McManus, Moore, Mott, Nelson, Perine, Pugh, Pulcifer, Schmitt, Stanton, Transue - 32.

[13] A gentleman who for a number of years has been identified with the reform element in the Assembly, writes of this feature of the machine's hold on the Legislature as follows: "One of the principal difficulties with the Legislature as it is now constituted and has been for many years past, is that the machine or organization always endeavors to secure the election of young men who haven't very fixed opinions and who are easily influenced; not knowing the machine tactics and the real object behind the legislation they do not seem to see the necessity for standing firm and for that reason are often led into voting for or against measures which they would not were they more familiar with the tricks of the machine men. A new grist of legislators is what the organization is always looking for. They want a certain number of old "stand-bys" who will do their dirty work for a mere pittance or some paltry reward, real or anticipated, and with these men to influence and control the younger members their purpose is easily, accomplished."

[14] See Passage of Wheelan Bills, chapter XVII; Passage of Change of Venue bill, chapter XVI. Examples of good bills defeated in the Assembly in the closing days of the session were the Judicial Column bill, and the Holohan measure removing the party circle from the election ballot.

CHAPTER IV.

The Machine in Control.

Deliberately Held Up Measures in Committees Until the Close of the Session, When Senate and Assembly Were Forced to Take Snap Judgment on
Hundreds of Measures - In the Confusion Thus Created, Good Bills Were Defeated and Bad Ones Passed.

The Legislature organized, the machine and anti-machine forces settled down to the work of the session. The situation was unique. The anti-machine element had a comfortable majority in the Assembly and at least a bare majority in the Senate. But the machine controlled the committees of both Houses, had selected the presiding officers, and had dictated the selection of the majority of the attaches. When, for example, it was suggested that in the event of a close vote in the Senate on the Anti-Racetrack Gambling bill, it might be found necessary to send the Sergeant-at-Arms after Senators who might attempt to dodge the vote, not a single attache of the Sergeant-at-Arms' office could be named who was in sympathy with the movement against the gamblers. Incidentally, however, it was discovered that the clerk of the important Senate Enrolling and Engrossing Committee had been an employee at Frank Daroux's notorious Sausalito poolrooms. These were disquieting discoveries for the reform element.

Although the machine controlled the strategic positions of the organization of the Legislature, it was still in the minority in each House. This meant that the machine could not, in open fight, pass a vicious or undesirable measure, or put through any of its schemes. The machine's course soon became apparent. If the machine could not put laws on the statute books to its liking, it could block the passage of good measures. Having crafty leaders in both Senate and Assembly, and, above all, controlling the committees, the machine was admirably prepared to do this. By employing delaying tactics which would have done credit to a specialist in criminal defense, the machine devoted the first two months of the session to the blocking of legislation.

The methods employed were very simple. As soon as a bill was introduced it was referred to a committee of the House in which it originated. The committee would hold the measure until the reform element gave indications of protesting[15]. The bill would then be returned. If possible it would be further delayed by amendment on second or third reading. If finally passed by the House of its origin, it would be sent to the other House, where it would be referred to a committee. In the majority of cases the committee could hold it indefinitely. In such cases as the committees were forced to report on measures that had passed the other House, the measure would be amended, which necessitated its being reprinted, and again acted upon by the House of its origin[16], all of which made for delay.

But it must not be thought that the Senate and Assembly were left in idleness during the first two months of the session. Such is by no means the case; Senators and Assemblymen never worked harder. The machine leaders during the first month of the session craftily kept the members wrangling in committees. During the second month the Senate was kept working day and night passing comparatively unimportant Senate bills, and the Assembly working as hard passing Assembly bills; but the Senate passed very few Assembly bills and the Assembly very few Senate bills. As a measure must pass both Houses to become a law, few bills were sent to the Governor for his approval. Thus during the first two months of the session many bills passed in one house or the other, but pitifully few passed the Legislature.

The reform element, working sixteen hours a day not unlike so many mice in a wheel, were apparently in complete ignorance of the situation which they were creating. Senators whose bills had passed the Senate began to complain that they could not get the measures out of the Assembly committee; Assemblymen whose measures had passed the Assembly were as loud in their charges that their bills were being held up in Senate committees. The machine actually turned this early dissatisfaction to its advantage. Soon it was being announced on the floor of the Assembly: "If Senate committees will not act on Assembly bills, then the Assembly committees will not act on Senate bills." The Senate made the same threats as to Assembly bills. So, for about a week, Senate committees openly slighted Assembly bills, while Assembly committees in retaliation slighted Senate bills. The situation was very amusing; it was, too, highly satisfactory to the machine.

About the first week in March - the Legislature adjourned March 24 - the anti-machine members awoke to the fact that in spite of their day and night sessions, little had been accomplished. The further disquieting discovery was made that the bulk of the Assembly bills which had passed the Assembly were being held in Senate committees, while the Senate bills which had passed the Senate, were apparently anchored in Assembly committees, and that the machine controlled the committees. The reform members of each House had good cause for alarm. Every Senator and Assemblyman has his "pet" measures. The reform Senators and Assemblymen found that to get their bills out of committees they would have to treat with the machine. Such a Senator or Assemblyman, with his constituents clamoring for the passage of a bill held up in a machine-controlled committee, had some claim to pardon if he turned suddenly attentive to the machine olive branch. And the machine, by the way, always has the olive branch out. Stand in with us, is their constant advance, and we will see you through.

As a result of these delaying tactics, literally hundreds of bills which had needlessly been held up in committees were forced upon the consideration of the Senate during the last three weeks of the session. Each House made records of passing more than 100 bills a day. There was little pretense of reading the measures as required by the State Constitution. The clerk at the desk mumbled over their titles; they were voted upon and became laws. In the rush to get through, as will be shown by example in other chapters, Senators and Assemblymen voted for measures to which they were openly opposed. The machine minority was merely reaping the benefits of a situation which the cleverness of its leaders had created.

Although machine-advocated and unimportant measures could be passed in such a situation, bills which the machine opposed could not be[17]. Machine-opposed measures were either held up in committees until their passage was out of the question, or they were denied consideration in Senate or Assembly, or their advocates worn out by the tactics of the machine leaders. Senate Bill 220, which removed the party circle from the election ballot, passed in the Senate after a bitter contest, was held up in the Assembly until five days before adjournment, and then denied a second reading. Boynton's Senate Bill 249, providing for the arrangement of judicial candidates on the ballot without designation of party affiliations, intended to take the Judiciary out of politics, which after a long contest passed the Senate, was held up in the Assembly until the day before adjournment, when it was denied passage. This bill was introduced in the Senate on January 12. So popular was it, such was the demand for its passage, that it was not openly opposed. It was finally defeated on March 23, the day before adjournment. Thus two months and eleven days were required to wear out its advocates.

About March 1, the machine began to crowd the anti-machine element for early adjournment. At that time not far from 2000 bills were recorded in the Senate and Assembly histories. The action had the effect of a good stiff push to a man sliding down hill; the anti-machine forces had the votes to prevent adjournment but the machine's adjournment plans added considerably to anti-machine discomfiture. Senator Wolfe actually gave notice that on Friday, March 5, he would move that the Legislature adjourn on March 13. This would have given a fortnight for consideration of nearly 2000 bills. At the time of Wolfe's motion, there were pending the Direct

Primary bill, the Railroad Regulation bills, the Commonwealth Club bills, the Islais Creek Harbor bills, and scores of other important measures, the passage of which had unnecessarily - albeit most cleverly - been delayed.

As a result of clever manipulation, dating from the first day of the session, the machine was thus in the closing days, in spite of the majority against it, able to pass, amend or defeat measures, pretty much as its leaders desired. The anti-machine forces, Republican and Democratic, were during those last days, merely reaping the harvest which they had sown when they permitted the Democratic-Republican machine to take the organization of the Legislature out of their hands.

[15] The Senate Committee on Election Laws, for example, held the Direct Primary bill for thirty-eight days, and finally reported it back so amended that it had to be rewritten. See chapters VI and VII on efforts of the machine to hold the Anti-Racetrack Gambling bill in committee.

[16] It was stated on the floor of the Assembly, that were the Ten Commandments to be adopted by the Assembly, the Senate would find some excuse for amending them.

[17] The most astonishing example of this was furnished by the passage of the Change of Venue bill in the Senate. See chapter XVI.

CHAPTER V.

Election of United States Senator.

Opposition to Perkins Overcome by the Dead Weight of the Machine - Movement Against His Re-election Failed for Want of Leadership - Proceedings Without Warmth or Enthusiasm.

No funeral was ever attended by greater somberness than was the re-election of George C. Perkins to the United States Senate, January 12-13, 1909. The nominating speeches were made without enthusiasm; not a cheer greeted Senator or Assemblyman charged with the task of putting the aged Senator in nomination. Pulcifer of Alameda, who made the nominating speech in the Assembly, was received with icy calmness. Even when the Alamedan referred to the veteran Senator as "one whose hair has grown white and whose eyes have grown dim in the service of his country," not so much as a ripple of applause stirred the chamber. When the speaker concluded his review of the Senator's life and political career, the incipient murmur of approval which somebody started died away for want of vitality.

In the Senate, the task of nominating Perkins fell to Stetson of Alameda. But Stetson's nominating speech was received with no more enthusiasm than was that of the shifty Pulcifer. The "system," the "organization," the "machine," have it as you will, returned George C. Perkins to the United States Senate. The people of California had no voice in it, nor, for that matter, the Legislature, although the majority of the Legislature was opposed to the machine. In carrying out the ignoble part prepared for them - prepared for them by the "machine" which a majority of them opposed - the members of Senate and Assembly went through the forms prescribed without a hand clap and without a cheer.

But it must not be thought that the re-election of Senator Perkins was without opposition. Indeed, it met with the same sort of honest but ineffective resistance that attended the election of Stanton to the Speakership of the Lower House. And like the campaign against Stanton the opposition to Perkins got nowhere because of the lack of leadership, organization and plan of action on the part of the resisting legislators.

The machine had been preparing for Perkins' re-election for months; but the opposition to Perkins made no move until after the November elections.

The first outward sign of opposition came from Assemblyman E. J. Callan of the Thirty-ninth District, the fighting reform district of San Francisco.

Callan, three or four weeks before the Legislature convened, fell into a trap which the wily Alameda County politician had set some time previous. Perkins had long before invited criticism of his "record," which meant his votes on issues that had been passed upon by the United States Senate. As a matter of fact, such votes mean little, for the misplaced "courtesy of the Senate," under which schemers betray the people, makes it possible for even recognized "reformers" to be forced to vote against most desirable measures. The other fellows of the Perkins stripe when brought to book on their "record" can always give in defense: 'Why, your reformer, Senator So and So, did the same thing.' To be sure, a La Follette does kick over the traces once in a while, in which event he usually votes alone, while the solemn victims of "courtesy" vote against him according to Senatorial custom, not to use the more expressive word, stupidity.

Thus, when Perkins craftily invited his opponents to attack him on his record, they dodged the trap gingerly, all save Callan. Callan didn't walk, he rushed into it, sending a scathing letter to Perkins on that gentleman's Senatorial record. Perkins' reply and explanation came as a counter blow. The fire was tempered out of Callan's letter. Callan had permitted Perkins to select the fighting ground, and Perkins had exhibited admirable judgment.

The attack on Perkins had better been made on his attitude toward the shipping interests of California - the development of the isthmian route to New York, for example; on his attitude toward the machine, whose strangle-hold upon the State is locked with federal patronage; on his attitude toward the so-called "Roosevelt policies"; on his attitude toward the Roosevelt administration, upon which he hung with the dead weight of crafty, persistent obstruction. There were plenty of vulnerable points in the Perkins armor, but naturally in selecting the point of attack, Perkins carefully avoided them. So Callan's bolt rebounded harmlessly, to the astonishment of the various well-meaning reformers, and the intense satisfaction of the machine, whose somewhat anxious leaders recognized full well that Callan's discomfiture would discourage attacks from other possibly effective sources.

The next move against Perkins came the week before the Legislature convened. A number of anti-machine Republicans met at San Francisco to canvass the situation, and formulate a plan to defeat Perkins if possible. It was found that on joint Senate and Assembly ballot, the Democrats would have twenty-nine votes and the Republicans ninety-one. Sixty-one votes are required for the election of a Senator. The Republicans at the meeting considered these twenty-nine votes as with them in the selection of an anti-machine Republican for Perkins' place. The anti-machine Republicans thus in revolt against the machine, themselves numbered twenty Senators and

Assemblymen, which made forty-nine votes against Perkins. In addition, an even dozen Republican Senators and Assemblymen were counted upon as willing to vote against Perkins if his defeat could be shown to be certain. This would have given the anti-Perkins element sixty-one votes, just enough to elect. For one of their number to fail, meant a deadlock; for two, if Republicans, to fail meant Perkins' election. It was a slender chance, but the possibility of success kept the movement alive until the hour of the Senatorial caucus.

Those who were promoting the movement were not at the time aware that six of the Democratic Assemblymen and one of the Democratic Senators were governed by such high conceptions of their duties as citizens and responsibilities as legislators, that they were to cast their votes in the Senatorial election for a San Francisco saloon keeper, on the ground that he is a "good fellow" and had "spent money liberally for the party." This of itself made the defeat of Perkins impossible.

The anti-Perkins forces were also handicapped by the fact that they had no candidate. The machine had been craftily booming Perkins for years; the reformers had boomed nobody[19]. They were, then, without material for a positive fight; all they could do was negative, which is always confession of weakness. In addition, aside from the Bulletin, there was no San Francisco publication that could be counted upon to back their movement. The Call was openly supporting Perkins. The movement against Perkins, while it admittedly represented the attitude of the majority of the electors of the State, and the feeling of a safe majority of both Houses of the Legislature, was without one element of real strength[20].

Under the United States Revised Statutes, the Legislature was called upon, to proceed on the second Tuesday after organization, to elect Senator Perkins' successor. As the Legislature had organized on January 4, the second Tuesday fell on January 12. The call for the Republican caucus to go through the form of selecting a candidate for the Senate, was circulated the third and fourth days of the session. The Republican Senators all signed it, not a few of them with the non-resistance of a wretch in the hands of a hangman.

More opposition developed in the Assembly. Callan and three or four others kept up their resistance to the last, but when the caucus assembled on Friday evening, January 8, all the Republican Senators and Assemblymen who could do so were in attendance[21].

The caucus was of course hopelessly programmed for Perkins. Nevertheless, the better element of the party endeavored to secure some expression from Senator Perkins as to his attitude toward the Western transportation problem. This led to a heated debate which kept the caucus in session until a late hour. The debate turned on the celebrated Bristow letter.

For years, the Southern Pacific Railroad Company has been able to prevent effective water competition by way of the Isthmus of Panama. The Government has a line of steamers running from New York to the Isthmus, and a railroad line across the Isthmus. With an additional line of steamers running from San Francisco to Panama, the Government would have a through line from San Francisco to New York. This would give genuine competition with the Southern Pacific system, and free the State from the grasp of the transportation monopoly.

In August, 1907, Hon. J. L. Bristow, now United States Senator from Kansas, was appointed a Special Panama Railroad Commissioner, to investigate the necessity and feasibility of putting on the Pacific line. Mr. Bristow, in a report that fairly sizzled with criticism of Southern Pacific and Pacific Mail Steamship Company methods, recommended that the government line be established. When Pacific freight rates were arbitrarily raised just before the Legislature convened, shippers of the State appealed, not to Senator Perkins or to Senator Flint, but to Senator Bristow from interior Kansas, asking that he concern himself with having government steamers put on the San Francisco-Panama route. Bristow replied that he would do what he could, that he was receiving many letters from Western shippers who favored the plan, but that the chief difficulty in the way was the opposition of the California delegation in the Senate.

This Bristow letter caused all the trouble at the Perkins caucus. The suggestion was made that Perkins owed it to the State to explain the charges brought against him by the Senator from Kansas. A resolution was accordingly introduced providing that a telegram be sent Senator Perkins calling upon him to state whether the charge made by Senator Bristow were true.

Immediately the pro-Perkins people assumed the dignified position that such a telegram would be an insult to the venerable Senator from California. Nobody seems to have taken the trouble to state that the Bristow charges were untrue, but that the requesting of the Senator to answer them would be an insult to that dignitary was made subject of the warmest oratory. So warm was it, that the opposition to Perkins melted away like wax - or putty, if putty melts - until but five members of the caucus had the courage to vote to ask Perkins to declare himself on the transportation problem. Callan of San Francisco voted for it, so did Drew of Fresno, so did Young of Berkeley and two others. But 77 members of the caucus voted against the resolution. Senator Perkins was permitted to maintain a dignified silence on the Bristow charges. After the vote on the resolution, Assemblyman Callan left the caucus.

But even with the Republican caucus nomination, Perkins did not receive the entire Republican vote. In the Assembly, Callan voted for Chester Rowell of Fresno, and Sackett for Thomas R. Bard of Ventura. Fifty-six of the Assembly votes, however, were cast for Perkins.

In the Senate, Perkins received thirty-two votes. The thirty regular Republicans voted for him, as did Senator Bell, the Independent-Republican, and Senator Caminetti, Democrat. Senator Caminetti voted for Perkins because Caminetti regarded Perkins, as nearly as could be determined, the choice of the electors to whom Caminetti owed his election. Caminetti believes that the United States Senator should be selected by the people of the State. The nearest he could get to this was to ascertain the wishes of the people of his district. He was convinced that the people of his district wished to see Perkins re-elected. So, regardless of partisan considerations, Caminetti the Democrat voted for Perkins the Republican. Caminetti's explanation of his vote is worthy of the most careful consideration[22].

The regular candidate of the minority for the Democratic complimentary vote was J. O. Davis, a gentleman of the highest character. But eight of the Democratic members voted against him. Seven of the eight, Assemblymen Black, Collum, Hopkins, Lightner, O'Neil and Wheelan and Senator Hare voted for Harry P. Flannery, a San Francisco saloon-keeper; the eighth, Senator Kennedy, voted for William H. Langdon. Six Democratic Senators and thirteen Democratic Assemblymen voted for Mr. Davis. They were: Senators Campbell, Cartwright, Curtin, Holohan, Miller, and Sanford; Assemblymen Baxter, Gibbons, Gillis, Irwin, Johnson of Placer, Juilliard, Maher, Mendenhall, Odom, Polsley, Preston, Stuckenbruck and Webber.

[19] It is interesting to note that when a good citizen gives effective resistance to the machine, that the machine invariably starts the cry - "He is a candidate for the United States Senate." The open candidacy - and liberal advertising - of a machine man for the Federal Senatorship causes no adverse comment. For an anti-machine man to so aspire - or the suspicion in machine breasts that he so aspires - is heralded as evidence of his complete unworthy and irresponsibility.

[20] But when the machine Republicans of a State unite with Democrats to elect a machine man to the Federal Senate, no such difficulties attend them. Note the election by a coalition of machine Republicans and machine Democrats in Illinois of "Billy" Lorimer, the notorious "blond boss" of the stockyards, to the United States Senate.

[21] Senator Bell, although a Republican, was excluded because he would not make his peace with Walter Parker, the Southern Pacific boss of the political district lying south of Tehachepi. See Chapter 11, Organization of the Senate.

[22] Caminetti's explanation of his vote, as printed in the Senate Journal, is in full as follows:

"Mr. President: During the campaign of 1906, in the Tenth Senatorial District, resulting in my election as Senator, I made the question of 'The election of United States Senators by direct vote of the people' one of the leading issues upon which I asked the suffrage of the people. I then pledged myself in all my speeches and in the press, to endeavor to secure the passage of a law by the Legislature in case of my election having that object in view, and in case of failure in the effort I would nevertheless follow that principle and vote for the choice of a majority of the qualified electors of that district in the selection of a Senator during my term of off cue.

"The last session of the Legislature failed to enact the necessary legislation on the subject, but the people of my district have nevertheless plainly indicated to me that Hon. George C. Perkins was at the last election, and now is, their choice for the United States Senatorship.

"Under these circumstances I feel in honor bound by my pledges to the people of the Tenth Senatorial District, to record the choice of a majority of the qualified electors thereof for Hon. George C. Perkins for United States Senator, hoping in so doing that it will never again be necessary for a member of the Legislature to vote the choice of the people of his district in this, or any other, indirect way, but that this Legislature will rise superior to partisanship and give to the people hereafter an opportunity, under suitable laws, to vote directly for candidates for that office. Should this Legislature fail in this high duty to the public, I trust that the people, in whom all power resides, will hereafter take up this matter in the way the people of the Tenth Senatorial District did two years ago, and thus be able in all legislative districts of the State to record their choice for the exalted office of United States Senator."

CHAPTER VI.

The Anti-Racetrack Gambling Bill.

Supporters of the Measure Knew What They Wanted, Drew a Bill to Meet the
Requirements of the Situation and Refused to Compromise with the Machine
Element - Suggestive Series of "Errors" Attended Its Passage.

Of the three principal reform measures considered by the Legislature of 1909 - the Direct Primary bill, the Railroad Regulation bill and the Anti-Racetrack Gambling bill - the last named was the only one to become a law untrimmed of its effective features. The Anti-Racetrack Gambling bill passed the Assembly, passed the Senate and was signed by the Governor precisely as it had been introduced; there was not so much as the change of a comma allowed. The result is an anti-gambling law on California statute books which if it work as well as it has in other States will prevent bookmaking and pool-selling, thus relieving horse racing of the incubus which has made the sport of kings disreputable[23].

Since the reform element succeeded in passing the Anti-Racetrack Gambling bill without amendment, there is widespread opinion that there was no opposition to its passage. As a matter of fact, nothing is farther from the truth. Before a legislator reached Sacramento, the pro-gambling lobby was on the ground, and continued its hold-up process until the Assembly, by a vote of 67 to 10, passed the measure, and by a vote of 57 to 19 refused to grant it reconsideration.

The writer remembers his first poll of the Senate on the anti-gambling issue, when only nineteen Senators could be safely counted for it[24]; twenty-one were necessary for its passage. To be sure, a number of the Senators not included in the list of the nineteen who were from the beginning safe for the measure, were pledged to vote for an anti-pool selling bill, but this did not necessarily mean the effective Walker-Otis bill which had been drawn to prevent pool selling and bookmaking. Not a few unquestionably figured on voting for a bill that would place them on record as against racetrack gambling, but do racetrack gambling little or no harm.

These uncertain ones were blocked in their plan of action because the proponents of the Anti-Gambling bill knew just what they wanted to do, namely, close up poolrooms and bookmakers' booths. They took the most effective way to close them up, namely, adapted to California Constitution and criminal practice, the Hughes anti-gambling law, the adoption of which

Governor Hughes forced in New York, and which in New York State had proved most effective.

The bill was drawn carefully and its backers in the Legislature and out of the Legislature let it be known that no amendment, not so much as to change a comma, would be tolerated. The measure was introduced in the Senate by Walker of Santa Clara, and in the Assembly by Otis of Alameda. It was known as the Walker-Otis bill.

This determined stand for the passage of the measure just as it had been drawn thoroughly alarmed the gambling lobby. "Reformers" who would not "compromise" proved a new experience. The machine never compromises until it is whipped. Accordingly, when public opinion demanded action on the Walker-Otis bill, the machine Senators began to talk of compromise. In fact, up to the hour of the vote on the bill in the Senate, Senator Wolfe did not stop whining compromise. In his speech against the passage of the bill, just before the final vote was taken he insisted: "There should have been a compromise measure agreed upon, a bill for which we all could have voted."

The moment before Wolfe had been warning the Senate that to pass the Walker-Otis bill would tend to wreck the Republican party in California. Just what the Walker-Otis bill had to do with Republican policies Mr. Wolfe would no doubt have difficulty in answering. But the measure did have much to do with machine policies. The machine had prevented the passage of the Anti-Gambling bill two years before, and was prepared to prevent the enactment of an effective anti-gambling law at the session of 1909. Senator Wolfe undoubtedly fell into the common error of mistaking the machine for the Republican party.

However, the spirit of no compromise which gave Senator Wolfe so much concern saved the Walker-Otis bill, and has given California an effective law. The lesson of the incident is that if effective laws are to be placed on the statute books, there can be no compromise with the machine. There was compromise with the machine in the direct primary issue, with the result that the Direct Primary law is in many respects a sham. But that is another story to be told in another chapter. The anti-machine element did not compromise with the machine on the Walker-Otis bill, with the result that an effective law was passed.

From the beginning, the anti-gambling element let it be known that no suggestion of compromise would be entertained. They announced boldly that if the machine succeeded in amending the measure, they, the anti-gambling Senators and Assemblymen, would work to prevent the passage of the amended bill. The position of these members of the Legislature who did not propose to be sidetracked by machine trickery is well illustrated by an interview with Senator Walker, which appeared in the Sacramento Bee on January 19.

"If the Hughes bill can not pass the California Legislature in the form that it was passed in New York," said Senator Walker, "I shall vote against the compromise or the amended bill. The people of California have made clear their desire that an effective anti-gambling law, such as New York enjoys, be placed on the statute books. To substitute anything else would be betrayal."[25]

So there was no compromise with the machine on the Walker-Otis bill, and the people were not betrayed, as they were to be later in the passage of the Direct Primary bill and the, Railroad Regulation bill, where there was compromise with the machine.

When the machine found there was to be no compromise, a curious series of mishaps became the lot of the Walker-Otis bill, particularly in the Senate. The measure, when introduced, was, in the ordinary course of legislation, referred to the Senate Committee on Public Morals. But it did not reach that committee until several days after its introduction. When the discovery was made that it had not reached the committee, a sensation budded but never bloomed. The facts, however, were brought out that the measure had been reposing in the pocket of a clerk instead of going to the committee. This "error" was corrected, and the bill turned over to its proper custodians.

Then came the discovery that the bill had not been properly printed; three words had been left out of the printed bill in the State printer's office. This "error," as soon as discovered by Senator Walker, was corrected. It was declared to be "trivial." But the "trivial" typographical and clerical errors in the Direct Primary bill in the final count gave the machine its opportunity to amend the measure to machine liking. The writer has no doubt in his own mind that the machine aimed to delay the passage of the Walker-Otis bill until the end of the session, as it did the Direct Primary bill, and then amend it to suit machine purposes or defeat it altogether.

Error even attended the recording of the passage of the bill. After a measure has passed the Senate, its title must be read and approved, and an order made transmitting it to the Assembly, all of which must be recorded in the Senate journal. The printed Senate journal of February 4, however, the day the bill was passed, merely recorded the passage of the bill. Nothing appeared about its title having been read, or that it had been transmitted to the Assembly. Walker discovered this "error," and a hasty inspection of the original minutes followed. The original minutes contained the proper record as follows: "Title read and approved. Bill ordered transmitted to the Assembly." But the two sentences had been omitted from the printed journal. The patient Walker had the correction made. None of these irregularities, however, resulted in serious delay. Those behind the measure watched their opponents closely, refused utterly to treat them with the "courtesy due Senators," in fact, acted under the assumption that the gambling element would stop at nothing to defeat the bill. This watchfulness is an important although comparatively minor reason why the bill was passed.

Then came the machine's move to pass "an anti gambling bill" as a substitute for the Walker-Otis measure. Martinelli in the Senate and Butler in the Assembly had introduced an Anti-Pool Selling, Anti-Book Making bill. The measure had much to commend it but was by no means so effective as the Walker-Otis bill. As a last straw, the gambling element grasped at the Martinelli-Butler bill, and threw their influence on the side of its passage. But here they again met with the uncompromising resistance of the reform element. There was nothing left for the machine to do but make its fight on the floor of Senate and of Assembly. And the fight came on in a way and with a suddenness which brought consternation upon the machine forces.

[23] The Walker-Otis bill is in full as follows:

Section 1. A new section is hereby added to the Penal Code to be known as Section three hundred and thirty-seven a thereof and to read as follows:

aye. Every person, who engages in pool selling or bookmaking at any time or place; or who keeps or occupies any room, shed, tenement, tent, booth, or building, float or vessel, or any part thereof, or who occupies any place or stand of any kind, upon any public or private grounds within this State, with books, papers, apparatus or paraphernalia, for the purpose of recording or registering bets or wagers, or of selling pools, or who records or registers bets or wagers, or sells pools, upon the result of any trial or contest of skill, speed or power of endurance, of man or beast or between men or beasts, or upon the result of any lot, chance, casualty, unknown or contingent event whatsoever; or who receives, registers, records or forwards, or purports or pretends to receive, register, record or forward, in any manner whatsoever, any money, thing or consideration of value, bet or wagered, or offered for the purpose of being bet or wagered, by or for any other person, or sells pools, upon any such result; or who, being the owner, lessee, or occupant of any room, shed, tenement, tent, booth or building, float or vessel, or part thereof, or of any grounds within this State, knowingly permits the same to be used or occupied for any of these purposes, or therein keeps, exhibits or employs any device or apparatus for the purpose of recording or registering such bets or wagers, or the selling of such pools, or becomes the custodian or depositary for gain, hire or reward of any money, property or thing of value, staked, wagered or pledged, or to be wagered or pledged upon any such result; or who aids, assists or abets in any manner in any of the said acts, which are hereby forbidden, is punishable by imprisonment in a county jail or State prison for a period of not less than thirty days and not exceeding one year.

[24] Had not the people of the Twenty-ninth and Thirty-first Senatorial Districts revolted against the machine at the general election of 1908, the Walker-Otis bill would probably have been defeated in the Senate. In the chapter dealing with the passage of the Miller-Drew Reciprocal Demurrage bill, it will be shown how the Democratic Senators Holohan and Campbell were elected in the Republican Twenty-ninth and Thirty-first Senatorial Districts, not because they were Democrats, but because the Republicans of those districts, recognizing the real issue before the State - the machine against the anti-machine element - voted for Holohan and Campbell, knowing them to be for good government and a "square deal" for all. Holohan and Campbell were from the beginning foremost in their support of the Anti-Racetrack Gambling bill. To be sure, at the final vote, only seven Senators voted against the measure. But it is generally conceded that when the session opened, the gamblers had nineteen Senators who could have been prevailed upon to vote against an effective anti-gambling bill. Had machine men sat in the seats occupied by Holohan and Campbell, the gamblers would have had twenty-one votes in the Senate, and the Walker-Otis bill would have been defeated.

[25] Much of the credit for this determined stand is due Earl H. Webb, president of the Anti-Racetrack Gambling League, who managed the fight for effective anti-racetrack gambling legislation not only during the session of the Legislature, but before the Legislature convened. Mr. Webb first convinced himself that the Walker-Otis bill would stop pool selling and bookmaking; and that the measure would stand the test of honest interpretation by the courts. Then he made his fight for it. To Mr. Webb, more than to any other one person, is due the credit for its passage.

CHAPTER VII.

Passage of the Walker-Otis Bill.

Anti-Machine Element Forced the Issue and Compelled Early Action on the
Measure - Evidence That Machine Planned to Defeat or Amend the Bill by Delaying Its Passage Until Toward the End of the Session.

As one looks back over the exciting first five weeks of the session, when the Walker-Otis bill was under consideration, it is plain that the machine would have preferred to have made its initial fight in the Senate. If defeated in the Senate, the enemies of the measure could have jockeyed for delay, prevented the passage of the measure until the closing hours of the session, and then killed it or forced its supporters to accept amendments.

But the initial fight did not come in the Senate. The Assembly was the battle-ground. The reason for this lies principally in the fact that while Assemblyman W. B. Griffiths, of Napa, raises fast horses, he is not a gambler, and is as much opposed to the bookmaking, pool-selling features of the track as Senator Walker himself. Griffiths was made chairman of the Assembly Committee on Public Morals. While this committee has sundry sins to answer for, nevertheless it made an astonishingly clean record on the Walker-Otis bill. On January 18, less than three weeks after the Legislature had assembled, Chairman Griffiths called his committee together to take up the Walker-Otis bill.

Of the nine members of the committee, seven were present, Mott and Mendenhall alone failing to answer to their names. Those present were: Griffiths, Cattell, Young, Dean, Perine, Fleisher and Wilson. The seven members went through the bill paragraph by paragraph and decided unanimously to recommend it for passage.

Had a dynamite bomb been set off under the Emeryville gambling establishment, greater consternation could scarcely have seized upon the pro-gambling element. The gamblers realized that the committee's prompt action threatened the machine's plan to delay action on the measure until the closing days of the session. For the moment all interest centered in Mott and Mendenhall, the two members of the committee who had been absent when the measure had been considered. Twenty-four hours developed the fact that Mendenhall sanctioned the action of his seven associates. This made eight of the nine committeemen for the bill. But the ninth member, Assemblyman Mott of Alameda County, was very much offended at what the committee had done.

Assemblyman Mott was elected as a Lincoln-Roosevelt League member. Probably the Lincoln-Roosevelt League does not like to be reminded of that unfortunate fact. But the lesson of Mr. Mott is so necessary for the Lincoln-Roosevelt League and all other reform movements that the conspicuous part which Mott played against reform policies cannot be too much insisted upon. To be sure, Mr. Mott voted for the bill when it was up for passage - the Lincoln-Roosevelt Republican platform of his county pledged him to it. But there is a deal of difference between supporting a measure and voting for it[26].

Mott was very much offended at what the committee had done and demanded that another meeting be held. Such a meeting, to accommodate Mr. Mott, was held - held in the office of Speaker Phil Stanton; held behind closed doors; held with Jerk Burke, Southern Pacific lobbyist, safely entrenched across the hall from Speaker Stanton's office in the back office of Sergeant-at-Arms Stafford[27].

But Mott failed to change the position of his eight associates. The further consideration of the measure by the committee which he demanded was denied. He accordingly took the fight for reconsideration to the floor of the Assembly. The fact that eight of the committee were against him, apparently had no weight at all with Mr. Mott.

Failing to force the committee to reconsider its action in recommending that the bill pass, Mott told his troubles to the Assembly. In the Assembly Mott moved that the measure be re-referred to the Committee on Public Morals, eight members of which had joined in recommending that it "do pass."

The motion was lost by a vote of 53 to 23. This was recognized as the test vote in the Assembly on the Anti Racetrack Gambling bill. That the opponents of the bill failed to make a better showing fairly paralyzed the pro-gambling lobby. Mott, chagrined and discomfited, retired in confusion[28].

Assemblyman Gibbons managed at this point to tie the bill up for another day, by giving notice that on the day following, he would move that the vote by which the bill was refused reference to the Committee on Public Morals be reconsidered. The day following Mr. Gibbons made his motion but was voted down, thirty Assemblymen supporting and forty-eight opposing him[29].

The Gibbons motion having been disposed of, Assemblyman Butler moved to amend the measure, by substituting for it the Martinelli-Butler bill. But again did the anti-gambling element force the issue. The motion was lost by a vote of 23 to 52.

Other proposed amendments having been voted down, Mr. Otis moved that the bill be put on its passage the next day, January 21. This was a final blow at the machine's purpose to delay the passage of the bill as long as possible, and was met with determined opposition. But the motion prevailed by a vote of 44 to 32.

The bill was on the following day put upon its final passage. The writer considers the real test vote on the bill was cast on Mott's motion to refer the measure back to the Committee on Public Morals. The vote on the passage of the measure counts for little under the circumstances. Sixty-seven Assemblymen voted for it; only ten - and every one of them from San Francisco - voted against it.

By consulting the table showing the six votes on this bill - Table "D" of the appendix - it will be seen that eleven of the twenty-three Assemblymen who voted for Mott's motion to refer the measure back to the Committee on Public Morals voted for its final passage. Two, Baxter and Schmitt, who had voted for the Mott resolution, were absent when the final vote on the bill was taken, leaving only ten who had voted for the Mott resolution to vote against the bill. The eleven who had voted for Mott's motion, but who switched to safety when the vote on the bill's passage came, were: Beardslee, Greer, Johnson of Sacramento[30], Johnson of San Diego, Johnston of Contra Costa, Moore, Mott, Nelson, Odom, Wagner, Webber - 11.

There was just one more parliamentary move by which the Walker-Otis bill could be delayed in the Assembly, to give notice of a motion to reconsider the vote by which the measure had been passed. Grove L. Johnson came to the rescue with the notice. This tied the bill up for another twenty-four hours. On the 2nd Johnson made his motion to reconsider but was defeated by a vote of nineteen to fifty-seven.

The table of the six votes on the Walker-Otis bill shows at a glance who voted consistently for the measure on all of the numerous roll calls; who voted consistently against it; and who were pulled backward and forward, voting one moment to satisfy the public demand that the bill be passed, and the next on the side of the gambling interests[31].

Public opinion was running high for the passage of the Walker-Otis bill by the time the measure reached the Senate, after passing the Assembly, but the bill might still have been held up in the Senate committee[32] had it not been for the ridiculous attack which Tom Williams, president of the California jockey Club, made upon all who supported the measure, or all who Williams thought supported it.

The occasion was a public hearing before the Senate Committee on Public Morals, at which Williams was asked to present the side of the opponents of the bill. The crowd that filled the Senate chamber expected from Williams some reasons why the measure should be denied passage, but it was disappointed.

Instead of giving reasons in support of his position, Williams introduced the methods of the barroom into the Senate chamber. He dramatically gave Rev. Frank K. Baker, of Sacramento, the lie, under conditions which stamped Williams as a bully and a coward. His uncalled-for attack on Dr. Baker would have killed his argument, but not content with this, he made probably the most astounding attack on the Protestant clergy of the country ever heard in California, certainly the most astonishing ever heard in the Senate chamber of the State[33].

The racetrack man's tirade did not give the reasons for continuance of gambling, which the people expected to hear from him. Finally, when Williams was swamped by questions which his insolence and tactlessness had provoked, Senator Frank Leavitt came to his rescue by moving adjournment. Leavitt's motion prevailed, but not until Williams had effectively settled the fate of the Walker-Otis bill.

The Committee on Public Morals reported the bill back the next day with the recommendation that it do not pass. The recommendation was that of Weed, Wolfe and Leavitt. While Kennedy and Savage failed to vote for the recommendation, they made no minority report. But even with the unfavorable report, the measure passed the Senate by a vote of 33 to 7. In the eleventh hour, uncertain Senators like Welch joined the winning side, but the showing made by the gamblers was, all things considered, better than could have been expected[34].

In the Senate and Assembly, out of a total vote of 120, the gambling element, which had year after year succeeded in preventing the passage of an anti-racetrack gambling bill, commanded on the measure's final passage but seventeen votes. The incident illustrates what aroused public opinion, when it finds expression in a definite plan of action, can compel.

But even with the measure's final passage, the delays that attended it continued. It passed the Senate on Thursday, February 4. By the following Saturday, the measure had been correctly engrossed, but could not go to the Governor until it had received the signature of Speaker Stanton of the Assembly. Stanton was out of town. As a result, it was February 10, six days after it had passed the Senate, before it went to the Governor. Governor Gillett took nine days to sign it, the Senate History showing that it was approved on February 19. Because of the delays the gamblers were enabled to complete their season at the Emeryville track.

[26] Of the six votes taken in the Assembly on the Walker-Otis bill issue, Mott in effect voted four times against the immediate passage of the measure. See Table "D."

[27] It was Jerk Burke's first appearance at the capital for the session. The danger which threatened the gambling element brought to the capital every machine lobbyist within reach, from Frank Daroux down. It was an anxious hour for the machine.

[28] This first test vote in the Assembly on the Walker-Otis bill was as follows:

For Mott's motion, and in effect against the bill: Baxter, Beardslee, Beban, Black, Coghlan, Collum, Cullen, Greer, Hopkins, Johnson of Sacramento (Grove L.), Johnson of San Diego, Johnston of Contra Costa, Macauley, McManus, Moore, Mott, Nelson, Odom, O'Neil, Pugh, Schmitt, Wagner, Webber. - 23.

Against Mott's motion, and in effect for the bill: Barndollar, Bratty, Bohnett, Butler, Callan, Cattell, Collier, Costar, Cronin, Dean, Drew, Flavelle, Fleisher, Flint, Gerdes, Gibbons, Gillis, Griffiths, Hammon, Hanlon, Hans. Hawk, Hayes, Hewitt, Hinkle, Holmquist, Irwin, Johnson of Placer, Juilliard, Kiwi, Leeds, Lightner, Maher, McClellan, Melrose, Mendenhall, Otis, Perine, Polsley, Preston, Pulcifer, Rech, Rutherford, Sackett, Silver, Stanton, Stuckenbruck, Telfer, Transue, Whitney, Wilson, Wylie, Young - 53.

[29] The several votes taken on the Walker-Otis bill will be found In the table "D" of the appendix.

[30] Johnson of Sacramento voted for the bill to give notice that he would the next day move for its reconsideration. Reconsideration can be secured only by a member voting with the majority. Had Johnson voted against the bill he could not have secured its reconsideration.

[31] Attention is called to the vote on reconsideration of Assemblyman Feeley, of Alameda, another Lincoln-Roosevelt member Mr. Feeley was absent when the vote on Mott's motion was taken. But Mr. Feeley voted for the bill when it was on final passage, thus keeping his record straight. But Mr. Feeley hastened to vote for reconsideration of the measure.

Mr. Feeley, like Mr. Mott, was nominated by the Lincoln-Roosevelt League because he could be elected. Mr. Feeley furnishes another example of the folly of which reformers are sometimes guilty, of nominating men whose best recommendation seems to be that they can be elected. To be elected is very important, to be sure; but if a man when elected to the Legislature is to vote against reform policies, why should the anti-machine element nominate him, thereby losing all the chance they, might have had of electing a man who would be in sympathy with their endeavors?

[32] In 1907, a measure similar to the Walker-Otis bill was killed in this way. It passed the Assembly and was in the Senate referred to the Senate Committee on Public Morals. The committee refused to report it back to the Senate, and friends of the measure could not secure enough votes on the floor of the Senate to compel the committee to act. The committee (1907) consisted of Senators Irish, Leavitt, Lynch, Wolfe and Kennedy. Irish and Lynch did not sit in the Senate of 1909, and could not be reappointed to the committee. But Lieutenant- Governor Porter distinguished himself by reappointing to the committee Wolfe, Leavitt and Kennedy. Weed and Savage were added to take the places left vacant by Irish and Lynch. Weed in 1907 voted with Leavitt, Wolfe and Kennedy against compelling the committee to release the Anti-Racetrack Gambling bill. Senator Savage (1907) voted for the bill's release, but Senator Savage at the opening of the session of 1909, was at least counted as opposed to the Walker-Otis bill. The gambling element had no complaint to make of the Committee on Public Morals which Lieutenant- Governor Porter had appointed.

[33] Williams was not the only gambler who injured the gamblers' cause that night. Frank Daroux, keeper of the notorious Sausalito poolrooms, interrupted A. J. Treat, of Sausalito, who was speaking for the Walker-Otis bill, to demand of him how it is that at the polls the gamblers of that city invariably defeat the anti-gambling element.

"You will remember, Mr. Daroux," came back Treat, "that at the last general election you and I discussed that question?"

"Yes," was the reply.

"And I asked you why you were in politics?" continued Treat.

"Yes," said Daroux.

"And you told me," insisted Treat, "that you were in politics for principle."

"Yes," admitted the pool seller.

"And I asked you how you spelt it then; and I ask you how you spell it now?"

The crowd that packed the Senate Chamber, even the scores of racetrack touts that had been rushed to Sacramento to give weight to the side of the gamblers, went wild at this. Treat was cheered to the echo. Daroux slunk back into his seat silenced and was not heard from again the whole evening.

[34] The vote was as follows:

For the bill: Anthony, Bates, Bell, Bills, Birdsall, Black, Boynton, Burnett, Caminetti, Campbell, Cartwright, Curtin, Cutten, Estudillo, Holohan, Hurd, Kennedy, Lewis, Martinelli, McCartney, Miller, Price, Roseberry, Rush, Sanford, Savage, Stetson, Strobridge, Thompson, Walker, Welch, Willis, Wright - 33.

Against the bill: Finn, Hare, Hartman, Leavitt, Reily, Weed, Wolfe - 7.

CHAPTER VIII.

The Direct Primary Bill.

Parallel Between It and the Walker-Otis Bill - Attempt to Placate the Machine Weakened Position of Its Supporters - Most Serious Criticism Came from Advocates of the Direct Primary Idea - What the Original Measure Provided - Machine's Plan of Campaign.

The parallel between the Walker-Otis Anti-Racetrack Gambling bill and the Wright-Stanton Direct Primary bill furnishes the most suggestive feature of the Legislative session. Each was based on a demand of a large majority of the people of the State for the correction of an abuse; the one to prevent the prostitution of the race-course in the interest of the gambling element; the second to prevent the domination in public affairs of the corrupt, corporation-backed political boss.

Each had been discussed in the public prints for months previous to the convening of the Legislature, and each had been made in the popular view of affairs a sort of test by which the Legislature was to be judged.

Each had the support of not only the better element of electors, but the better element of each House of the Legislature. Each had the determined secret opposition, and so far as it dared, the open opposition of the machine.

The campaign which the machine planned against the bills was practically the same in each instance - to amend the measures into a condition of ineffectiveness, and then pass them as sop to The People. This would have given The People a Direct Primary law without a direct primary; an Anti-Gambling law that would neither close poolrooms nor interfere with bookmaking.

And here the parallel ends.

The proponents of the Anti-Gambling bill introduced an Anti-Gambling measure, showed that it was the best that could be drawn, and let it be known that they (the supporters of the measure) would, if it were amended by the machine, vote against it.

The proponents of the Direct Primary bill, on the other hand, seemed possessed of the notion that they must placate the machine if any Direct Primary bill were to be passed.

The backers of the Anti-Gambling bill treated the machine leaders as recognized enemies of the measure, with whom there could be no compromise. The backers of the Direct Primary bill treated the machine leaders as friends and allies, inviting them to offer suggestion and advice.

The results of the two campaigns speak for the effectiveness of the two methods. The Anti-Gambling element put through an effective Anti-Gambling bill, refusing to compromise on so much as the change of a comma. But in the case of the Direct Primary bill, the machine not only had the last word, but in the feature of the nomination of United States Senators, the real bone of contention, amended the measure very much to its liking.

Long before the Legislature convened it was common talk at San Francisco that the backers of the Direct Primary bill were willing to accept any sort of a bill, so long as a direct primary measure be passed. Inasmuch as it is quite possible that a legislative enactment called Direct Primary law may be a trifle worse than no Direct Primary law at all, the jelly-fish attitude of the leaders in the movement caused no little unfavorable comment.

It did not seem to occur to the self-constituted leaders that their proper course was to draw up the most effective measure possible, let its effectiveness be known to the people - as was done in the case of the Anti-Gambling bill - and insist that the Legislature go on record for or against it.

Instead, they endeavored to satisfy everybody, apparently attempted to come to a compromise understanding with the machine, or at least to please machine leaders. Their theory seemed to be that if the measure were not made too effective, the machine would not seriously oppose its passage, thus insuring a glorious and at the same time, easy victory.

However unwarranted this assumption from appearances may be, such hidebound machine men as Wolfe and Leavitt were consulted and flattered, apparently with the idea that although they had been abused like pickpockets on previous occasions, they could be won over to the Direct Primary cause.

The stupidity of this policy was shown at the end of the session, when Wolfe and Leavitt dictated the terms under which the Direct Primary bill should pass. Had the supporters of the Anti-Gambling bill pursued the same policy, and treated the machine leaders as possible friends instead of recognized enemies, Wolfe, Leavitt and the other machine leaders would unquestionably have dictated the provisions of the Anti-Gambling bill, and have forced that compromise which Wolfe in his speech on the Walker-Otis bill regretted so bitterly had not been made.

The purpose of the Direct Primary is primarily to take away from the political bosses the monopoly which the convention system gives them in naming candidates for office, and to place such nomination in the hands of

The People. To this end, under the Direct Primary laws that have of recent years been adopted, the boss-controlled convention is done away with, and the candidate for office nominated by the direct vote of The People.

The play of the machine was to make the direct nomination difficult and impracticable and, if possible, entirely ineffective. The real supporters of the Direct Primary idea aimed to make the nomination as simple as possible, and easily attained, that genuine expression of the choice of the electors could be secured.

But instead of aiming at simplicity and direct methods, the Direct Primary bill, introduced in the Senate by Wright and in the Assembly by Stanton[35], threw a confusing mass of partisan detail about the selection of the primary candidate. It was made practically impossible for an independent citizen believing in the principles of a given party, but withholding his right to exercise the citizen's judgment at the polls, to become a primary candidate. Throughout, the measure made it smooth sailing for the mere partisan and extremely hard for independent Republican or independent Democrat to secure party nomination[35a].

For example, the candidate for party nomination, was, according to the terms of the bill, required not only to set forth the name of the party under which he might seek nomination, but to make affidavit "that he affiliated with said party at the last preceding general election, and either that he did not vote thereat, or voted for a majority of the candidates of said party at said next preceding general election, and intends to so vote at the ensuing election."

Thus, no citizen who had not supported the majority of his party candidates at the previous election, and who was unwilling to take an oath before their nomination, to support a majority of the candidates at the next ensuing election, was to be eligible for primary nomination to office.

But this, and similar unfortunate provisions were practically lost sight of in the fight made over the provisions for the nomination of United States Senators, and remained in the measure as it was finally enacted into law.

It may be, as the machine element contends, that provision for the nomination of United States Senators has no place in a Direct Primary law, but the fact remains that The People have inseparably linked with the direct primary idea the selection of United States Senators by direct vote.

The Federal laws provide that United States Senators shall be elected by the Legislature. But in States where Direct Primary laws have been adopted, provisions have been made by which the names of candidates for the United States Senate are placed on the primary ballot the same as the name of any other candidate for a State office. The same Direct Primary laws give candidates for the Legislature opportunity to pledge themselves to accept The People's decision, and as members of the Legislature to cast their votes for such candidate for the United States Senate as The People may have named.

The Legislature is thus made to abide by The People's will in electing United States Senators, precisely as the Electoral College is made to abide by The People's will in the election of the President.

To be sure, no candidate for the Legislature need take the pledge if he does not care to do so, but it is recognized that where it is possible for the voter to express a choice for United States Senator, the legislative candidate who fails to pledge himself to respect The People's choice would stand slim chances of election.

The Direct Primary law adopted by Oregon[35b] represents the highest development of the plan for popular selection of United States Senators. In that State the candidate for the United States Senate is nominated the same as any other candidate, the names of each successful primary nominee going on the regular ballot the same as that of any candidate for State office.

The Senatorial candidate who receives the highest number of votes is not, of course, elected to the United States Senate, but candidates to the Legislature are given opportunity to pledge themselves to respect the wishes of the voters and elect to the Senate the candidate who is thus endorsed. The Legislative candidate may sign such a pledge, or he may sign a statement that he will regard the popular vote for United States Senator as merely advisory and not binding.

But it is noticeable that in Oregon and other States where such wholesome direct primary measures have become laws the legislative candidate signs the pledge to abide by the mandate of the electors.

Unquestionably The People of California expected some such provision in the California Direct Primary law. Unfortunately, however, Senator Wright, who had charge of the bill, is not at all in sympathy with the Oregon plan. It is claimed that the framers of the bill were as little in sympathy with the Oregon plan as Senator Wright himself. At any rate, the bill, as a sort of compromise, gave the electors opportunity to express their choice for United States Senator within party lines. The candidate for the Legislature was to be given opportunity to pledge himself to abide, not by the selection of the electors of the State, but by the selection of the electors of his party[36].

The name of a candidate for the United States Senate did not, under the original Wright-Stanton bill, go on the final ticket. His choice was confined to the primaries and was at best to be regarded only by the legislators of his own political faith. The People of California were not to be given a direct vote in the selection of United States Senators, as are The People of Oregon.

If the framers of the Wright-Stanton Primary bill thought that their compromise on the United States Senator feature of the measure would placate the machine, they were much disappointed. The machine fought the arrangement for popular selection of United States Senators within party lines as positively as it would have combated the Oregon plan itself.

Under either plan, the machine recognized there was always danger that the selection of a United States Senator would actually be made by The People. This would mean loss to the machine of Federal patronage, and Federal patronage is the sure rock upon which the machine in California is founded. Indeed, had either plan been incorporated into law, the re-election of Senator Frank Flint would have been made practically impossible. So the machine fought the Wright-Stanton plan as stubbornly as it would have opposed the Oregon plan.

On the other hand, the best supporters of the Direct Primary idea were much disappointed that the Oregon plan had not been incorporated into the bill. Not a few of them grew lukewarm in their support of the measure. The extreme partisanship of its provisions and the failure to provide for popular selection of United States Senators hurt the measure with its friends, and failed to placate its enemies. From the beginning the most effective arguments against the bill were found in the bill itself.

This was demonstrated at the public hearing, held January 26th, to consider the various provisions of the measure. The principal speakers were Hiram Johnson and Judge John F. Davis.

Mr. Johnson dealt with the Direct Primary in a general way. He spoke of it in its relation to practical politics, showing that an effective Direct Primary would place this Government of ours back into the hands of The People. That is what was wanted. Every point Johnson made was received with applause from the crowd that packed the Senate Chamber. And when Johnson concluded with an appeal for "a Direct Primary law that shall be a Direct Primary law in substance and not in form alone," he was cheered to the echo.

Judge Davis was not so fortunate in his text as was Mr. Johnson. Davis was there to discuss the details of the bill. He had scarcely begun before he found himself between a cross fire of questions from those on the one side who wanted an effective measure passed and on the other from those who wanted no Direct Primary at all. The opponents of the Direct Primary scored few points; the believers in the measure did.

To save himself from a ridiculous position, Davis had to evade the question whether he would rather see an able and effective Democrat elected to the United States Senate than a vicious and corrupt Republican. He failed as miserably in attempting to justify the extreme partisan features of the bill. And the questions which Judge Davis could not answer came from men who wanted to see an effective Direct Primary measure enacted, not from the opponents of the Direct Primary theory.

Of course this dissatisfaction of the advocates of an effective law encouraged the machine to action. The measure was deliberately left with the Committee on Election Laws. The Anti-Gambling bill had passed both Houses by February 4th, one month after the session had opened. But on that date, the Committee had just begun consideration of the measure. To be sure, the Election Laws Committee had been stacked against the Direct Primary bill, but the Public Morals Committee had been stacked against the Anti-Gambling bill as well. But the opponents of racetrack gambling were satisfied with the Walker-Otis bill, while the proponents of the Direct Primary for California were by no means satisfied with the Wright-Stanton bill.

So the machine dared do with the Direct Primary bill what it did not dare do with the Anti-Gambling bill. The Walker-Otis bill had a standing which the Wright-Stanton bill did not have.

That the Committee on Election Laws did not act early in the session on the Direct Primary bill was not because of the purpose of Senator Estudillo, Chairman of the Committee. Time after time did Estudillo call meetings for consideration of the bill, and repeatedly, he found only himself, and Senators Stetson and Wright in attendance. Finally, in February, Senator Estudillo succeeded in getting his committee together for consideration of the all-important measure.

That the machine proposed to make the bill inoperative was recognized from the moment the committee was called to order. The manner in which this was to be done developed as rapidly. The machine's plan was as follows:

(1) As to candidates:

The machine proposed to amend the bill so that either a majority or a high plurality vote should be required to nominate candidates at the primary election. In the event of no candidate for a given office receiving a majority or the required plurality, the nomination was to be made by a nominating convention as under the old convention system. With such a provision it would have been easy for the machine to introduce a large number of candidates at the primaries, thus making it impracticable for any one of them to receive a majority or even a high plurality vote. This would have thrown nominations into a convention. Thus, while the State would have had a Direct Primary law, it would have been practically impossible to nominate a candidate under its provisions.

(2) As to United States Senators:

To deny The People a voice in the election of United States Senators, the machine had two plans:

(A) To cut all provisions for the election of United States Senators out of the bill.

(B) Failing in this, to amend the bill so that candidates for the Legislature would be required to regard the choice of the electors of their several districts as advisory. The vote was in no way to be held binding, nor was a legislative candidate to be required to sign a pledge to regard in any way the wishes of the electors. Under this arrangement there could be as high as 100 candidates for the United States Senate endorsed at a single election - eighty from Assembly, twenty from Senatorial districts. The effect would be, of course, the endorsement of at least several candidates, with the result that the Legislature would in the end be left to choose as under the present system. Thus, while the State would have a law which apparently gave The People a voice in the naming of Federal Senators, there would be no change whatever in the manner in which the Federal Senators were nominated and elected.

[35] In addition to the Wright-Stanton bill, Senator Roseberry introduced a measure providing for a postal primary. In the appendix will be found Senator Roseberry's views on the postal primary plan.

[35a] The writer has been reliably informed that this concession was made to the machine before a member of the Legislature reached Sacramento.

[35b] Senator Caminetti introduced a separate bill providing the Oregon plan for the popular choice of United States Senators. He was requested not to press its passage BECAUSE IT MIGHT INJURE THE CHANCES OF PASSAGE OF THE DIRECT PRIMARY BILL. The machine claquers is never at a loss for an excuse for the defeat of a meritorious measure.

[36] The original Wright-Stanton bill provided two pledges, which the candidate for the Legislature was given opportunity to sign. The first pledge bound him to abide by the choice of the electors of his party for United States Senator. It read as follows:

"I further declare to The People of California and to The People of the .... (Senatorial or Assembly) District that during my term of office, without regard to my individual preference, I will always vote for that candidate for United States Senator in Congress who shall have received for that office the highest number of votes cast by my party at the September primary election next preceding the election of a Senator in Congress."

If the legislative candidate did not care to sign this pledge, he was given the alternative of signing the following:

"I further declare to The People of California and to The People of the ... (Senatorial or Assembly) District that during my term of office I shall consider the vote of The People at any primary election for United States Senator as nothing more than a recommendation, which I shall be at liberty wholly to disregard, if I see fit."

CHAPTER IX.

Machine Defeated in the Senate.

Reform Forces, Regardless of Party, Unite to Secure the Passage of an Effective Direct Primary Law-Agree on a Compromise Measure and Succeed in Forcing It Through the Senate - Machine Badly Beaten.

Senator Leroy A. Wright of San Diego introduced the Direct Primary bill in the Senate on January 17th, and during the month that it slumbered in the Senate Committee on Election Laws there was no reason to believe that Senator Wright was not in sympathy with the provisions of the measure. On February 1st, however, Senator Wright made the astonishing confession before the Committee on Election Laws that he was not in sympathy with that provision of his bill which gave legislative candidates opportunity to pledge themselves to abide by the choice of the electors of the State for United States Senator. From that moment began Senator Wright's fight against his own bill, which finally landed him in the camp of Leavitt, Wolfe and the other machine Senators.

At the meeting of the Senate Committee on Election Laws, held February 1st, the solid six on the Committee, Leavitt, Wolfe, Savage, Hartman, Kennedy and Hare, had voted two amendments into the bill which rendered it absolutely useless for practical purposes.

The first amendment provided that a majority instead of a plurality vote should nominate, a provision as unconstitutional as impracticable. The second amendment cut out of the measure all provision for popular vote for United States Senators.

This decided action on the part of the machine had brought consternation upon Estudillo and Stetson who wanted to see an effective measure passed. Wright in this crisis took the floor to state his position.

"For my part," said Wright, "I would never sign a pledge to vote for the candidate for United States Senator in Congress who shall have received for that office the highest number of votes cast by my party. I do believe, however, that the people of this State demand a partisan Direct Primary law. But I think that the people of Oregon recognize that they have made a mistake in going so far as they have. Under the pledge required of candidates for the Legislature in the measure before us (the Wright bill) a member of the Legislature might find himself compelled to vote for a candidate whom the voters of his district opposed. I opposed this provision when the bill was drawn, but my objection was overruled. I now stand for the bill as it has been introduced."

Wolfe, Leavitt and the rest of the machine Senators grinned exultantly as Wright stated that he did not approve the provisions of his own bill. But the faces of Estudillo and of Stetson, who had been looking upon Wright as their leader in the pro-primary fight, fell. To employ the famous expression of Speaker Stanton of the Assembly, they felt the ground slipping from under their feet. There was a sensation of farther slipping, when Wright, author of the measure, pro-primary leader and Call-heralded reformer, offered an amendment as substitute for popular State-wide choice for United States Senator, by making the vote for United States Senator advisory only[37].

The grin of satisfaction on the faces of the machine Senators broadened as Wright read his amendment while the faces of Estudillo and Stetson grew blanker. But the machine Senators were in no hurry. Things were coming their way; there was no reason for them to rush matters. So they lazily took twenty-four hours to think it over. Then they bluntly rejected Wright's compromise, the solid six, Wolfe, Leavitt, Savage, Hartman, Kennedy and Hare voting against its acceptance.

Estudillo and Stetson voted to accept the compromise. They explained their votes. Their explanations showed their earnestness in working for the best Direct Primary measure that could be passed - which indicates what might have been done under other leadership - and a loyalty to Wright, the accepted leader in the Direct Primary fight, which, to say the least, was misplaced.

"With this amendment," said Senator Stetson, in explaining his vote, "the bill is not one-half so strong as it was before. I do not like it. But I must train with one side or with the other, and for that reason shall vote for Senator Wright's substitute."

Senator Estudillo stated that he voted for the amendment against his better judgment.

"I don't believe in your amendment, Senator Wright," said Estudillo, turning to that gentleman. "I don't think it amounts to anything. I vote with you against my better judgment. I do not believe that this amendment will give The People what they want - an opportunity to vote directly for candidates for the United States Senate. My opinion is that we should pass a good bill or no bill at all. I shall, however, yield to Senator Wright, who is the recognized leader in this Direct Primary fight, and vote for his amendment."

And then the six machine members rejected the amendment.

There wasn't much left of the Direct Primary bill. The measure was, on February 16th, two weeks after the application of the committee's pruning knife, reported back to the Senate with all reference to election of United States Senators stricken from it, and the unconstitutional and impracticable majority vote required for the nomination of candidates for office, instead of the constitutional and practical plurality vote, as originally provided in the bill.

The fact should not be lost sight of that the two Senators on the Committee on Election Laws who led the fight against the Direct Primary bill, Leavitt and Wolfe, in the Committee on Public Morals led the fight against the Anti-Gambling bill. Nor should it be forgotten that two of their most docile followers in the Committee on Election Laws, Kennedy and Hare, are "Democrats." There was no partisanship shown in the ranks of the opponents of the Direct Primary bill; machine Democrats and machine Republicans united for its defeat. But when anti-machine Republican and anti-machine Democrats united for its passage, Wolfe and Leavitt were shocked beyond measure.

Machine Senators denounced the anti-machine Republicans as mongrels, enemies of the Republican party, and insisted that if the anti-machine Republicans persisted in continuing with the anti-machine Democrats to secure the passage of an effective Direct Primary law, the Republican party in California would go to smash.

The arrogant course of the machine members of the Election Laws Committee, had at least one good effect it drove the anti-machine Republicans and the anti machine Democrats together as a matter of self-defense. The anti-machine Republicans and Democrats saw the machine Democrats and Republicans united to defeat the passage of an effective Direct Primary measure. So the anti-machine Republicans and Democrats organized that they might successfully combat the organized machine Democrats and Republicans. For the first time in the history of the California Legislature, so far as the writer knows, the Senate divided on the only practical line of division for the enactment of good measures and the defeat of bad ones - with the anti-machine Senators on one side and the machine Senators on the other.

The "band-wagon" Senators of the Welch variety, and the doubtful Senators, were left for the moment to herd by themselves.

The anti-machine forces held meetings - caucuses if you like - to decide upon the course to be pursued. They numbered at first twenty members, fifteen Republicans and five Democrats. The Republicans were Bell, Birdsall, Black, Boynton, Burnett, Cutten, Estudillo, Hurd, Price, Roseberry, Stetson, Strobridge, Thompson, Walker and Wright; the

Democrats, Caminetti, Campbell, Cartwright, Miller and Holohan. George Van Smith, of the San Francisco Call, credited with being an expert on Direct Primary legislation, was admitted to the deliberations of the twenty.

Senator Price, however, became alarmed at the irregularity of anti-machine Republicans meeting with anti machine Democrats, gathered his virtuous partisan skirts about him and fled in dismay.

Senator Caminetti also left the meeting. Caminetti is a strong advocate of the Oregon plan for the election of United States Senators. When Caminetti found Senator Wright, the accepted leader of the pro-primary forces, opposed not only to the Oregon plan, but to any plan that would give electors a State-wide vote for United States Senators, he refused to go to Wright's assistance. Later on, however, when Wright went to Caminetti pleading for support, Caminetti agreed to abide by the decisions of the anti-machine caucus. Curiously enough, after the machine had worn the anti-machine forces out, Caminetti was the only Senator who refused to accept the machine's amendments to the bill which the anti-machine caucus had agreed upon.

With Price and Caminetti out, the anti-machine forces were reduced to eighteen Senators, although it was known that Rush sympathized with the movement but was not present because he had been unavoidably detained.

The eighteen organized by electing Senator Estudillo chairman, and Senator Boynton secretary. Senator Wright made a short address in which he virtually threw up his hands. He told what the Wolfe-Leavitt element had done with the bill in committee, and stated that unless the anti-machine forces got together, the machine would amend the measure into ineffectiveness. Following Wright's address the anti-machine Senators considered the original Wright-Stanton bill under three heads:

(1) Shall a mere plurality, or a majority, or a high plurality be required to nominate at a primary election?

(2) Shall the partisan features be eliminated from the measure?

(3) Shall the provisions of the measure be extended to the election of United States Senators?

The first question was brought up on Stetson's motion that a twenty-five per cent plurality be required to nominate. The machine aimed to fix the plurality at forty per cent, but even the twenty-five per cent compromise was denied. The motion received but four votes, in its favor.

Then came discussion of the clause quoted in the previous chapter, which requires of each primary candidate that he make affidavit that he supported his party ticket at the previous election, and proposes to support it at the coming election. It was understood by all who had any thing to do with the Direct Primary bill that the clause made it impossible for a primary candidate to run on two primary tickets. Cartwright moved that the clause be stricken from the bill. The motion was lost by a vote of 14 to 4. Senators like Black of Santa Clara voted against the motion in the interest of harmony, although personally they favored the elimination of all partisan features.

The question of primary nomination of candidates for the United States Senate was then taken up. Senator Wright moved that the vote for Senators be advisory only, and that it be by Assembly and Senatorial districts instead of State-wide, as the original bill provided. The vote was as follows:

For Wright's motion - Burnett, Wright - 2.

Against Wright's motion - Bell, Birdsall, Black, Boynton, Cartwright, Cutten, Holohan, Miller, Roseberry, Stetson, Strobridge, Walker - 12.

Excused from voting - Campbell, Estudillo, Hurd, Thompson.

A scene of great confusion followed. Campbell, who had refused to vote because he insisted upon the Oregon plan of electing United States Senators by direct vote of The People, insisted that the provision be incorporated into the bill. He refused to be bound by any plan that would restrict the election within party lines. So they blocked Campbell in one corner of the room with a table, and reasoned with him. Twenty-one votes were required to pass the Direct Primary bill in the Senate. At that time counting Rush, who was not present at the caucus, the anti-machine forces had only nineteen. They could not afford to lose even one of their number.

Above the confusion, Senator Holohan managed to make his voice heard.

"Gentlemen," he said, "I would like to have the Oregon plan incorporated into this bill, But that seems to be impracticable at this time. Eventually, I am sure California will adopt the Oregon plan of naming the United States Senator, which to my way of thinking is the most common sense, the fairest, the most American plan. But if we are to pass a Direct Primary measure at the present session, we must reach a basis of compromise. Let us now get together and stand together on a measure upon which we can all agree. Let us pledge ourselves to abide by the decision of this meeting, and stand or fall by the bill which we have agreed upon."

Holohan's counsel prevailed. The Senators present pledged themselves to abide by the decision of the meeting and to stand or fall by the bill which they had agreed upon. And Senator Leroy A. Wright was among them and was bound in honor as every Senator present was bound in honor to stand by the bill which had been agreed upon.

The uniting of the anti-machine Senators to fight the combined machine Democrats and Republicans called down upon the anti-machine element the denunciation of the machine press. The Catkins newspapers, for example, sputtered their condemnation of Republican Senators who would unite with Democratic Senators in "rump caucus."

On the other hand the San Francisco Call, at that time warmly supporting the anti-machine movement in the Senate, was extreme in denouncing Lieutenant-Governor Porter, presiding officer of the Senate, Leavitt, Wolfe, and all others who were opposing the passage of the Direct Primary measure as it had originally been introduced by Wright, and as it had been agreed upon in the reform caucus[38].

The fight in the Senate came on the second reading of the bill February 18th. On the 16th, however, the setting for the contest had been fixed by the majority of the Committee on Election Laws, which reported with favorable recommendation the measure as the Committee had cut it to pieces. The minority of the Committee, Estudillo, Stetson and Wright, reported back the bill agreed upon by the non-partisan caucus of anti-machine Senators.

But the fight did not come over either report. When the bill came up on the 18th for second reading and amendment, Senator McCartney, on behalf of the machine forces, introduced a resolution over which the contest waged. McCartney's resolution provided that the bill should be so amended that the primary vote for United States Senator should be by districts and advisory only, and that for county and local offices a vote of 25 per cent and for State offices a vote of 40 per cent should nominate[39].

The debate was over this resolution. The motion for its adoption was defeated by a vote of twenty-seven against to thirteen for[40].

Incidentally, the debate settled one of the most important questions affecting the bill, namely, the percentage of votes to be required for primary nominations. The machine, to render the measure inoperative, was contending for a majority or at least a high plurality vote, while the anti-machine element was contending for a mere plurality. The debate developed the fact, that any provision for other than a mere plurality vote would be unconstitutional. This service was performed by Senator Cutten of Humboldt[41]. Senator Cutten's clear presentation of this much discussed point, settled the vote percentage question right there. When the measure was under consideration by the Assembly Election Laws Committee, Grove L. Johnson did suggest that a 40 per cent plurality be required to nominate. But no serious attempt was made so to amend the bill, after Cutten's speech, and the defeat of the McCartney amendment.

Naturally, the anti-machine forces felt warmly encouraged by this complete defeat of the machine. The San Francisco Call, the recognized advocate of the Direct Primary bill, the next day, February 19th, said of the outcome:

"Twenty-seven Senators at Sacramento stood true to their party pledges, and voiced the will of the people in their votes on the Direct Primary bill yesterday. Thirteen other Senators wrote into the record conclusive proof of their unfitness for the offices they hold, when they voted against the Wright-Stanton bill, and for the corrupt political machine which is the Southern Pacific Railroad. Every man of these thirteen confessed corruptionists knew what he was doing, knew whose will he was putting above The People's. Every one of these thirteen betrayers of the public weal has written the epitaph of his political tombstone."

The Call was as generous in its praise of the anti-machine Democrats and Republicans as it was bitter against the machine Senators who had endeavored to force the McCartney amendment into the bill. While that paper printed the names of the thirteen in bold, black type on the first page under the heading, "These Men Voted for the Machine," in type just as bold and just as black it printed in an honor column the names of the twenty-seven who had voted against the McCartney amendment, under the heading, "These Men Voted for the People."

Said the Call in its admirable report of the defeat of the McCartney amendment, of the original nineteen anti-machine Senators who had organized to resist the machine:

"Genuine manhood has been on tap at every conference of the independents. They have not squabbled for partisan advantage. They have worked together to give The People an honest and genuine Direct Primary measure. Senator Wright won a brilliant fight. He won it with and through the earnest co-operation of the unbossed Democrats and Republicans."

Said the Call of the measure itself in its issue of February 18th - the day of the defeat of the machine Senators:

"The Direct Primary bill is The People's bill. Such men as Dooling, Wright, Stanton, Davis and Cartwright made it. There is no honest argument against it, there will be no honest Senators against it."

Such was the view of the Call on February 18. Few were willing to believe on that date that within a month the Call would have thrown its influence on the side of Leavitt and Wolfe and Warren Porter in an attempt to force part of the McCartney amendment into the Direct Primary bill. It did not seem possible then that within a month the Call would be denouncing, ridiculing and misrepresenting Senators whose efforts had resulted in the defeat of the McCartney amendment because of the refusal of these anti-machine Senators to join with the machine Senators whom they had once defeated, and accept the amendment which they had once rejected. It did not then seem possible that on March 18th the Call would be behind the thirteen "betrayers of the public weal," itself betraying the Senators whose "genuine manhood" had on February 18 appealed to its editors so strongly.

But such was to be. And, too, the combination of Calkins Syndicate, Lieutenant-Governor Porter, Senator Leroy A. Wright, the San Francisco Call and the thirteen "betrayers of the public weal" proved too much for the little band of anti-machine Senators. And what is more, backed by the Call, the machine leaders finally amended the Direct Primary bill, which on February 18th the Call had stated very positively no honest Senator would be against.

[37] Wright's amendment had been carefully typewritten before the meeting. It read as follows,

"Party candidates for the office of United States Senator shall have their name placed on the official primary election ballots of their respective parties in the manner herein provided for State Office, provided, however, that the vote for candidate for United States Senator shall be an advisory vote for the purpose of ascertaining the sentiment of the voters in their respective parties."

[38] On February 17th the Call said of Senator Eddie Wolfe's opposition to the bill:

"The fight (Direct Primary) promises to be both spirited and bitter. Eddie Wolfe of San Francisco, picked by the machine to make its fight for the garroting of the Direct Primary bill, by the injection of a majority nominating clause, has served notice that he proposes to tear the reformers to pieces."

Of Leavitt and other machine Senators, the Call on the same date said:

"Leavitt, who bossed the fight against the Otis-Walker bill, will furnish the brains for the fight against the Direct Primary bill, and every one of the seven who voted against the Otis-Walker bill, are more or less frankly against the primary bill. Savage, who did not vote against the Walker-Otis bill because his vote would have done no good, and Hartman and Hare, who did vote against the Otis-Walker bill, have gone on record against honest direct Primaries, as members of the majority of the Senate Committee on Election Laws. Savage is frank enough to admit that he is opposed to any direct primary law."

[39] The McCartney resolution was in full-as follows:

"Resolved, That Senate Bill No. 3, and all pending amendments thereto, be and the same is hereby referred to the Committee on Elections and Election Laws, with the following instructions:

"1. Amend the bill so as to give an advisory vote by districts on United States Senators."

"2. Amend the bill by providing for a percentage of votes before nomination by direct vote of the people, as follows: If the highest candidate for any county or local office receive less than 25 per cent of the vote of his party, and if the highest candidate for a State office receive less than 40 per cent of the vote of his party, that the nomination shall be referred to a convention of delegates elected at the same time that candidates are voted on by direct vote."

"3. Amend the bill by providing that the convention aforesaid shall prepare the platform of the party and perfect party organization."

[40] The vote in full was as follows:

Against the McCartney amendment and in effect for the bill agreed upon by the anti-machine Senators: Anthony, Bell, Birdsall, Black, Boynton, Burnett, Caminetti, Campbell, Cartwright, Curtin, Cutten, Estudillo, Holohan, Hurd, Lewis, Martinelli, Miller, Price, Roseberry, Rush, Sanford, Stetson, Strobridge, Thompson, Walker, Welch, Wright - 27.

For the McCartney amendment and in effect against the bill agreed upon by the anti-machine Senators: Bates, Bills, Finn, Hare, Hartman, Kennedy, Leavitt, McCartney, Reily, Savage, Weed, Willis, Wolfe - 13.

[41] Cutten showed that Section 13, Article XX of the State Constitution provides that "a plurality of the votes given at any election shall constitute a choice where not otherwise directed in this Constitution."

Senator Cutten then proceeded to demonstrate that a primary election is an election within the meaning of the terms used. The Supreme Court of Indiana has so declared, and, coming nearer home, Cutten showed that the California Supreme Court has so held also.

In The People vs. Cavanaugh, 112 California, the Supreme Court held that any primary election that should become mandatory becomes an election and only those primaries that may be optional with a party as to whether or not they should be held, are not elections.

The Wright-Stanton bill and the Direct Primary amendment to the Constitution make the direct primaries mandatory, nor is there anything in the State Constitution providing that anything other than a plurality vote shall be required to nominate. For the Legislature to have yielded to the machine's demand that a majority or high plurality vote be required to nominate and inserted such a provision in the Direct Primary bill, would have been to render that measure unconstitutional, for under the plain provisions of the Constitution only a plurality vote can be required to nominate.

Were a majority or even high percentage plurality vote required to nominate, the Direct Primary law would have been made unconstitutional, because:

1. A plurality might not be equal to the percentage or majority.

2. A percentage or majority contemplates a convention to nominate in case the candidate does not receive the percentage or majority, and a convention, the best authorities hold, is prohibited under the constitutional amendment providing for the primary election.

CHAPTER X.

Fight Over Assembly Amendments.

Machine Succeeds in Amending the Direct Primary Bill in the Assembly - Assemblyman Pulcifer at Critical Moment Votes with the Machine - Senate, Although Held Up By Machine Element for a Week, Refuses to Concur in Assembly's Action.

The machine Senators, having failed to amend the Direct Primary bill on its second reading, apparently accepted their whipping, and allowed the measure to go through third reading and final passage without opposition[42].

Twenty-seven Senators at the final roll call voted for it; not one vote was cast against it. Even Leavitt and Wolfe voted for it. The anti-machine Senators had won "a glorious victory."

But the victory was one tempered with grave misgivings on the part of careful observers of machine trickery. The fact that the bill as it had passed the Senate contained several serious clerical and typographical errors, and that its title was unsatisfactory if not defective, worried the genuine supporters of the bill not a little. The bill had been loosely drawn to begin with, and as originally introduced contained most unfortunate clerical errors, which bobbed up at most inopportune times.

At every stage of its passage in the Senate such errors were uncovered, and after it had passed second reading, no less than eight serious errors were discovered to be still in the bill. The only way these errors could be corrected was by amendment.

The errors were called to the attention of Senator Wright and of George Van Smith of the Call, who were urged to have them corrected in the Senate that the bill might go to the Assembly letter perfect, and without necessity of amendment[43]. But both Van Smith and Wright were of the opinion that time would be gained by leaving the Assembly to make the corrections.

The bill as it finally passed the Senate was a defective bill, the defects of which could be corrected in the Assembly only by amendment. In the end the fate of the measure was made to hinge on these clerical and typographical defects.

The Assembly Committee on Election Laws had been stacked against the passage of a Direct Primary bill, precisely as the Senate Committee had been. At the first meeting held by the Committee to consider the measure, it became evident that the majority of the Committee would, if it could, put the McCartney amendments, which had been defeated in the Senate, into the bill.

Leeds, Chairman of the Committee, moved that the primary vote for United States Senator be made advisory and by districts only, while Grove L. Johnson, in spite of the fact that such a provision is impracticable and unconstitutional, stated that he wished a provision in the bill requiring a 40 per cent plurality to nominate, instead of a mere plurality.

Leeds and Johnson, taken together, stood for precisely what the machine had stood for in the Senate, namely, an advisory, district vote for United States Senators and a 40 per cent plurality vote to nominate.

Speaker Stanton, although not a member of the Committee, was present at the meeting, and although he had introduced the bill in the Assembly, announced that he was for so amending the measure that the vote for United States Senator should be made merely advisory and by districts. This was pretty strong intimation that there was trouble ahead for the Direct Primary bill. Stanton was in effect throwing down his own bill.

After several meetings, the Committee adopted amendments providing for the Leeds - suggested advisory district vote for United States Senators, providing for correction of the clerical and typographical errors, and providing an oath from primary candidates that they would abide by the platform of their party to be adopted after their nomination. This last amendment was defeated in the Assembly.

The only real opposition in the Committee to the machine's plan to make the primary vote for United States Senators advisory only and by district, came from Assemblymen Hinkle of San Diego and Drew of Fresno. Drew was ill most of the time and could not attend the meetings. The brunt of the fight for a State-wide vote for United States Senators, therefore, fell on Hinkle.

He fought well.

Every effort was made to pull him down. He was told that his bills would be "killed."

He was deliberately misrepresented in papers which were endeavoring to force into the bill the advisory district vote amendment, which, as introduced in the Senate by McCartney, had been rejected by the anti-machine Senators. Leavitt and Wolfe and Warren Porter were for the amendment, but the anti-machine Senators continued against it as they had on February 18th, the day of their "glorious victory" over the machine in the Direct Primary fight.

But, astonishing as it may seem, the San Francisco Call[44], which up to the passage of the bill in the Senate had fought the machine Senators so valiantly, was giving indication of siding with Wolfe and Leavitt. In its issue of March 6th, the Call stated that Hinkle was alone of the Assembly Committee battling for the bill as it passed the Senate. In another sentence the Call said: "Leeds, Rech, Hinkle and Pugh voted for the advisory vote amendments."

That sentence was shown about the Capitol, and on it was based the story that Hinkle had "fallen down," and would vote with the machine. All this added to the confusion of the situation.

But Hinkle had not "fallen down." He was in the fight just as hard as ever, and with Assemblyman Bohnett organized the reform element in the Assembly to fight the machine amendments.

Those who were endeavoring to force the advisory district plan for nomination of Senators into the bill took the most astonishing methods to force it upon the anti-machine Senators. For example, the San Francisco Call of March 4th said of it:

"The amendments proposed by Leeds and supported by Stanton are not even remotely related to the McCartney proposition, which was voted down in the Senate."

The Call's statement was easily disproved, but it unquestionably confused the anti-machine legislators, who were insisting upon retaining the provision for State-wide vote for Senators in the bill[45].

And then came the cry that those who were opposing the Leeds-McCartney amendment were enemies of the Direct Primary, for the Assembly, it was alleged, was overwhelmingly in favor of the amendment, and would not pass the bill without it. Jere Burke, John C. Lynch, and other patriots of their ilk were most insistent in expression of this fear. But such men as Bohnett, Hinkle, Drew and other recognized anti-machine leaders in the Assembly were not to be bluffed in this way. They stood firmly for the passage of the bill as it had passed the Senate.

The fight on the floor of the Assembly came over Leeds' motion to amend the bill by making the vote for United States Senator advisory only and by districts. The vote on Leeds' motion was 37 to 37. The "overwhelming majority" favoring the amendment, in spite of the use of every pull at the command of the machine, had not materialized. As a majority vote was necessary to read the amendment into the bill, a moment more and Speaker

Stanton would have been forced to declare the amendment lost. This would have meant final defeat for the machine, and the Direct Primary bill as it had passed the Senate would have gone to final passage.

At this critical moment in the bill's history, however, Assemblyman Pulcifer[46], the Lincoln-Roosevelt League member from Alameda county, got into action. He had voted against the amendment. But with his vote really meaning defeat for the machine element, he promptly changed his vote from no to aye. This made the vote 38 for the amendment and 36 against it. The amendment which the anti-machine Senators had fought so valiantly and so effectively was finally read into the bill[47].

The amendments necessary to correct the typographical and clerical errors which had been permitted to remain in the bill as it passed the Senate, together with a number of ridiculous amendments - which were finally rejected by both Houses - were then adopted, and the bill sent to the Senate[48].

The fact developed almost immediately that if the Senate refused to concur in the Assembly amendment forcing the advisory district vote into the bill the Assembly would recede from the amendment. As a matter of fact Assemblyman Collum, who voted for the amendment March 9th, voted on March 22d to recede from it. Had the anti-machine forces in the Assembly been held together, as they could have been had the question of receding been put up to them fairly, few other changes with Collum's would have been sufficient to assure success for the anti-machine forces.

But in spite of the situation in the Assembly, Senator Wright, who was by this time working openly with Wolfe, Leavitt and Warren Porter to secure the adoption of the Leeds amendment (which as the McCartney amendment the Senate had already rejected), was insisting that the Assembly would not recede, and that unless the Senate concurred with the Assembly amendment, nothing could save the Direct Primary bill from being cut to pieces in Free Conference Committee.

Nevertheless, the Senate by a vote of 19 against to 20 for concurrence, did refuse to concur, 21 votes being necessary for concurrence.

Senator Stetson was absent when the vote was taken, being ill at his home in Alameda county. Had he been present he would have voted against concurrence in the amendments. This would have made the vote 20 to 20.

Originally, on February 18th, twenty-seven Senators had voted against the Leeds-McCartney amendment, but when Senator Wright switched to the machine, Senators Hurd and Burnett wobbled along after him. The four band-wagon Senators, Lewis, Martinelli, Price and Welch, tagged along after them. This made the vote:

Against concurrence in the amendment and for the bill as it passed the Senate - Anthony, Bell, Birdsall, Black, Boynton, Caminetti, Campbell, Cartwright, Curtin, Cutten, Estudillo, Holohan, Miller, Roseberry, Rush, Sanford, Strobridge, Thompson, Walker - 19.

For concurrence in the amendment and against the bill as it originally passed the Senate - Bates, Bills, Burnett, Finn, Hare, Hartman, Hurd, Kennedy, Leavitt, Lewis, Martinelli, McCartney, Price, Reily, Savage, Weed, Welch, Willis, Wolfe, Wright - 20.

Every one of the thirteen Senators who opposed the bill when it was first before the Senate, voted to concur. Wright, Welch, Price, Martinelli, Lewis, Burnett and Hurd joining them, made their number twenty.

Under the rules which govern the Senate, in the event of a tie vote, all the Senators voting, the President of the Senate, in this case Warren Porter, has the casting vote.

Had Senator Stetson been present, he would have voted with the anti-machine Senators. This would have made the vote 20 to 20. Warren Porter would then have had the deciding vote. He would have voted to concur. Senator Stetson's illness temporarily saved the Direct Primary bill.

In the ordinary course of legislative business, the Senate having refused to concur in the Assembly amendment, the bill would have gone back to the Assembly, the Assembly would have receded from the amendment, and the machine's defeat would have been final. But the quick-witted Wolfe saw a way to prevent such action. He promptly moved that the Senate reconsider the vote by which it had refused to concur in the Assembly amendment. Wolfe commanded twenty votes of the Senators present, the anti-machine element nineteen. Wolfe required, however, twenty-one to compel reconsideration. But when the question came up, Wolfe still lacked the one vote necessary for reconsideration, the anti-machine element was still without the necessary twenty votes to tie the Senate, thus giving Warren Porter the deciding vote. Wolfe, however, with his twenty votes, postponed consideration of his motion to reconsider the vote by which the Senate had refused to concur. A somewhat extraordinary parliamentary situation, to say the least. But it answered the machine's purpose. For a week[49a] the machine was able to hold the Senate in deadlock. All business was practically suspended. For hours the reform Senators were compelled to sit in their seats waiting the pleasure of President Porter and President Pro Tem. Wolfe to call the Senate to order. The folly of permitting the machine to organize the Senate was forced home to every good-government man present. The machine because it controlled the Senate organization could and did arrogantly override the rights of the Senate, giving the ultimatum that no business should be transacted until the anti-machine Senators had concurred in the machine amendments to the Direct Primary bill.

The machine's play was to bully, bluff or beg one of the anti-machine Senators to desert to the machine, which would have given the machine twenty-one votes, enough for concurrence, or, failing in this, to force the attendance of Senator Stetson, which would have tied the Senate, thus giving Warren Porter the deciding vote. But before Senator Stetson, pale and plainly on the verge of breakdown, could be brought to Sacramento, Senator Black became very ill and was obliged to go to his home at Palo Alto. Thus when Stetson returned, the vote stood 20 to 19, precisely where it had been before. Performer Porter was still denied the privilege of casting the deciding vote. For once the machine found itself squarely against a stone wall, with the sympathy of the public strongly against its creatures and methods. Night after night as the fight went on, the Senate gallery was packed with interested spectators, who cheered the anti-machine Senators to the echo. There were no cheers for the machine, but on one occasion at least the machine was hissed, when one of its creatures attempted an attack on Senator Black.

Never did the machine work harder to switch anti-machine Senators to its side. Jere Burke had characteristic corner conferences, Johnny Lynch labored with anti-machine Senators openly on the floor of the Senate chamber, as did Warren Porter. From a southern county came the Chairman of the Republican County Committee to tell his Senator who was voting with the anti-machine element what a mistake he was making. P. H. McCarthy "happened in" and worked with George Van Smith of the Call and Eddie Wolfe in the fruitless attempt made to "pull down" Senator Anthony[49]. Anti-machine Senators found their pet bills being held up in Assembly Committees.

But the nineteen anti-machine members stood firm, in spite of the fact that Senator Wright, who had originally led them, and George Van Smith, of the Call, who had originally advised them, and the Call, which had originally backed them, were all working on the side of Leavitt and Wolfe and Porter and the thirteen Senators of whom the Call had said on February 19, when they had voted for the amendment which they were still supporting, "Every man of these thirteen confessed corruptionists knew what he was doing - knew whose will he was putting above The People's will. Every one of these thirteen betrayers of the public weal has written the epitaph of his political tombstone."

And then the machine forces attacked Senator Black. Although Senator Black was lying ill at his home at Palo Alto, the Call on March 18 stated that he was in hiding in Sacramento.

The Call on the same date expressed its deep regret for and its utter condemnation of, the "asinine filibuster, designed to prevent a tie vote which would be decided by the Lieutenant-Governor, Warren Porter, in favor of concurrence in the Assembly amendment to the Direct Primary bill."

On February 18 the Call had objected very strenuously to Porter's attitude toward the Direct Primary bill. The Call on that date said:

"To-day the wolves (a pet name for the machine Senators), urged by their masters, will make their last stand in the Senate against a people determined to be free. Warren Porter, the Lieutenant-Governor of the fatted soul, who professes all the virtues and practices all political evil, will be the whipper-in."

One month later, March 18, the Call was complaining bitterly that the anti-machine Senators would not permit the same "Lieutenant-Governor of the fatted soul" to whip them into line for the amendment to the Direct Primary bill, which they had rejected on February 18, and for which the Call had praised them generously. The Call's special representative at Sacramento, George Nan Smith, was by this time working openly with Porter, Wolfe, Leavitt, Hartman, Lynch and Burke to compel Senate concurrence in the Assembly amendments, while Senators Boynton, Black, Miller, Campbell, Holohan, Stetson and the other anti-machine Senators whom the Call had formerly backed in their efforts against the machine, had become "pin-head politicians," in the columns of the Call, intent upon defeat of the Direct Primary bill.

The Call's extraordinary change and outrageous condemnation of the anti-machine Senators of course brought its protest. The people of Palo Alto met in mass meeting on March 21st, and adopted resolutions condemning the Call's course[50]. Senator Black from his sick bed wrote a letter showing the Call's insincerity and breach of faith with the pro-primary Senators[51]. The paper was bitterly denounced on the floor of the Senate.

But throughout the State the newspapers which stand for good government, and incidentally for an effective direct primary law, were firm in their support of the anti-machine Senators. Just before Senator Black was taken ill, for example, at the time when Senator Stetson was unable to be at the capital, the Sacramento Star, in an editorial article under the heading, "Illness a Blessing," cleverly put in a nutshell what the people were thinking and the reform press was saying. "We do not desire to wish Senator Stetson any bad luck," said The Star, "but if his slight indisposition should continue for a few days, or, in lieu of that, if some other solon of the same faith as regards the Primary bill can only contract some minor ailment, there will be more joy than sorrow among the people who want something approaching a real direct primary."[52]

Matters were brought to a climax when the performers through Senator Weed - who was, by the way, Chairman of the Committee on Public Morals, which reported adversely on the Walker-Otis bill-introduced a resolution, authorizing the Sergeant-at-Arms to bring Senator Black to Sacramento, even though a special engine and coach be chartered for the purpose[53]. The resolution brought forth indignant protest from the anti-machine Senators, and a telegram from Senator Black to Warren Porter, denouncing the unwarranted proceedings[54]. Nevertheless, Doctor Douglass W. Montgomery of San Francisco, in spite of the fact that four reputable physicians, Dr. Howard Black, Dr. H. B. Reynolds, Dr. J. C. Spencer and Dr. R. L. Wilbur, had certified that Senator black's physical condition did not permit of his being removed to Sacramento, went to Palo Alto with the Sergeant-at-Arms to investigate the sick Senator. Montgomery's investigations seem to have been confined to the outside of Senator Black's house[55]. At any rate he did not see Senator Black. The performance was given its sordid feature by Montgomery charging the Senate $400 for his services.

The Montgomery incident demonstrated clearly that the machine was whipped[56]. Senator Wolfe accordingly on Monday, March 22, after holding the Senate in deadlock more than a week, moved that the vote whereby the Senate had refused to concur in the Assembly amendment to the Direct Primary bill, be reconsidered. This, the Senate as a matter of courtesy, at Senator Wolfe's request, did. It then refused to concur in the Assembly's objectionable amendment. For the second time, the Senate went on record against the machine's advisory district-vote plan for the election of United States Senators. For the second time the anti-machine element in the Senate, in its efforts to secure the passage of an effective direct primary measure, had, fighting fair, and in the open, and above board always, defeated the machine. The machine thereupon met the anti-machine element with a trick that completely turned the tables, a trick by which the anti-machine forces were defeated, and the machine element placed in a position to amend the bill as it might see fit.

[42] Senator Wolfe, on the day of his defeat in the Senate, told the writer that he would offer no further opposition to the passage of the bill.

[43] Charles R. Detrick of Palo Alto, for example, called the attention of both Wright and Van Smith to the errors, and offered his services for their correction, but his offer was declined.

[44] The Call's course is all the more reprehensible from the fact that it had for two years been declaring for an effective Direct Primary law, and, indeed, assumed all the credit for the agitation for the reform.

[45] The Leeds amendment, which the Call stated was in no way related to the McCartney amendment, read as follows:

"Party candidates for the office of United States Senator shall have their names placed on the official primary election ballots of their respective parties in the manner herein provided for State officers, provided, however, that the vote for candidates for United States Senator shall be an advisory vote for the purpose of ascertaining the sentiment of the voters of the respective Senatorial and Assembly Districts in the respective parties."

The McCartney amendment of that section of the bill dealing with the nomination of Senators read:

"Amend the bill so as to give an advisory vote by districts on United States Senators."

It will be seen that the Leeds amendment and the McCartney amendment were not remotely, but very closely related; were, in effect, the same.

[46] A similar example of Pulcifer's trickiness attended the defeat in the Assembly of Boynton's Senate bill providing for a nonpartisan column on the election ballot for candidates for the Judiciary. The measure had the backing of the reform element, and passed the Senate with but little opposition. At that time it would have had even easier sailing in the Assembly. But the machine succeeded in preventing action on the measure In the Assembly until a few hours before adjournment. In the rush of the close of the session, the measure, it is alleged, was made subject of pretty vicious trading. But when it came to a showdown thirty-five votes were cast for the measure and twenty-nine against. Six more votes would have passed it. Had there been full attendance the bill would have been passed. A call of the House was ordered to compel such attendance, but was finally discontinued, by Pulcifer, who had voted for the bill, voting for discontinuance, thus tying the vote. This gave Speaker Stanton an opportunity to end proceedings under the call of the House, by casting the deciding vote against continuance. Stanton, with Pulcifer's assistance, thus cast what was practically the deciding vote that killed the bill. Had the call of the House been continued until all the Assemblymen were brought in, the measure would probably have been passed.

[47] The vote in full was as follows:

For the amendment and against the bill as it had passed the Senate: Barndollar, Beatty, Beban, Black, Butler, Coghlan, Collier, Collum,

Cronin, Cullen, Feeley, Greer, Hammon, Hanlon, Hans, Hawk, Grove L. Johnson, Johnson of San Diego, Johnston of Contra Costa, Leeds, Lightner, Macauley, McClellan, McManus, Melrose, Mott, Nelson, O'Neil, Perine, Pugh, Pulcifer, Rech, Rutherford, Schmitt, Stanton, Transue, Wagner, Wheelan - 38.

Against the amendment and for the bill as it passed the Senate:
Beardslee, Bohnett, Callan, Cattell, Cogswell, Costar, Dean, Drew, Flint, Gerdes, Gibbons, Gillis, Griffiths, Hayes, Hewitt, Hinkle, Holmquist, Irwin, Johnson of Placer, Juilliard, Kehoe, Maher, Mendenhall, Moore, Odom, Otis, Polsley, Preston, Sackett, Silver, Stuckenbruck, Telfer, Whitney, Wilson, Wyllie, Young - 36.

[48] When a bill passed by the Senate is amended in the Assembly the measure goes back to the Senate. If the Senate concur in the amendments, that settles the matter. But if the Senate refuse to concur, then the bill goes back to the Assembly, where that body may recede from its amendments or refuse to recede.

If the Assembly recede, the measure goes to the Governor just as it passed the Senate. If the Assembly refuse to recede, the measure is referred to a conference committee of six, three appointed by the Speaker of the Assembly and three by the President of the Senate.

The Conference Committee may consider only the amendments adopted by the Assembly. If the Conference Committee fail to agree, or if either Senate or Assembly reject its report, then the bill goes to a Committee on Free Conference. The Committee on Free Conference is permitted to make any amendment it sees fit. If its report be rejected by either Senate or Assembly, the bill gets no further; is dead, without possibility of resurrection.

Such was the maze of technicality into which Lincoln-Roosevelt Leaguer Pulcifer threw the Direct Primary bill when he changed his vote from no to aye on the Leeds amendment.

[49a] The postponements were made from hour to hour. The reform Senators would be informed that the matter would be taken up at eleven o'clock in the forenoon. At that hour, the machine would postpone consideration until three o'clock in the afternoon. At three o'clock, further postponement would be ordered until eight o'clock. At eight o'clock there would be postponement until the next morning. Twenty-one votes were necessary for concurrence in the Assembly Amendments, but a majority of those voting was sufficient to secure postponement. The machine on this issue controlled twenty votes, one short of enough for concurrence, but one more than the nineteen controlled by the anti-machine element, and

hence enough to postpone from hour to hour consideration of Wolfe's motion.

[49] It is very amusing less than three months later to see those partners of the Direct Primary fight, P. H. McCarthy and the San Francisco Call, in fierce political conflict at San Francisco.

[50] The resolutions adopted at Palo Alto read: "Resolved, That we note with disapproval the changed attitude of the San Francisco Call upon the Direct Primary bill, and its attempt to discredit Senator Black and other friends of good government in the Legislature."

[51] Senator Black's letter covered the situation fully. It was addressed to the press of the State, and was as follows: "No decent primary law would have been possible but for the combination of thirteen Republicans and seven Democrats in the Senate who have stood together throughout this whole fight. Senator Wright and the 'Call' were powerless in the contest until these twenty Senators got behind them.

"One of the conditions of this combination was a State-wide vote on United States Senator, and the 'Call' fought with us against Senators Wolfe and Leavitt on this proposition. Immediately after the bill left the Senate and got into the Assembly the 'Call' began to display a lack of interest in the primary fight. If it had maintained its attitude in favor of the original bill these amendments never would have been proposed by the Assembly."

"When the question of concurring in the Assembly amendments comes up, we find the 'Call' and Senator Wright deserting the men who made the primary fight in the Senate and going over to the camp of the 'push' politicians, who have always favored the district plan of nominating United States Senators."

"I take issue with the 'Call' when it says: 'As a matter of fact, the whole question of the United States Senatorship is of little importance to the people of California,' etc."

"The United States Senatorship is the most important office to be filled by the people of California under the provisions of the proposed Direct Primary law. The so-called district plan for nominating United States Senators is worse than a makeshift. it provides for no pledge on the part of candidates and would be purely a straw vote, binding on nobody."

"The stubborn fact remains that the 'Call,' after leading in the fight for an honest Direct Primary law for two years and a half, has deserted the cause of the people at the most critical moment of the struggle."

"MARSHALL BLACK."

[52] The Star's clever editorial article is worth preserving. It was in full as follows: "There are times, it appears, when the illness of a statesman is good for the people. We do not desire to wish Senator Stetson any bad luck, but if his slight indisposition should continue for a few days, or, in lieu of that, if some other solon of the same faith as regards the Primary bill, can only contract some minor ailment, there will be more joy than sorrow among the people who want something approaching a real direct primary.

"As explained in The Star's news columns, had Senator Stetson not been ill, a tie vote on the proposition to concur with the Assembly in amending the primary bill, presumably in the interest of Senator Frank Flint and generally to machine advantage, would have occurred. And then - it's unkind to say such things - any person with a grain of sense would know that Mr. 'Performing' Porter, our honored and distinguished Lieutenant-Governor, would break the tie by casting his vote for the machine.

"The evident intention of Senators who stand for the Wright bill in its original form, which is a start toward a real direct primary (and that doesn't include Senator Wright, more's the pity) to dodge the possibility of the tie vote by absenting themselves without leave is regrettable - regrettable only because it is necessary. Their action, with the aim of serving the best interests of the people, is highly honorable compared with the tactics of the powers that be, even unto the Governor himself, who have been trying every means to club legislators into line to stand by the 'organization' and defeat the will of the people.

"It's hard to be very sorry just now over Senator Stetson's illness, but he deserves a vote of thanks for contracting that cold. And another for being on the right side."

[53] The Weed resolution reads as follows: "Resolved, By the Senate of the State of California, That the President of the Senate be and he is hereby authorized to instruct the Sergeant-at-Arms to Proceed at once to Palo Alto with a competent physician, to be named by the President of the Senate, for the purpose of ascertaining whether it is safe for Senator Black to proceed at once to Sacramento, to attend as a member of the Senate the thirty-eighth session of the California Legislature, and

"Be it further resolved, That in the event that such examination results in disclosing a state of health wherein it will be safe for Senator Black to be present, then the Sergeant-at-Arms shall bring him at once to Sacramento and, if necessary, to secure an engine and coach for that purpose."

[54] Black's answering telegram was in full as follows: "I beg to inform you (Lieutenant-Governor Porter) and through you the Senate of California that I regard the resolutions adopted last Saturday in reference to my absence, as

discourteous, as a reflection on my honor and integrity and as proposing an infringement on my privileges and rights as a Senator and citizen. I have, therefore declined to see the persons sent here under that resolution, and shall continue to decline to see them until my physicians inform me that I can with safety return to Sacramento.

"Ample evidence of my physical condition has been presented to your representatives by four reputable physicians, and these physicians have furnished and will furnish evidence of my condition from time to time as requested by you or by the Senate.

"MARSHALL BLACK."

[55] Dr. Montgomery's $400 report will be found in the appendix.

[56] The schemes resorted to to get Black back to Sacramento are almost beyond belief. It was even intimated to him that his bills would be held up if he did not return. The following telegram scarcely requires comment:

Sacramento Cal Mch 20-09
Hon. Marshall Black,

Palo Alto, Cal.

Your bill to issue bonds for general improvement fund before me. I would like to have you here to explain its provisions and the necessity for it. 12-50Pm J. N. GILLETT.

CHAPTER XI.

Machine Amends Direct Primary Bill[57].

By Trick Prevents Senate From Concurring in Amendments to Correct Clerical and Typographical Errors, Thus Creating a Situation Which Threw the Measure Into a Committee on Free Conference With Power to Amend.

It is a very good rule to be sure that your rattlesnake is dead before placing yourself in a position to be bitten. The reform Senators neglected this rule, with the result that after they had the machine element whipped on the direct primary issue, they placed themselves in a position where the "performers" struck at them viciously, and snatched victory from them.

As was shown in a previous chapter, the Direct Primary bill, after it had originally passed the Senate in the face of machine opposition, was allowed to go to the Assembly containing several serious clerical and typographical errors. The Assembly corrected these errors by a series of ten amendments. It was necessary for the Senate to concur in these amendments to get the bill into proper form. The amendments added in the Assembly to which the anti-machine Senators took exception, were seven in number and dealt principally with the changing of the method of electing United States Senators, from the plan of State-wide vote, to that of district, advisory vote. The seven were known as the "vicious amendments"; the ten correcting the typographical errors were called the "necessary amendments." There is no good reason why the ten necessary amendments should not have been made before the bill was first sent to the Assembly. But they were not, and the errors which were thus left in the bill served the machine most advantageously when the final fight came. After Wolfe had given up hope of compelling the reform Senators to concur in the vicious amendments read into the bill in the Assembly, his play was to bring about a situation by which the bill would be thrown into a Committee on Free Conference. The committee would be appointed by President Porter of the Senate, and by Speaker Stanton of the Assembly. Such a committee would, of course, be in sympathy with machine policies, and could be counted upon to amend the bill to the machine's liking. There is little doubt that the machine leaders in the Senate and the machine leaders in the Assembly acted in conjunction in the proceedings which followed Senator Wolfe's action in abandoning his efforts to force the anti-machine Senators to support the so called vicious Assembly amendments.

Wolfe's first move was to ask as a matter of courtesy that the Senate adopt his motion to reconsider the vote by which it had the week before refused to concur in the Assembly amendment. This request the reform element granted, purely as a matter of courtesy. Wolfe then edged up a step nearer.

No sooner had he received the courtesy of reconsideration than both he and Leavitt were to the fore with a suggestion that the Senate should refuse to concur in all the amendments and let them be threshed out in the Assembly. The purpose of the two machine leaders was apparent.

Had the Senate concurred in the ten Assembly amendments made necessary to correct typographical errors, and refused to concur in the seven objectionable amendments, all that would have been necessary would have been for the Assembly to recede from its objectionable amendments. But if Wolfe could so engineer matters that the Senate would refuse to concur in all the amendments, then it would be necessary for the Assembly to recede from all its amendments, including those intended to correct typographical errors, or send the bill to a conference committee, to be selected by Stanton and Porter. From a Committee on Conference to a Committee on Free Conference, also to be appointed by Stanton and Porter, and with full power to amend the bill to its liking, was but a step. The Committee on Free Conference was Wolfe's aim. He eventually got it.

Boynton and Walker were quick to see the trend of Wolfe's requests, however, and Walker moved to vote on the seven vicious amendments on one roll call, and on the ten correcting the typographical and clerical errors on a second.

As a substitute Wolfe moved that the seventeen amendments be passed upon under one roll call.

At first Senators Cutten and Stetson apparently could not see the trend of Wolfe's scheming. In the debate that ensued Wolfe pretended indignation that his motives were being questioned.

There was very good reason for questioning Senator Wolfe's motives, but Cutten and Stetson and even Walker assured Wolfe that no reflection upon him was intended. What these men should have done was to have denounced Wolfe right there as a trickster and made no bones about it. But on the absurd assumption that a member of the State Senate is necessarily a gentleman, the much deserved denunciation did not come.

However, Wolfe's motion did not prevail and the amendments were taken up one by one. Six of the seven vicious amendments were rejected, the first of the six by a vote of 19 to 20.

This brought the Senate to the amendments intended to correct typographical and clerical errors. And here the vote switched. The reformers had up to this time been voting to reject the amendments, because the amendments were objectionable, while the programmers in the first instance voted for concurrence. But when it came to amendments intended to correct typographical and clerical errors only, Wolfe and his following, with the exception of Burnett, who refused to stand for any such dastardly piece of work, voted to refuse to concur in the amendments, while the anti-machine Senators, of course, voted to concur in them.

Burnett, voting with the anti-machine element, gave them twenty votes, leaving Wolfe and his following only nineteen. But twenty-one votes were necessary for concurrence. The machine, while it could not force the Senate to concur in the vicious amendments, could prevent the Senate's concurrence in the amendments to correct the clerical and typographical errors. The bill was accordingly sent back to the Assembly with the typographical and clerical amendments still in dispute.

Even before the bill had reached the Assembly, Senator Frank Leavitt and George Van Smith of The Call were on the floor of that body, fighting to prevent the Assembly receding from its amendments.

When the Assembly grasped the fact that the Senate had refused to concur in the amendments necessary for correction of typographical errors, those who were working for an effective Direct Primary bill were thrown into the greatest confusion. Speaker Stanton's rulings which followed, were not calculated to relieve the situation. Speaking from the desk, Stanton said:

"If you recede from some of these amendments and not from others where will your bill be? It will be dead. The only thing that you can do to save the Direct Primary bill now is to recede from all the amendments and let the typographical errors remain in the bill, or refuse to recede from any of the amendments and let the bill go into conference. If you recede from some of the amendments and not from others, your bill is dead. We cannot send this bill back to the Senate saying that the Assembly has receded from some of the amendments and not from others."

Assemblymen Preston, Bohnett and others who were standing for an effective measure, were amazed at the position which Stanton had taken.

"I cannot for the life of me," said Preston, "see why we cannot recede from part of the amendments and refuse to recede from the others. Some of these amendments are really necessary for the good of the bill. Others should be rejected. Give me fifteen minutes and I will guarantee to dig up authorities which will show us the course to be pursued."

Assemblyman Bohnett confessed himself unable to understand why the Assembly could not send part of the amendments to conference and not the others.

By this time matters had got so warm in the Assembly that Senator Leavitt found it necessary to lend dignity to the occasion by taking his seat at the side of Speaker Stanton, whom he engaged in conversation. The conference was, of course, carried on in whispers.

Assemblymen Young, Bohnett and others, finding that it would be impossible under the assumption of the Speaker to refuse to recede from part of the amendments while receding from the others, advised the good government members to refuse to recede from all the amendments, and pass the bill, typographical errors and all.

It was demanded of Bohnett if this would not lead to the practical defeat of the measure. Bohnett insisted that it would not; that the typographical errors, while deplorable, did not materially affect the bill.

However, many of the better element of the Assembly did not dare to take the risk, and the motion to recede was lost by a vote of 29 to 42[51].

Assemblymen who unquestionably stood for a good bill voted against receding. Had the vicious amendments alone been under consideration, they would have voted to recede. Among these were such men as Assemblyman Drew of Fresno. The Assembly, having refused to recede from its amendments, the bill went to a Committee on Conference, appointed by Speaker Stanton and President Porter. The machine had gained its point.

The Conference Committee consisted of Senators Wolfe, Leavitt and Wright, and Assemblymen Leeds, Johnson of Sacramento, and Hewitt. Of the Committee, Hewitt[59] was the only member who favored a Statewide vote for United States Senator, and opposed the advisory district vote. The committee had scarcely been missed from Senate and Assembly chambers before it was back to report that no agreement could be reached.

The same members were thereupon appointed as a Committee on Free Conference, which gave them power to amend the bill. As a Committee on Free Conference they recommended the advisory district vote plan for the nomination of United States Senators[60].

Senator Wolfe, having got the bill in shape to his liking, with a suave smirk upon his face, stated that he trusted that all the Senators present would vote for the measure.

"Not on your life," came Caminetti's protest.

And Caminetti did not vote for the Free Conference Committee's report.

But in spite of Caminetti's protest, both Senate and Assembly adopted the Conference Committee's report. They had to do so or defeat the bill entirely. Caminetti was the only Senator who voted against it. The machine, after a fight of nearly two months, in which it was twice defeated in the Senate, and escaped defeat in the Assembly by only one vote, that of Pulcifer, had carried its point, had succeeded in denying the people of California the privilege of casting a practical, State-wide vote for United States Senators.

What the anti-machine Senators[61] thought of the outcome is best expressed in the little speech which Senator Stetson made his fellow-Senators in explaining his vote to accept the report of the Committee on Free Conference.

"Before voting on this matter," said Stetson, "lest any one in the future may think that I have been passed something and didn't know it, I wish to explain my vote, and wish to say that this permission accorded a candidate to go on record to support that candidate for United States Senate, who shall have the endorsement of the greatest number of districts, comes from nobody and goes to nobody. It means nothing - mere words - idle words. The only way in which a candidate could have been pledged would have been to provide a pledge or instructions to the Legislature. The words 'shall be permitted' mean nothing and get nowhere. I shall vote for this report, not because I want to, but because I have to if we are at this session to have any Direct Primary law at all."

[57] The plain citizen will marvel at the lengths to which the machine went to prevent a provision being incorporated into the Direct Primary bill for the selection by State-wide vote of United States Senators. The plain citizen does not, however, look upon a United States Senator through the same eyes as the machine. To the plain citizen that United States Senator is desirable who represents policies beneficial to his country and his State; to the machine that United States Senator is desirable who will in effect turn his Federal patronage over to the machine. The election of United States Senators by State-wide vote would take their appointment out of machine hands, which would mean loss to the machine of Federal patronage. For this reason the almost unbelievable lengths to which the machine went to prevent the provision for State-wide vote for the election of United States Senators being incorporated into the Direct Primary bill.

[58] The vote was as follows:

Ayes: Messrs. Bohnett, Callan, Cattell, Cogswell, Collum, Costar, Flavelle, Gerdes, Gibbons, Gillis, Hinkle, Holmquist, Irwin, Johnson of Placer, Juilliard, Kehoe, Maher, Mendenhall, Odom, Otis, Polsley, Preston, Sackett, Stuckenbruck, Telfer, Whitney, Wilson, Wyllie and Young - 29.

Noes: Messrs. Barndollar, Beardslee, Beatty, Beban, Black, Butler, Coghlan, Collier, Cronin, Cullen, Drew, Feeley, Fleisher, Flint, Greer, Griffiths, Hammon, Hanlon, Hans, Hawk, Hewitt, Johnson of Sacramento, Johnson of San Diego, Leeds, Macauley, McClelland, McManus, Melrose, Moore, Mott, Nelson, Perine, Pugh, Pulcifer, Rech, Rutherford, Schmitt, Silver, Stanton, Transue, Wagner, Wheelan - 42.

[59] Hewitt voted against the amendments the day they were read into the bill.

[60] The Free Conference Committee's amendment was in full as follows:

"By nominating petitions signed and filed as provided by existing laws party candidates for the office of United States Senator shall have their names placed on the official primary election ballots of their respective parties, in the manner herein provided for State offices, PROVIDED, HOWEVER, THAT THE VOTE FOR CANDIDATES FOR UNITED STATES SENATORS SHALL BE AN ADVISORY VOTE FOR THE PURPOSE OF ASCERTAINING THE SENTIMENT OF THE VOTERS IN THE RESPECTIVE SENATORIAL AND ASSEMBLY DISTRICTS IN THE RESPECTIVE PARTIES, and the Senatorial and Assembly nominees shall be at liberty to vote either for the choice of such district expressed at said primary election, or for the candidate for United States Senator who shall have received the endorsement of such primary election in the greater number of districts electing members of his party to the Legislature."

[61] Stetson was not the only Senator to protest. Senators Campbell, Holohan and Miller sent to the Secretary's desk the following explanation of their votes: "We voted for the Direct Primary bill because it seems to be the best law that can be obtained under existing political conditions. We are opposed to many of the features of this bill, and believe that the people at the first opportunity will instruct their representatives in the Legislature to radically amend the same in many particulars, notably in regard to the election of United States Senators, and the provisions that prevent the endorsement of a candidate by a political party or organization other than the one that first nominated such candidate."

A second protest, signed by Senators Curtin, Cartwright and Sanford, was also printed in the Journal. It reads as follows: "We voted to adopt the report of the Committee on Free Conference on Senate Bill No. 3, not because we believe it to be what is desired by the people of this State, but because we believe it to be the only bill that can be adopted at this late hour, as the Legislature is about to adjourn."

CHAPTER XII.

The Railroad Regulation Issue.

Recent Increase in Freight Tariff Had Brought About a Condition Which Required Action - Senate Divided Into Supporters of an Effective and Supporters of an Ineffective Measure - Manipulation by Which Measures Were Placed in Hands of a Machine-Controlled Committee.

Some one has very well said that the real test of a Legislature is its action on railroad measures. The Legislature of 1909, if estimated by this standard would not appear to advantage. But to condemn the Legislature of 1909 for its failure to give the State an effective railroad regulation law, is to condemn every Legislature that has sat in California since the present State Constitution went into effect thirty years ago. The Constitution empowers the Legislature to pass effective railroad regulation measures, but up to the session of 1909, the machine, or system, or organization - one name is as fragrant as another - had prevented the passage, if we exclude the ineffective Act of 1880, of any railroad regulation law at all. The machine has ever moved against the interests of the people and in the interest of its dominating factor and at the same time its chief beneficiary, the Southern Pacific Railroad Company. It has so manipulated the nomination and election of Railroad Commissioners as to keep in that office men utterly dominated by railroad influences.

With weak and corrupt men as Railroad Commissioners, and machine-dominated Legislatures which have neglected to pass laws which would have made the Commission effective, or even provide funds for the Commission to carry on its work, even had the Commissioners been so inclined, California has been left helpless to oppose any extortion which the railroad might see fit to exact. The system of charging all that the traffic will bear has governed utterly. For this the Southern Pacific Company can thank, and the People of California condemn, the machine.

The cost to the people has been enormous. It was pretty conclusively shown at the Legislative investigation into the cause of recent advance of freight rates, that upwards of $10,000,000[62] a year has in this one instance been added to the freight charges exacted from the people of the Pacific Coast. The added burden falls upon the Pacific Coast manufacturer, merchant, farmer, fruit grower, consumer. All from the highest to the lowest help pay the tribute. Thirty years is a long period, and the arm of the railroad tribute-taker far-reaching. The vast sums which, unrestricted, the Southern Pacific has been able to exact run into enormous totals. From a dollar and cent standpoint, it has paid the Southern Pacific Company to control the machine.

But the railroad's absolute domination of the State could not continue forever without protest that would eventually force a hearing. This protest came toward the close of 1908. The increase in freight rates made just before the Legislature of 1909 convened emphasized the necessity for the enactment of a law that should galvanize the Railroad Commission into activity; ensure the enforcement of constitutional provisions for the protection of the public against dominant transportation companies; in a word, provide effective railroad regulation.

Governor Gillett in his biennial message to the Legislature, and Attorney General Webb in his biennial report gave expression to this aroused public sentiment.

General Webb, after reviewing railroad conditions in California, on page 13 of his report says: "It is thus apparent that the shippers of the State are practically helpless."

"I believe," continues the Attorney General, "that this review of the situation will show the imperative necessity of prompt legislation on this subject, and under the Constitution of this State, the Legislature has ample authority to enact the required legislation."

Governor Gillett, in his biennial message, takes practically the same stand as does Attorney General Webb.

"Our State," says the Governor on page 12 of his message, "has not kept pace with the majority of the States of the Union in the enactment of laws regulating railroads in their business as common carriers."

"I can virtually promise you," said General Webb at a meeting of the Senate Committee on Corporations, held on the evening of January 25th, "that in the event of this (the Stetson Railroad Regulation bill) becoming a law, and the Railroad Commission refusing or neglecting to act under its provisions, the Governor will call the Legislature together in extraordinary session for their impeachment."[63]

There was no question of the aroused public sentiment in favor of the passage of a railroad regulation measure. Even before the Legislature convened it became evident that some sort of a measure would have to be passed; even the railroad lobby saw that. The Legislature accordingly divided on the question. As the fight was carried on in the Senate - the Assembly in the rush of the closing hours of the session merely putting its "O. K." on what the Senate had done - the division in the Senate alone will be considered. The division in that body was:

(1) The minority, made up of the out and out machine Republicans and Democrats, who were prepared to pass a measure which under the name railroad regulation would leave the railroads practically independent of effective State supervision.

(2) The majority, which stood for the passage of an effective law.

The minority had the best captains in the Senate and was backed by the machine lobby made up principally of Southern Pacific attorneys.

The majority was poor in generals. But it had the backing of the shippers of - the State, who sent able counsel to Sacramento to present the shippers' side.

And in the end the machine minority wore out and defeated the majority. A comparatively effective railroad regulation bill was rejected and an ineffective measure passed.

Three railroad regulation measures were introduced in the Senate, their authors being Campbell, Stetson, and Wright.

The Campbell bill had much to commend it, but was rejected without much consideration by either side. Campbell was not in the program of either railroad or shippers. But before the session was over Campbell had made himself felt. He had, too, introduced a Constitutional Amendment for the correction of railroad abuses, which was to figure later on, but his bill was scarcely considered. The attorney for the shippers, in speaking before the Senate Committee on Corporations, confessed that he had not read the Campbell bill.

The attorney for the Southern Pacific Company, however, attempted to split the anti-machine forces by praising the Campbell bill, and setting the anti-machine Senators to disputing over the relative merits of the Campbell and Stetson bills. But nothing came of this graceful little coup. Campbell and his followers were too sensible to be caught by any such trickery. They gave their loyal support to the Stetson bill, and the Campbell bill was allowed to die in the Senate Judiciary Committee. This narrowed the fight down to the Stetson bill and the Wright bill.

The Stetson bill had been prepared in the office of Attorney General Webb, and at the instigation of Governor Gillett. As originally introduced it contained certain defects, which were afterwards corrected, but such Senators as Cutten, Caminetti, Black, Campbell, Miller, Cartwright, Bell and Thompson, admitted that the measure could be made the basis of as effective a law as could be prepared under the present constitutional provisions for the regulation of transportation companies.

The original measure was particularly weak in the section providing for demurrage charges. This was finally corrected by the passage of a separate reciprocal demurrage bill, which had been introduced by Miller. Another weakness in the Stetson bill as originally introduced was that the Railroad Commission was made a sort of barrier between the Courts and those who had grievances against the transportation companies. This objection was corrected by amendments.

Numerous other amendments adopted from time to time made the Stetson bill probably as effective as a California railroad regulation law can be made, under the Constitutional provision which places extraordinary powers in the hands of the State Board of Railroad Commissioners.

Just where the Wright bill originated nobody seems to know for certainty. But Senator Wright introduced it. Senator Wright was well selected for the job. For two years he had been groomed as the reformer who would introduce the State-saving Direct Primary Bill. So a railroad regulation measure introduced by Senator Wright might at least be calculated to bear the stamp of respectability.

Like the Stetson bill, the Wright bill was based on the constitutional provisions which make the State Board of Railroad Commissioners the center of railroad regulation in California. And here the parallel ends.

Comparison of the two measures is not at all to the advantage of the Wright bill.

The Stetson bill provided fine and imprisonment as penalty for infringement of its provisions; the Wright bill provided fine only.

The Stetson bill had a definite anti-pass provision; the Wright bill as originally introduced had no such provision.

The Stetson bill authorized not only the Attorney-General, but the District Attorney of any county of the State to proceed to enforce its provisions; the Wright bill granted the Attorney-General alone such authority.

The Stetson bill required the Railroad Commissioners to meet at least once in every two weeks; the Wright bill provided that such meetings should be held monthly.

The Stetson bill gave the Railroad Commissioners authority to make physical valuation of railroad properties; the Wright bill contained no such provision.

The Stetson bill recognized all discriminations to be unjust; the Wright bill provided that no interference should be instituted unless the discriminations complained of were shown to be unjust.

And finally, the Stetson bill provided that the State Board of Railroad Commissioners should have power to fix absolute rates, thus insuring stability of rate schedules, while the Wright bill provided that the Commissioners should fix maximum rates only, thus permitting the famous "fluidity" of schedules advocated by machine lobby and Southern Pacific attorneys.

The contest between the supporters of the Wright and the supporters of the Stetson bill, finally narrowed down to the question of providing for absolute or maximum rates.

The provision for the maximum rate in Senator Wright's bill, authorized the railroad regulating Commission to fix the highest charge which a railroad may exact from a shipper. This is called the maximum rate. The transportation company is authorized to lower the rate at will, but it cannot charge a rate beyond the maximum as fixed by the Commission. This leaves the railroads to fix a sliding schedule of rates, so long as they do not exceed the maximum. It gives the railroads the advantage of that "fluidity" of schedules, which railroad attorneys insist is necessary for railroad prosperity.

The maximum rate is provided in the Interstate Commerce Act, but the Interstate Commerce Commissioners, finding it impracticable, have for years been clamoring for Congress to authorize the fixing of absolute rates. The cry of the Interstate Commerce Commission has been taken up by the shipping interests, and from one end of the country to the other there is growing demand that authority be placed somewhere to make railroad rates, when fixed by a regulating Commission, absolute.

The absolute rate, or the fixed rate as it is better called, which was provided in the Stetson bill, can neither be lowered nor raised by the railroads. Once fixed by the regulating Commission, it must remain until the Commission grants permission for its change. The railroads cannot lower it any more than they can raise it.

The advantages of the absolute rate are many. In the first place, where the absolute rate is established, there can be no discrimination, because the rate is known, it can neither be raised nor lowered, and the railroads have no opportunity to favor one shipper at the expense of another.

In the second place, the shipper is guaranteed a stability of rate schedules which is deemed necessary for settled business conditions. The merchant, for example, includes transportation charges in the cost price of the goods in which he deals. But if the transportation charges on the same class of goods are subject to frequent change, the merchant can never tell when his competitor is to be given the advantage of a sudden lowering in freight rates. This uncertainty unsettles business. The merchant holds that transportation rates should be just as stable as tariff rates. On this account, the merchant advocates fixed rates and stability of schedules as against maximum rates and constantly shifting schedules.

The supporters of the Stetson bill, then, backed the shipping and merchant classes; while the supporters of the Wright bill backed the contentions of the transportation companies.

The Campbell and the Stetson bills had been originally referred to the Senate Judiciary Committee, while the Wright bill had been referred to the Senate Committee on Corporations. For the first few weeks of the session, no particular note had been taken of the Wright bill, attention being centered on the amendment of the Stetson bill.

Things were going swimmingly with the Stetson bill, when the machine lobby awoke to the fact that something was wrong in the Senate. There was at least some indication that the Senate would pass an effective railroad regulation measure.

And then, before the advocates of the Stetson measure could tell exactly what was happening, the railroad regulation measures were taken from the Judiciary Committee and placed in the hands of the Committee on Corporations.

A glance at the personnel of the two Committees at least suggests why this was done.

The members of the Judiciary Committee were Willis, Wolfe, Wright, McCartney, Savage, Boynton, Anthony, Burnett, Cutten, Estudillo, Martinelli, Roseberry, Stetson, Thompson, Curtin, Cartwright, Caminetti, Miller, Campbell.

The nine Senators whose names are printed in Italics, when the issue came to vote on the floor of the Senate, voted against the Stetson bill and for the Wright bill; nine of the ten whose names are printed in ordinary letters voted for the Stetson bill and against the Wright bill. The tenth, Roseberry, was absent, but when he found that the vote had been taken, stated that had he been present he would have voted for the Stetson bill and against the Wright bill.

Furthermore, Estudillo, who finally voted for the Wright bill, did not approve the measure and voted for it because he feared the absolute rate feature of the Stetson bill to be unconstitutional.

Thus at the time the Stetson and the Campbell bills were taken from the Judiciary Committee, the Committee was regarded as standing:

For the Wright bill - 8.

Against the Wright bill - 11.

For the Stetson bill - 11.

Against the Stetson bill - 8.

It was certainly not in the interest of the Stetson bill that the measure was taken from the Judiciary Committee and sent to the Committee on Corporations.

A glance at the personnel of the Committee on Corporations reveals a significant state of affairs. The Committee consisted of the following Senators: Bates, Welch, Wright, McCartney, Burnett, Bills, Walker, Roseberry, Finn, Miller, Kennedy.

When the test came on the floor of the Senate, the nine of the eleven Senators whose names are printed in italics voted for the Wright bill and against the Stetson bill. The two members whose names are printed in ordinary letters, voted for the Stetson bill, and against the Wright bill.

The line-up of the Committee on Corporations, when the measures were taken from the Judiciary Committee and sent to the Committee on Corporations, was then:

For the Wright Bill - 9.

Against the Wright Bill - 2.

For the Stetson Bill - 2.

Against the Stetson Bill - 9.

The change was certainly not made in the interest of the Stetson bill.

The incident stirred up Campbell and other anti-machine Senators to the fighting pitch. An arrangement was made, however, by which the measures were to be sent back to the Judiciary Committee after the Committee on Corporations got through with them that the Judiciary Committee might pass upon their constitutionality. The arrangement had two effects - it silenced the unquieting protest of the anti-machine Senators, and it delayed consideration of the bills. But, as the sequel showed, the arrangement did not help the Stetson bill in the least.

[62] The testimony was that of George J. Bradley, traffic manager of the Merchants' and Manufacturers' Traffic Association of Sacramento. It was as follows:

It is estimated on conservative figures that the increase in eastbound California products, or Pacific Coast products, I should correctly say, which is composed of canned fruits, canned vegetables and canned salmon, of which there are several million cases, go from the North Pacific coast through either San Francisco or through the North Pacific coast, the minimum being forty thousand pounds to the car, and the increase being ten cents per hundred pounds, means forty dollars a car increase. Now, taking the number of cars of all those products that are shipped, it amounted to about - and leather and other products - it amounted to about four million dollars eastbound. Now, when the question of westbound comes out, of course, it is practically impossible for any man to say just exactly what that increase will mean in dollars and cents, and the only way, therefore, to arrive at it is to take the percentage of proportion now in their westbound tariff, which is composed of about between eight hundred and a thousand items. They have raised the rates from 10 to 25 cents on over two hundred articles, all of which move in quantities; in other words, the process by which the tariff has been amended has been that in every instance where there was a commodity moving in quantities the rate has been advanced; wherever there was no movement and they wished to encourage a movement, they reduced the rate. Now, you take the five transcontinental lines that operate on the Pacific Coast, namely, the Northern Pacific and the Great Northern on the north and the Canadian Pacific; the Southern Pacific and the Santa Fe and the San Pedro and Los Angeles on the south, give you six trunk lines operating on the Pacific Coast. If you will take their gross earnings, which amount to over four hundred millions, segregate that by allowing fifty per cent of that to passenger service, which is a very conservative estimate, because the passenger service does not amount to that, leaves two hundred million dollars of gross freight earnings. Take five per cent of that for terminal business, and business is based on terminal rates from the coast, plus the local back, because the rate, of course, is felt everywhere, the rates to the interior points are made on the terminal rate, plus the local back. Take five per cent of that and their increase in every instance has been 10 per cent, and in some cases 16 2/3 and 20 per cent; but take a very liberal conservative estimate and put it at five per cent and you have ten million dollars; now, split that in two and take two and a half per cent of it and you have got five millions of dollars. Now, that and your four million dollars on eastbound freight and you have nine millions of dollars increase in freight rates, and I believe that that is a conservative estimate. I don't see how you could get at it any closer, because every man, it doesn't make any difference where he is, every man that buys pays that ten to twenty per cent increase.

[63] Senator Caminetti on February 12 introduced a concurrent resolution calling for the removal of the present Board of Railroad Commissioners from office. The Committee on Corporations reported adversely, and on March 15th the resolution was finally rejected.

CHAPTER XIII.

Machine Defeats the Stetson Bill.

Southern Pacific Attorney Succeeds in Clouding the Issue - Railroad Claquers Active in Advocating the Maximum Rate, Which Was Designated as
Little Better Than No Rate At All - No Fight Over the Bill in the Assembly.

Having succeeded in transferring the railroad regulation measures from the Senate Judiciary Committee, the majority of whose members were anti-machine, to the Committee on Corporations, the majority of whose members were machine, the machine proceeded to discredit the Stetson bill, by making it appear that the State Constitution by implication prohibits the fixing of absolute railroad rates, and provides that the Railroad Commissioners may fix maximum rates only. Peter F. Dunne was brought to Sacramento to make this argument before the Senate Committee on Corporations.

Dunne, in his address, showed greater ability than integrity. When he had finished, even the anti-machine members of the Committee were completely befuddled. Walker, one of the members of the Committee who is not a lawyer, groped in utter darkness thereafter, until he finally stumbled into the arms of Eddie Wolfe and Frank Leavitt and Jere Burke, when the final vote on the railroad bills was taken. It was Walker's only stumble of the session. But for his unfortunate vote against the Stetson bill and for the Wright bill, Walker would have made an exceptionally clean record.

Not only did Dunne befog the lay Senators of the Committee, he shook the faith of men like Miller and Roseberry - both lawyers - on the constitutionality of the absolute rate. Miller recognizes that the absolute rate is the only practical rate; but until the end of the session he was not prepared to say that it could be constitutionally established. Dunne certainly did a good job. To be sure, his address was a mass of misrepresentations, but of misrepresentations cunningly put. He shattered the implicit faith of the anti-machine Senators in the absolute rate. And that was what he had been sent to Sacramento to do. The evil that Dunne did lived long after he had left the capital.

Curiously enough, neither the term "absolute rate" nor "maximum rate" appears in the State Constitution.

Article XII, Section 22, of the Constitution, provides that the Railroad Commissioners "shall have the power and it shall be their duty to establish rates of charges for the transportation of passengers and freight by railroad or other transportation companies."

Further on in the same section, it is provided that "any railroad corporation or transportation company which shall fail or refuse to conform to such rates as shall be established by such Commissioners, or shall charge rates in excess thereof, * * * shall be fined not exceeding $20,000 for each offense."

The dispute between those who stood for maximum rates - that is to say, the members of the machine lobby, the machine Senators, the Southern Pacific attorneys and those who wanted absolute rates - namely, the anti-machine Senators and the attorneys representing large shipping interests - waxed hot over the words in the above quotation which are printed in Italics.

The advocates of the absolute rate held, with at least apparent reason, that the words "fail to conform to such rates" mean just what the dictionaries say they do: That the railroad charging a rate in excess of that fixed by the Railroad Commissioners, or a rate less than that fixed by the Commissioners, is not conforming to the rates. Such, at least, seems reasonable construction of a very simple phrase.

But not so, insisted the railroad lobby. That aggregation of patriots skimmed over the words "fail to conform to such rates," and saw only, "or shall charge in excess thereof." Inasmuch, the pro-railroad element held, as the Constitution says that the railroads shall not charge in excess of the rates fixed by the Railroad Commissioners, the railroads are at liberty to reduce the rates as fixed by the Commissioners at will. In other words, according to the pro-railroad element, the Constitution authorizes the fixing of maximum rates only.

The pro-railroad claquers even went so far as to claim that the Supreme Court has decided that the maximum rate is the only rate that can be fixed under the State Constitution. They referred the doubtful to the notorious decision in the Fresno passenger rate case known as the Edson decision.

But no question of maximum rates was involved in the Edson case. To be sure, Chief Justice Beatty took occasion to say in his opinion in that case that his understanding had been that the State Constitution provides for the maximum rate. But this had no place in the decision, was purely dictum, and is so regarded.

Attorney-General Webb has an ingenious but very plausible explanation of Judge Beatty's much-discussed observation. General Webb points out that previous to the adoption of the present State Constitution - 1879 - Justice

Beatty had been engaged in the active practice of the law in this State. Up to the time of the adoption of the Constitution of 1879 the maximum rate had prevailed in California. About that time, Judge Beatty went to Nevada and was absent from the State for several years. Returning to California, after the State Constitution had been adopted, Judge Beatty found no case in which the duties of the Railroad Commissioners had been involved, until the Edson case came up.

"I am of the opinion," said General Webb in discussing this point, "that when the Chief justice spoke of the maximum rate in the Edson case he was governed by mental impressions received previous to 1879, when the maximum rate was indeed the rule in California."

All this was a very pretty theory. To the common-sense mind "conform to the rates fixed" might mean conform to them; the normal man might be unable to dig out of the Constitution any prohibition of absolute rates. But the confusion caused by the raising of the question got the Stetson bill very much in the air.

During all the discussion, however, the Wright bill was not considered at all. Nobody was thinking of the Wright bill - that is to say, nobody outside of those scheming for its passage. Like a mongrel duck's egg under a respectable hen, it was left to incubate undisturbed, to surprise everybody at the hatching.

Finding themselves unable to clear away the doubt which raising the question of the constitutionality of the absolute rate had created, the anti-machine Senators and the attorneys of the shippers finally, after the Wright bill had been forced into prominence, put the case something like this:

"If the Courts decide that the maximum rate only is constitutional, then the Wright bill, which provides for the maximum rate, will be constitutional, and the greater part of the Stetson bill will also be constitutional.

"But if the Courts decide that an absolute rate is the only rate justified under the Constitution, then the Wright bill will be unconstitutional and all the Stetson bill constitutional."

This somewhat loose argument unquestionably kept certain Senators who recognized the impracticability of the maximum rate, but feared for the constitutionality of the absolute rate, in line for the Stetson bill.

With the situation thus confused, all was in readiness to bring the Wright bill before the public. This was done on February 17th. Up to that date the writer honestly believes that not two minutes had been devoted to public discussion of this measure, although the Stetson bill had been discussed paragraph by paragraph, line by line, every word weighed carefully.

The ceremony of giving the Wright bill prominence took place behind the closed doors of an executive session of the Senate Committee on Corporations. These executive sessions, by the way, are seldom held when the best interests of the public are to be conserved. The proceedings were evidently pre-arranged. Senator Wright opened by moving that the policy of the Committee should be that the Railroad Regulation measure to receive favorable consideration from the Committee must provide for the maximum rate.

The vote was as prompt as it was decisive. Senator Wright's motion carried by a vote of 7 to 3. The vote was as follows:

For the maximum rate - Bates, Welch, Wright, McCartney, Bills, Finn, Kennedy.

Against the maximum rate - Walker, Roseberry, Miller.

Burnett, the eleventh member of the Committee, was absent.

Gradually it dawned upon Walker, Miller and Roseberry that this meant the favorable recommendation of the Wright bill. The next moment that fact was hammered into them by the Committee deciding by the same vote, 7 to 3, to recommend that the Stetson bill do not pass; and that the Wright bill do pass.

The machine had won the opening skirmish in the railroad regulation controversy. Incidentally it had come out in the open squarely for the Wright bill. From that moment the machine Senators labored openly for the passage of the measure. However, the machine was not yet out of the woods with its Railroad Regulation bill. The Senate Judiciary Committee had still to pass upon it, and the majority of the Judiciary Committee was anti-machine.

Wright followed the same course in the Judiciary Committee as he had taken in the Committee on Corporations, namely, moved that it be the sense of the Committee that the Railroad Regulation bill to be favorably considered by the Committee should provide for the maximum rate.

Wright's motion was, however, lost by a vote of 8 to 10. The Committee not only rejected the maximum rate, but endorsed the absolute rate, thus reversing the Committee on Corporations. The vote by which this was done was as follows:

Against the maximum rate, against the Wright bill and for the Stetson bill - Campbell, Cutten, Miller, Stetson, Thompson, Caminetti, Boynton, Roseberry, Curtin and Cartwright - 10.

For the maximum rate, for the Wright bill and against the Stetson bill -
Anthony, Martinelli, McCartney, Wright, Willis, Wolfe, Burnett and
Estudillo - 8.

Absent - Savage - 1.

Thus the Stetson bill after two months of machine effort against it, went to
the floor of the Senate from the Judiciary Committee with the
recommendation that it "do pass." Of the forty Senators, nineteen were
lawyers, and every one of the nineteen was a member of the Senate
Judiciary Committee. Thus the majority of the lawyers of the Senate, in
spite of the confusion which the machine claquers had created, were willing
to take their chances on the constitutionality of the Stetson bill.

But in fairness it must be admitted that members of the Judiciary
Committee who voted for the absolute rate provision of the Stetson bill
were still in the befuddled condition in which Peter F. Dunne's sophistry
had left them. Senator Miller, for example, in explaining his vote for the
absolute rate, said:

"I take this stand, not that I am convinced that the Supreme Court will
decide the absolute rate to be constitutional; I fear that it may not. But the
maximum rate is little better than no rate at all. I wish the absolute rate
provided in this bill, that the Supreme Court may be given opportunity to
pass upon it."

Senator Roseberry, who voted for the absolute rate, confessed himself as
much at sea as was Senator Miller. Senator Estudillo, who voted for the
maximum rate, insisted that he had not been able to make up his mind
which should be adopted.

On the other hand, Senator Cutten, himself a lawyer and a close student of
the legal questions involved, stated that while he had thought originally that
the maximum rate is the only constitutional rate that can be fixed, he had
been forced to come to the conclusion that the absolute rate alone is
constitutional.

But in the end the Wright bill and not the Stetson bill passed the Senate. It
passed after a day of debate in which the issue became clouded, if anything,
worse than at any stage of the proceedings. Leavitt and Wolfe, with Wright
chipping in with a me-too word now and then, led the debate in favor of
the Wright bill. Senators Stetson, Boynton, Cutten, Roseberry and Miller
led the fight for the Stetson bill. Significant enough was the fact that the
line-up of Senate leaders was precisely the same as that in the fight which
the machine carried on against the Direct Primary bill.

Miller's argument in favor of the Stetson bill showed the confusion under which the advocates of effective railroad regulation were laboring:

"If we adopt the Wright bill," said Miller, "the railroads will be satisfied and never dispute it in the Courts. Whereas, by the adoption of the Stetson bill the railroads will almost be compelled to appeal to the Courts, and then we shall have a quick decision on the question in which we are all interested. If the Courts sustain the Stetson bill, we shall have a law that will do all we want for the present."[64]

The debate on the measures was on a motion by Stetson that the Stetson bill be substituted for the Wright bill. In this Stetson made a serious mistake. He staked his whole bill on one issue, that of absolute or maximum rates. On all other points, the Stetson bill was better than the Wright bill. It was a mistake in policy for Stetson to stake the fate of his measure on a single issue.

Stetson's motion was lost by a vote of 16 to 22; the Stetson bill was accordingly not substituted for the Wright bill, and the Wright bill, which had come from the Judiciary Committee with a minority report back of it, went to third reading and final passage.

The vote by which Stetson's motion was defeated, was as follows:

To substitute the Stetson bill for the Wright bill - Bell, Birdsall, Black, Boynton, Caminetti, Campbell, Cartwright, Curtin, Cutten, Holohan, Lewis, Miller, Sanford, Stetson, Strobridge, Thompson - 16.

Against substituting the Stetson bill for the Wright bill - Anthony, Bates, Bills, Burnett, Estudillo, Finn, Hare, Hartman, Hurd, Kennedy, Leavitt, Martinelli, McCartney, Price, Reily, Savage, Walker, Weed, Welch, Willis, Wolfe, Wright - 22.

Senators Roseberry and Rush were absent from the room when the vote was taken but both were for the Stetson bill, which would have made the vote 22 to 18 in favor of the Wright bill.

The twenty Senators whose names are printed in Italics are the twenty who voted with Leavitt and Wolfe to maintain the deadlock on the Direct Primary bill that the measure might be so amended that the electors of California would be denied a practical, State-wide vote for United States Senators. But one of the twenty, Lewis, voted for the Stetson bill, while nineteen of them voted for the Wright bill.

On the other hand, only three of the Senators, Estudillo, Anthony and Walker, who stood out for an honest Direct Primary law, voted against the Stetson bill and for the Wright bill. Walker had supported the Stetson bill in the Committee on Corporations, but stumbled into the machine ranks when it came to final vote. Had the anti-machine had an organization, such as the machine Democrats and Republicans maintained, Walker's blunder could have been prevented. Probably, too, Estudillo and Anthony would have remained with the anti-machine forces[65]. This would have given the Stetson bill twenty-one votes, and assured its passage.

Another vote that should have been saved to the reformers was that of Burnett. Burnett was clearly tricked into voting for the Wright bill. When the Stetson bill received the favorable recommendation of the Senate Judiciary Committee, machine claquers filled the air with the indefinite promise that in the event of the Wright bill becoming a law, a constitutional amendment would be adopted, by which all ambiguity in the State Constitution on the question of maximum and absolute rates would be removed. The amendment was then pending before the Senate Judiciary Committee, which finally reported it favorably.

After the Wright bill had been passed, the amendment was defeated by machine votes, as will be shown in the next chapter.

In the closing days of the session, when Burnett was urging that steps be taken for investigation into the increase of freight rates, he called attention to the fate of that railroad-regulation amendment.

"I was led to vote as I did for the Railroad Regulation bill," he said, "on the understanding that that constitutional amendment would be adopted. As you know, it was defeated. My attitude on the regulation bill would have been very different had I known that the amendment was to be rejected."

The Wright bill met with practically no opposition in the Assembly, being rushed through the Lower House in the closing hours of the session. Had the Stetson bill passed the Senate, the machine would have tried to block and amend it in the Assembly as was done with the Direct Primary bill, but the measure would probably have been passed.

Had the anti-machine forces in the Senate been organized, the Stetson, and not the Wright bill, would have passed that body. Without organization, or even definite policy, in the face of organized machine opposition, it is astonishing - and at the same time most encouraging - that eighteen of the forty Senators stood by the Stetson bill to the end.

[64] The question to which Senator Miller referred was: Has the Legislature power under the Constitution to authorize the Railroad Commissioners to fix the absolute rate? a question upon which the machine does not propose the Supreme Court shall be required to pass.

[65] Walker and Estudillo were bitterly condemned for their vote for the Wright bill. Incidentally, the writer has been roundly criticized for offering

the excuse in their behalf that these two men indicated by their attitude on other measures throughout the session that they would have continued with the reform element in the matter of railroad regulation, had the anti-machine Senators been organized to give effective resistance to the machine. Perhaps the sanest of this criticism, certainly the most reasonable, is from a gentleman who was a close observer of the work of the session. He says:

"The course of the railroad rate bill from my point of view looked somewhat different in many details, at any rate, from your account of it. I cannot bring myself to think that it was defeated by any chance at the hands of a friendly Legislature. I think that what chances there were were mostly added to the number of votes the bill got and that the attitude of men like Walker and Estudillo on that bill was fundamental and to have been expected from the start. Of course what you say about the woeful lack of organization amongst the individual men was only too apparent. That phenomenon reaches back still deeper and is based upon the quality of human nature which exerts itself more persistently and more energetically and with soldier-like rhythm of compact organization when private selfish interests are involved, than when the general interest and somewhat vague uncentered end of public welfare is concerned."

But in spite of this very reasonable view, from a very reasonable gentleman, the fact remains that in the Committee on Corporations, Walker stood out against the machine on this very issue, and that in the direct primary fight both Walker and Estudillo stood out against the machine to the end. Had the anti-machine element been organized, the Stetson bill and not the Wright bill would in all probability have been passed.

CHAPTER XIV.

Railroad Measures.

Constitutional Amendment to Clear the Way for an Effective Railroad Regulation Bill Defeated - Rate Investigation Delayed Until Too Late for Effectiveness - Resolution to Continue Investigation Defeated - Reciprocal Demurrage Bill Becomes a Law - "Error" in the Full Crew Bill.

The anti-machine members of the Legislature had not proceeded far in their efforts to pass an effective railroad regulation law, before they became convinced that at best only a make-shift measure is possible, until certain alleged ambiguities of those sections of the State Constitution prescribing the powers and duties of the State Board of Railroad Commissioners have been removed. Where, to the common sense mind, no ambiguities exist, machine claquers and Southern Pacific attorneys can read them into the Constitution very easily, as in the dispute as to whether the absolute or the minimum rate is constitutional.

Advised by the attorneys representing the shipping interests, the anti-machine members undertook to simplify the language of the sections in dispute, so that a wayfaring man though a Judge on the bench or a machine legislator need not err in the construction thereof.

Early in the session, Senator Campbell had introduced a constitutional amendment to that end. The amendment went to the Judiciary Committee on January 14th. The majority of the committee, openly against the machine, favored the submission to the people of such an amendment. But it was not until February 22d that the amendment - or rather a substitute for it - was reported back to the Senate.

The day following, February 23d, Senator Campbell had the measure re-referred to the committee, that an amendment better calculated to meet the needs of the State might be prepared. The committee took until March 5th to make its report. The anti-machine Senators on the committee had to fight for every inch of the way toward securing a report upon an effective amendment. This, however, they finally succeeded in doing. The second substitute amendment smoothed out the ambiguities and the alleged ambiguities of the Constitution, of which the machine legislators made so much during the session, and of which it is feared the courts may make much later on. For the long list of constitutional powers and duties of the Railroad Commissioners, which are so worded as to confuse the legal mind, the framers of the amendment substituted the following:

"The Commission (Railroad) and each of its members shall have such powers and perform such duties as are now or may hereafter be provided for by law." Under that simple permission there could have been no question of the authority of the Legislature to empower the Railroad Commissioners to fix a system of absolute rates. Section 23, Article XII., of the Constitution, which at least confused the lawyers employed by the railroads to prevent the passage of the Stetson bill, was repealed entirely. The adoption of the amendment, would, had it been approved by the people at the general election of 1910, have removed every impediment which railroad attorneys claim to be in the way of an effective railroad regulation law for California.

Curiously enough the machine Senators who had been so much exercised over the alleged ambiguities of the Constitution when the Stetson bill was under consideration were found opposed to the submission of the amendment to the people. Every Senator who voted against the amendment had voted against the Stetson bill and had voted for the Wright bill. Burnett, who had been led to believe when he voted for the Wright bill that the amendment would be submitted to the people, voted for the amendment. Walker also switched back from the machine. Wright and McCartney, who had voted against the Stetson bill, also went on record for the amendment. The remaining fourteen Senators who voted for it, to a man, had voted for the Stetson bill and against the passage of the Wright bill. But a two-thirds vote of the Senate was required for the amendment's adoption. This meant twenty-seven votes. The amendment was defeated, the vote being nineteen for submission of the measure to the people, and sixteen against[66].

This ended all hope of a model railroad regulation law for California until 1913, for the Constitution must be amended before such a law can be realized. If a satisfactory amendment be adopted in 1911, it must before going into effect be ratified by the people. This ratification would come in 1912. The Legislature of 1913 would then be able to proceed with the passage of the model statute.

An attempt to investigate the causes and the necessity of the arbitrary increase in transcontinental freight rates failed as completely as did the attempted amendment of the Constitution.

Early in the session, on January 18, to be exact, Senator Caminetti introduced a resolution which directed the Senate Committee on Federal Relations to inquire into the cause of the increase in freight rates, and to report its findings to the Senate. Two days later Caminetti introduced a second and companion resolution, which provided that investigation should be made into the causes for the increase in express charges. On

Senator Leavitt's motion this last resolution was made a special order for January 22, when the first resolution was to come up. The Senate on the 22d re-referred the resolutions back to the committee.

The Senate Committee on Federal Relations was, by Caminetti's clever; tactics in having the resolutions go to that body, forced into a prominence which evidently worried the machine. It consisted of Burnett, Black and Sanford. Black, Republican, and Sanford, Democrat, were working openly against the machine. Burnett, while he managed to land on the machine side of things at critical points in the progress of the session, was by no means a machine coolie. Had it been known that the Committee on Federal Relations was to be charged with an investigation into railroad affairs, a very different committee would unquestionably have been appointed. The machine's problem was to correct the blunder made when the anti-machine forces were given a majority on what had become a committee charged with the handling of an important railroad issue. The ease with which the blunder was corrected speaks volumes for the machine's resourcefulness.

The air at the capitol suddenly became permeated with the idea that a committee of three was altogether too small to conduct so important an investigation as that proposed in the Caminetti resolutions. Accordingly the Committee on Federal Relations very readily recommended, when it reported the resolutions back to the Senate with the recommendation that the investigation be held, that two Senators be added to the committee, making it a committee of five. Had the machine observed the unwritten rules of Senatorial courtesy[67], which machine Senators insist upon so loudly, the anti-machine element would have been safe enough in doing this. Senatorial courtesy required that the author of the resolutions, Caminetti, be made one of the two additional members. This would have given the anti-machine element at least three members of the enlarged committee, a condition which did not line with machine purposes at all. So Senatorial courtesy was thrown to the winds, Senator Caminetti was ignored, and Senators Wolfe and Bills were named as the additional members of the committee. The machine seldom blunders, but when it does, usually covers its blunders with astonishing directness and dispatch. A glance at the records made by Senators Wolfe and Bills, which will be found in Table "A" of the Appendix, will show the truth of this statement.

The machine's next move was to delay the investigation. For one reason and another the investigation was delayed. Finally, on February 19, Caminetti gave notice that on the following Tuesday, he would move that the committee be discharged and a second committee ordered to carry out the instructions contained in the resolutions. This declaration of war stirred the machine to action - machine action. Assurances were given that the investigation would be held, but it was March 12, almost two months after the resolution had been introduced, and only twelve days before adjournment, before the committee placed its first witness on the stand.

At that time the Senate was in the midst of the Direct Primary fight, and in addition, the machine after months of planning was sending literally hundreds of measures into Senate and Assembly for final action. There was no time nor were the members of the committee in a condition to conduct the investigation which the anti-machine element had contemplated. But hurried hearings were held, and a mass of evidence of railroad and express company extortion brought into the open. The interested reader will find the testimony printed in the Senate journal of March 23, 1909.

Men of the standing of Edwin Bonnheim[68], treasurer and manager of Weinstock, Lubin & Co.; Russell D. Carpenter, auditor of Hale Brothers, Inc.; J. O. Bracken, manager of the California Commercial Association; C. H. Bentley of the California Fruit Canners Association; all testified that the increase in express and freight charges has worked great hardship upon the State. They showed that in the final analysis the consumer pays the increased charges. Furthermore, testimony was produced which at least indicated that the transportation companies, if economically not to say honestly managed, would receive fair returns on their legitimate investments, were even lower freight rates to be charged than those exacted prior to the increase of 1908. It was also shown that the State of California could institute and conduct an examination into railroad affairs before the Interstate Commerce Commission[69]. It was clear to all that thorough investigation under the Caminetti resolutions would prove of enormous benefit to the State. That the committee could do little or nothing in the short time remaining before adjournment was also recognized. Burnett had come out for thorough investigation, giving the anti-machine forces a majority of the committee. Witness after witness representing the large shippers and importers of the State urged that the investigation be carried on even after the Legislature had adjourned. Burnett as chairman of the committee was urging this course, but it was March 23, the day before adjournment, before he could get his committee report ready, and filed with the Senate, as basis for a resolution to continue the investigation after the Legislature had adjourned. There were but eleven dependable anti-machine Senators in addition to Burnett who were within reach of the capitol. But the machine had a safe majority within call. Burnett's resolution was defeated, the investigation denied, by a vote of twelve for to sixteen against[70].

But two important railroad measures were finally passed by the Legislature. The first of these was the "Full Crew bill," which required adequate manning of railroad trains. After being held-up as long as the machine dared, the bill was finally passed. But the "Full Crew bill" met with one of those unfortunate "errors"[71] which played such important parts in the passage of the Anti-Gambling bill and the Direct Primary bill. When the Legislature had adjourned this error was discovered, and Governor Gillett refused to sign the bill because of it.

The second important railroad measure passed was the Reciprocal Demurrage bill, introduced in the Senate by Miller, and in the Assembly by Drew. As finally passed the bill provides that railroad companies which fail to supply shippers with cars when proper requisition has been made for them, shall pay the injured shipper demurrage at the rate of $5 per car per day. On the other hand, shippers who fail to load or unload cars after a stated time, are required to pay the railroad $6 daily as demurrage. The extra dollar which the shippers are required to pay the railroads is exacted to compensate the railroads for rental of the car.

Similar laws up to the time of the passage of the Miller-Drew bill had been adopted by seventeen States of the Union, including Oregon and Texas. During the recent car shortage, it is alleged that empty cars needed in California, were sent into Oregon and into Texas, that the railroads might escape the demurrage charges exacted in those two States. California, without a demurrage law, was helpless. At the session of 1907, however, the machine, in complete control of the Senate, defeated a reciprocal demurrage bill. To be sure the demurrage was higher in the measure proposed in 1907 than in that passed at the session of 1909, but it was the principle of demurrage, not its amount, that the machine was against in 1907. In 1909, however, not a Senator voted against the bill. And in this connection there is a story told which unquestionably had its bearing upon the fate of the Reciprocal Demurrage bill at the 1909 session. The story deals with a political adventure in the life of one Henry Lynch.

Mr. Lynch voted against reciprocal demurrage in 1907. He voted neither for nor against reciprocal demurrage in 1909, for he was not at Sacramento to vote. Mr. Lynch was not at Sacramento to vote in 1909, for one reason at least, because he did vote against reciprocal demurrage in 1907.

Mr. Lynch hailed from the Thirty-first Senatorial District, which takes in San Benito and San Luis Obispo counties. These counties are intensely Republican; they are also farming communities. And since the one-time Senator Lynch voted against the Reciprocal Demurrage bill, the farmers have seen tons upon tons of their products rot in the fields because they could not get cars to move their crops.

But while the farmers of San Luis Obispo and San Benito counties were watching their products rot for want of cars to move them, it is alleged that cars were being sent from California to Oregon to meet the requisitions of Oregon shippers. Oregon had a reciprocal demurrage law on her statute books; California had not.

Senator Lynch's vote against the Reciprocal Demurrage bill was made a sort of issue in San Benito and San Luis Obispo counties at the election of 1908. A. E. Campbell, Democrat, was running against Mr. Lynch, Republican, for the State Senate. Right or wrong - the reader may judge which - the farmers of the two counties credited the defeat of the Reciprocal Demurrage bill not to the Republican Party, but to the Republican machine, or better described perhaps as the Republican-Democratic machine, that dominates the State, a machine which the people of California are just now engaged in smashing.

Being good Republicans, the people of Mr. Lynch's district gave Mr. Taft a plurality of more than 1,700; remembering the defeat of the Reciprocal Demurrage bill, they gave Mr. Campbell, Democratic candidate for the Senate, a plurality of 416. The fact that a United States Senator was to be elected didn't influence the Republicans of San Luis Obispo County at all. They elected a Democrat to the State Senate because they knew him to be free from machine domination - a machine maintained for the purpose of defeating good measures, such as the Reciprocal Demurrage bill, and furthering the passage of bad ones.

But the influence of Lynch's vote against the Reciprocal Demurrage bill was not confined to San Luis Obispo and San Benito Counties. It spread over into the adjoining Twenty-ninth District, which takes in Santa Cruz and San Mateo Counties. These counties are also intensely Republican. They gave Taft a plurality of 2,799. But they gave the Democratic candidate for the State Senate, James B. Holohan, a plurality of 677. Holohan ran 3,476 votes ahead of his ticket in a district where only 9,483 votes were cast for State Senator. Holohan was known to be free of machine influences. He could be counted upon to vote for a Reciprocal Demurrage bill without first consulting the Southern Pacific's political agent, Jere Burke. And the Republican whose place he took in the Senate had voted against the Reciprocal Demurrage bill of 1907.

The election of Holohan and Campbell unquestionably had its influence on the passage of the Demurrage, bill. Not a member of the Senate cast his vote against it, although several of the Senators who had voted against the bill two years before, sat in the Senate of 1909. Among these were ten Senators who, during the session of 1909, were conspicuously on the wrong side of most questions. They were Senators Bates, Hartman, Leavitt, McCartney, Reily, Savage, Weed, Willis, Wolfe and Wright. The ten, for example, constituted half the twenty Senators who opposed the plan to give The People State-wide popular vote in the selection of United States Senators. Only seven Senators voted against the Anti-Racetrack Gambling bill. Five of the seven - Hartman, Leavitt, Reily, Weed and Wolfe - had voted against reciprocal demurrage in 1907. But there was a harkening to the demand of The People in 1909, which had been wanting two years before. Seven of these ten Senators, who voted against reciprocal demurrage in 1907 - Bates, Hartman, McCartney, Savage, Willis, Wolfe and Wright - voted for reciprocal demurrage in 1909. Three of them - Leavitt, Reily and Weed - did not vote at all.

[66] The vote was as follows:

For the amendment: Bell, Birdsall, Boynton, Burnett, Caminetti, Campbell, Cartwright, Curtin, Cutten, Holohan, McCartney, Miller, Roseberry, Rush, Strobridge, Sanford, Thompson, Walker, Wright - 19.

Against the amendment: Anthony, Bills, Estudillo, Finn, Hartman, Hurd, Kennedy, Leavitt, Lewis, Price, Reily, Savage, Weed, Welch, Willis, Wolfe - 16.

[67] Machine Senators habitually exact the utmost consideration and courtesy from the anti-machine Senators, and habitually repay it with deceit and trickery. The curious feature of this is that the anti-machine Senators continue to extend the courtesy and continue to be tricked and imposed upon. A shutting off of "Senatorial courtesy" would go far toward solving the problem of machine domination of the Legislature.

[68] Mr. Bonnheim testified that prior to the new schedule of express rates enforced between New York and the city of San Francisco, the rate was $8.00 per hundred for shipments of from 10,000 to 20,000 pounds; $9.00 per hundred for 5,000 to 10,000 pounds; $10.00 per hundred for 2,000 to 5,000 pounds; $11.00 per hundred from 1,000 to 2,000 pounds. and $12.00 from 500 to 1,000 pounds; $13.50 from 100 to 500 pounds.

That the withdrawal of the bulk rates in December, 1908, resulted in an advance of 35 per cent by the withdrawal of the 2,000 pound rate, and an advance of 50 per cent by the withdrawal of the 5,000 pound rate; an advance of 66 3/4 per cent by the withdrawal of the 10,000 pound rate, and that the withdrawal of the 20,000 pound rate amounted to an advance of 92 8/10 per cent.

[69] Senator Cartwright actually introduced a resolution calling upon the Attorney-General to institute proceedings before the Interstate Commerce Commission:

To determine whether existing rates are reasonable or unreasonable.

To ascertain, fix and establish a reasonable schedule of freight rates, and to enforce the same.

To determine whether or not any existing rate is discriminatory.

And to prevent further discrimination between persons or places.

The resolution carried an appropriation of $25,000 to ensure competent legal and expert assistance.

The resolution was introduced on February 4. It went first to the Committee on Federal Relations, then to the Judiciary Committee, then to the Committee on Finance, from which it emerged March 1 with the recommendation that it be adopted. On March 2 it was sent back to the Committee on Finance and was never heard from again. The enormous benefit to the State if such an investigation could be honestly and effectively carried on, will be recognized.

[70] The vote was as follows:

For the resolution: Bell, Birdsall, Boynton, Burnett, Caminetti, Cutten, Estudillo, Holohan, Roseberry, Rush, Sanford, Thompson - 12.

Against the resolution: Anthony, Bates, Bills, Finn, Hartman, Hurd, Kennedy, Leavitt, Lewis, Martinelli, Reily, Savage, Weed, Willis, Wolfe, Wright - 16.

[71] E. F. Mitchell, Executive Secretary to Governor Gillett, makes the following statement regarding this particular error:

The electric companies which run interurban trains, also claimed that the bill, as prepared, applied to them, and would place upon them an unnecessary burden and expense.

"There is no doubt that section three of the act applies to motor cars and electric cars. The language is very plain. Section one of the bill describes passenger trains, section two refers to freight trains, and section three says "all other trains not propelled by steam locomotives." Now, there are only two classes of cars that are not propelled by steam locomotives, and those are motor and electric cars. In the Governor's opinion, an error was made in endeavoring to amend it, so it would not apply to motor cars and electric cars. The amendment was prepared, and we had here in the office, during the argument on the bill, the original committee amendments proposed. The amendment was to be made after the word "train" on the second line and had this amendment been made as contemplated, it would have excluded motor cars and electric cars, but instead of having been made on line two, as expected, it was carried into line three, where it gave the bill an entirely different meaning, It was one of those unfortunate things that crept into legislation through an oversight of somebody, which could have been readily corrected if the bill had been watched. The insertion of this amendment in the wrong place, instead of excluding motor cars and electric cars, as intended, included them. This error was not discovered until the bill came up before the Governor for consideration."

CHAPTER XV.

Defeat of the Commonwealth Club Bills.

Drawn By Committees of the Ablest San Francisco Attorneys Not Under Retainer of Prison-Dodging Captains of Industry - Measures Not Allowed to Reach Senate or Assembly, but Killed in Committees - Grove L. Johnson's Keen Opposition.

The graft prosecution at San Francisco not only brought the fact squarely before the public that large corporations sometimes catch the easiest way to achieve their purposes by bribing public officials, but that it is a deal easier to pass a camel through the eye of a needle than a millionaire offender through the legal cobwebs of technicality to a cell at San Quentin or Folsom[72].

That the technical defense in criminal cases was subject to grave abuses had been generally recognized. But it took the graft cases at San Francisco to fairly rub this unpleasant fact into the law-abiding element. Because for the first time in the practice of criminal law in California, unlimited wealth was available to employ the best legal talent to defend men under indictment.

The defending lawyers took advantage of every technicality. They emphasized the most trivial of them. Gradually it began to dawn upon The People that here were legal refuges, based upon the most absurd of technicalities, the sweeping away of which would in no way injure the substantial rights of a person charged with crime, refuges which were available to the rich man but denied to the poor or moderately well-to-do.

To be sure, any person accused could make his technical defense if he had the means to employ the necessary counsel. But in face of the astonishing performances going on in the courts at San Francisco, it soon became apparent to the thoughtful, that no man, whose fortune was expressed in terms of less than five ciphers could make such a defense.

Thus the unpalatable truth was forced home, that we have in California a technical defense available for the rich man charged with crime, which is in effect denied even those of the so-called middle classes.

With this conviction came demand of reform of the criminal laws to ensure:

(1) A prompt trial of an accused person on the merits of the case.

(2) A prompt judgment in the case of a verdict of guilty.

(3) A prompt hearing of the case in the Court of Appeal.

The machine was, of course, against any such "wicked innovations," as Assemblyman Grove L. Johnson would have called them.

However, at San Francisco, three considerable bodies, the Bar Association, the Commonwealth Club and the Citizens' League of Justice, took the matter up, and for months had the ablest lawyers of the State - at any rate the ablest not retained for the defense of capitalists under indictment - at work wrestling with the problem of simplifying the criminal codes and doing away so far as possible with technical defense, except in such cases as the substantial rights of the defendant might be involved.

A committee consisting of J. C. McKinstry, J. J. Dwyer, Lester H. Jacobs, Oscar Cushing and Warren Olney Jr. was appointed for this purpose by the Citizens' League of Justice. The Commonwealth Club appointed Beverly L. Hodghead, Orrin K. McMurray, Alex. G. Eells, Fairfax H. Wheelan, Sidney V. Smith, Lester H. Jacobs and Joseph Hutchinson. One would go far before finding more representative or more public-spirited bodies of citizens, or more able exponents of the law.

The labors of the several committees resulted in what may in a broad way be regarded as two sets of bills being prepared.

The first, known as the Commonwealth Club bills, were sixty-five in number, and were introduced in the Senate by Campbell, and in the Assembly by Butler. The second set was known as the Bar Association bills. They were introduced in the Senate by Burnett. They were nine in number, and while apparently covering much of the ground of the Commonwealth Club bills, were in no respects so complete as to method or detail. The Bar Association bills pin-pricked an abuse; the Commonwealth Club bills drove the knife in deep.

The sixty-five Commonwealth Club bills were readily divided into three groups, those dealing with Grand Juries and indictments, with trial juries and verdicts, and with appeals to the higher courts.

The general purpose of the measures dealing with Grand Juries was to make those bodies purely accusatory, to make their findings conclusive and not subject to attack. The basis of the proposed amendments and additions to the laws governing Grand Juries was that Grand Juries are primarily required to investigate secret offenses, and should be regarded as purely accusatory bodies. On this theory the Commonwealth Club bills made the indictment of a Grand Jury as binding as the action of a committing magistrate who holds a defendant to answer. Had the Commonwealth Club bills become laws there would have been no more placing of Grand Jurors on trial for having found indictments against persons able to employ crafty criminal lawyers.

But lest the defendant under investigation might be wronged, the Commonwealth Club measures so amended the codes that a Grand Juror in any way biased against the defendant was required to absent himself from the Grand Jury room when the defendant's case was under consideration. Under the proposed laws each Grand Juror was required to take oath "not to participate in the inquiry as to any matter or affecting any person as to which or whom he is biased or could not vote freely either way that the evidence presented would in justice require him to vote."

The Commonwealth Club amendments regarding trial juries dealt with the problem in the same broad spirit. The chief object sought was to avoid the trying of citizens called for jury service[73]. The proposed laws obviated this by leaving it with the Judge to determine the qualifications of the juror, that is to say, the examination of jurors in criminal cases was to have been taken out of the hands of the lawyers and required of the Judge. To compensate the defendant for whatever substantial disadvantage he might suffer, the number of his peremptory challenges was materially increased.

To prevent the setting aside of judgments on trifling technicalities, the proposed amendments provided that the Judge should fix the legality of the jury panel by general order, after which challenges could not apply to the whole panel, although they still held as to individual jurors.

One of the most important of the provisions regarding trial jurors was that the reading of mere newspaper reports of a case should not disqualify a trial juror, unless it were shown that the newspaper article purported to be a true copy of the official testimony.

The fact that under the present law the term "reasonable doubt" is not given legal definition paves the way for frequent miscarriages of justice. The Judge is required to define the term for the jury. The defendant may take exception to the definition, thus paving the way for technical defense in the upper Courts. The Commonwealth Club bills defined "reasonable doubt" to be, "that state of the case which, after the entire comparison and consideration of all the evidence in the cause, leaves the minds of the jurors in that condition that they cannot say they feel an abiding conviction to a moral certainty of the truth of the charge."

Amendments were also proposed to the law governing instructions to juries. Under the present rule, each side presents a long list of instructions for the Judge to give to the jury. If the Judge refuse to give the instructions as requested, objections to his refusal can be taken and made basis for a technical defense[73a]. Under the proposed amendments objection could be made only to such instructions as were given, not to those which were not presented to the jury.

In none of those proposed amendments could the substantial rights of the defendant be said to be encroached upon. But the proposed laws did clear away a mass of technicalities which has kept many a scamp out of jail.

The proposed amendments dealing with appeals in criminal cases aimed at prompt judgment and sentence after conviction, prompt appeal and conclusion of the case.

To this end, the measures provided that upon conviction the defendant must be sentenced forthwith, and if appeals were taken, taken on the judgment. Instead of the cumbersome bill of exceptions, which required weeks and sometimes months to prepare, it was provided that the entire testimony given at the trial, together with the complete minutes of the proceedings, should be sent to the higher tribunal. This would place before the Appellate and Supreme Courts all the facts and testimony which the Lower Court had considered. This feature of the Commonwealth Club bills was also covered by the measures which had been prepared by the Bar Association.

Under the proposed Commonwealth Club amendments, the defendant was not permitted to appeal on questions referring to the trial jury panels or the Grand jury, nor on any error not affecting his substantial rights. Error in an immaterial issue, or of not sufficient importance to affect the substantial rights of the defendant, was not, under the provisions of the Commonwealth Club bills, to be held ground for reversal.

"We believe," said the Committee which drew up the Commonwealth Club bills, "that what we have proposed is in no way revolutionary and deprives the accused person of no substantial right. The amendments proposed are merely designed to make the present law more effective, to relieve the Courts from the necessity of considering trivial matters and to aid in determining more promptly whether a person accused of crime is innocent or guilty."

The bills as introduced in the Assembly were referred to the Assembly Judiciary Committee. In the Senate, the bills went to the Senate Judiciary Committee.

The promoters of the Commonwealth Club bills made the mistake of treating the machine Senators and Assemblymen as men who could be won over with reason and plain statement. Instead of fighting for their bills and demanding their passage, the agents of the club were willing to listen courteously to suggestions from tricksters intent upon the defeat of the measures, who were only playing for time.

Carroll Cook was at Sacramento lobbying against the bills, as were others of that gentleman's view of affairs. Cook actually appeared before the Assembly Judiciary Committee on invitation of one of its members. The courtesy shown him by Grove L. Johnson, chairman of the Committee, was touching or nauseating, as one might view it. Johnson, who was in effect the Committee, took occasion on the day of Cook's appearance to denounce the measures as revolutionary, unconstitutional, vicious.

It is interesting to note that sixty-three of the sixty-five bills as introduced in the Assembly never got beyond Johnson's Committee. They died right there. The two exceptions got out of the Committee in the closing days of the session, one on March 10th, the other on March 20th. They were reported out with the recommendation that they do pass. It was then too late to take any action on them. They died on the Assembly file.

Those who were making a fight for the measures were kept running between the Judiciary Committee of the Assembly and that of the Senate. The Senate Committee, while a majority of its members were against the machine, was led by men who were not at all in sympathy with any plan that was calculated to clear away legal cobwebs. On the pretext that the reforms proposed were covered by the Bar Association bills, or that the measures were duplicated by other bills, or that they were loosely drawn, on any pretext, in fact, the Senate Committee recommended that fifty-two of the sixty-five measures be withdrawn. And they were withdrawn. Of the thirteen remaining, seven stuck in the Committee, died there; five, just before the session closed, were referred back to the Senate with the recommendation that they do not pass. They didn't. Of the sixty-five bills, the Senate Committee gave only one favorable recommendation. This lone recipient of Committee approval got back to the Senate on March 5th. It died on the files.

Such was the fate of the measures prepared under the direction of the Commonwealth Club for reform of the methods of indictment, trial and appeal in criminal cases. The Bar Association bills received somewhat better treatment.

Of the nine so-called Bar Association bills, eight passed the Senate; the other died in the Senate Judiciary Committee. Of the eight which got through the Senate, two were defeated in the Assembly, while six passed that body and went to the Governor.

Four of the six Bar Association bills which passed dealt with the repeal of those sections of the code which provide for bills of exceptions in criminal cases and substituted the plan, described in considering the Commonwealth Club bills, of providing the higher Court with complete record of the testimony and the proceedings in the trial Court.

One of the two remaining measures requires sentence to be imposed upon a convicted felon in not less than two nor more than five days after the verdict or plea of guilty, with the right reserved for the Court of extending the time to ten days. The sixth measure defines "a motion in arrest of judgment."

Such was the outcome of the effort made by reputable lawyers and public spirited laymen to eliminate quackery from the practice of the criminal law. But measures calculated to make the practice of the criminal law even more involved and technical than it is were granted more consideration. Many of them passed both houses. How they were passed and what they are will be considered in another chapter.

[72] No sooner had the indictments been returned in the San Francisco cases than the validity of the indicting Grand Jury was attacked. For months that issue occupied the attention of the Courts. One by one the members of the Grand Jury were dragged into Court, and in effect placed on trial that technical disqualification if such existed might be established. The greater part of a day was, for example, consumed in thrashing over the question whether one or three motions had been made in nominating the stenographer to the Grand Jury.

Then came appeals to the higher Courts which occupied more months and all but endless labor and expense.

When the attacks on the Grand Jury had been met and disposed of, and the defendants brought to the trial Court, the Prosecution found its labors scarcely begun. Every trial juror was placed on trial. Weeks and even months were required, because of technical objections, to secure a trial jury.

Just before the Legislature convened, Abe Ruef, had, as example, been convicted by a jury in the securing of which the metropolis of the State had been raked as with a fine-tooth comb for talesmen who were not technically disqualified to serve. Thousands were available who would have given the defendant a fair trial, but in all San Francisco very few could be found who were not because of one technical reason or another disqualified.

After conviction came the defendant's appeal, in which the Most trivial reasons were accepted for freeing the defendant whose technical defense had failed him in the lower Courts. Former Mayor Schmitz of San Francisco, after conviction of extortion, and Abe Ruef, after having pleaded guilty to the charge, were given their freedom under circumstances which, to put it mildly, shocked the whole State.

[73] A prominent San Francisco attorney told the writer recently that "the criminal lawyer too often questions a talesman needlessly, not so much to disqualify him, as to get technical error into the record."

[73a] It was on a technicality of this kind that the District Court of Appeals found excuse for reversal of the judgment in the case of Louis Glass, convicted of bribing a member of the San Francisco Board of Supervisors. E. J. Zimmer, the auditor of the Pacific States Telephone Company, of which Glass was an official, refused to testify at Glass' trial. The trial court refused to instruct the jury to disregard the refusal. The Appellate Court held this to be a fatal error.

CHAPTER XVI.

How the Change of Venue Bill Was Passed.

Slipped Through the Assembly Without Serious Opposition in Closing Days
of the Session - Passed by Trick in the Senate Although a Majority of That Body Were Opposed to Its Passage - Typical Case of Machine "Generalship."

Given the presiding officers of the Senate and Assembly and the appointment of the Committees of both bodies, the machine minority in the Legislature had comparatively little difficulty in preventing the passage of desirable measures. Thus, the Commonwealth Club bills to simplify and expedite proceedings in criminal cases, or, if you like, to prevent quackery in the practice of the criminal law, were, by clever manipulation, defeated, although if fairly presented to Senate and Assembly they undoubtedly would have become laws[74].

But when it came to passing vicious measures in the face of the opposition of the unorganized majority of both Houses, the machine had a harder job on its hands. A majority vote of each House is required for the passage of a measure. To get through its bills, then, the machine had to create a situation in which vicious measures could be rushed through without the unorganized reformers knowing what was being done. By preventing action on a large majority of the measures pending before the Legislature until the end of the session, such a situation was created. In the confusion of the closing days of the session, not only were good bills denied passage, but vicious bills, in spite of the opposition of a majority of the Legislature, were passed. Some normally anti-machine members in such a situation become worn out, get discouraged and vote for machine policies to secure machine support for measures, the passage of which their constituents at home are demanding. Others, in the confusion of a whirlwind close of the session, vote for measures which they have no time to read, and which they cannot understand. Thus, even with a majority of Senate and Assembly against machine policies, the clever machine leaders often slip through measures which could not be passed early in the session, when the members have opportunity to study the bills upon which they are called upon to act, and before the ranks of the reform element have been broken.

This was very well illustrated at the Session of 1909 by the passage of the so-called Change of Venue bill[74a]. This measure was introduced in the Assembly by Grove L. Johnson. Under its provisions a person charged with crime would have been permitted upon his whim or caprice to allege bias and disqualify the Judge before whom he was to be tried. The Legislature of 1907 was admittedly controlled by the machine, but even the Legislature of 1907 did not dare pass the Change of Venue bill. The reform Legislature of 1909, however, did pass it. The manner in which it was passed is a lesson in machine methods. To the credit of Governor Gillett let it be said, however, that he vetoed the measure[75].

Grove L. Johnson having introduced the bill, it was referred to Johnson's committee, the Judiciary Committee of the Assembly. The Committee held it until February 5, when it was referred back to the Assembly with the recommendation that it "do pass." On March 13, eleven days before adjournment, it passed the Assembly, by a vote of 42 to 15, 41 votes being required for its passage. Assemblymen like Drew, Telfer, Wilson and Stuckenbruck, men who fought the machine and machine policies from the beginning to the end of the session, voted for the bill. The negative vote of any two of them would have defeated it[76].

The passage in the Assembly of an important reform measure as late as March 13, would have meant its defeat in the Senate. Though in the majority the anti-machine Senators could not have forced a reform measure through the machine-controlled committees, machine-controlled even when a majority of a committee was anti-machine[77]. Measures of the Change of Venue bill stamp, however, had a clear way. The Change of Venue bill was on March 15 referred to the Senate Judiciary Committee. On March 16, twenty-four hours after, the Committee returned the bill with the recommendation that it do pass. On March 19, with twenty-two Senators opposed to its passage, and eighteen favoring it, with twenty-one votes necessary for its passage, the bill passed the Senate. This apparently impossible feat was, in the last two weeks of the session, a comparatively easy task for the machine.

To begin with, Senator Black, who opposed the bill, was ill at his home at Palo Alto. This left twenty-one Senators against the measure and eighteen for. The line-up was as follows:

For the Change of Venue bill - Anthony, Bates, Bills, Finn, Hare, Hartman, Hurd, Leavitt, Martinelli, McCartney, Price, Reily, Savage, Weed, Welch, Willis, Wolfe, Wright - 18.

Against the Change of Venue bill - Bell, Birdsall, Boynton, Burnett[76a], Caminetti, Campbell, Cartwright, Curtin, Cutten, Estudillo, Holohan, Lewis, Kennedy, Miller, Roseberry, Rush, Sanford, Stetson, Strobridge, Thompson, Walker - 21.

On the face of it, the outlook for the passage of the Change of Venue bill in the Senate was not good. The machine, however, planned to pass the bill on March 19.

The machine leaders went at the job systematically. When the Senators took their seats that Friday morning, they found that at Senator Bates' request, Assembly Bill 6 (the Change of Venue bill) had been put on the Special Urgency File. The Special Urgency File was to be considered at 8 o'clock Friday evening. Senator Bates stated in an interview that he had placed Assembly Bill No. 6 on the Special Urgency File "at the request of a fellow Senator." Who the fellow Senator was, Bates refused to say. Bates insisted, however, that he knew nothing about Assembly Bill No, 6, and could give no reason why it should be made a matter of "special urgency." Senator Bates has since the Legislature adjourned been given a position of trust in the United States Mint.

With the Change of Venue bill on the Special Urgency File, the next step was to get it considered at the moment most favorable for machine purposes. Along about 11 o'clock in the forenoon - the reader should keep in mind that in the ordinary course of the Senate's work the Special Urgency File would not have been considered until 8 o'clock that evening - Senator Wolfe moved that the Special Urgency File be taken up out of order. But before the Change of Venue bill could be reached, Senator Wright, who favored the passage of the measure, was found to be absent from the Senate chamber. On Senator McCartney's motion, the Change of Venue bill was temporarily passed on file. With the constant coming and going of Senators, there was no time while the file was under consideration, that the eighteen Senators counted on to vote in a solid block for the bill, were all present. The Senate concluded consideration of the Special Urgency File, and still the Change of Venue bill had not been taken up. The Senate then took up the second reading of Assembly bills, and then the Special File of Appropriation bills. A communication from Dr. Howard Black and Dr. Harry D. Reynolds was read setting forth that Senator Black was too ill to leave Palo Alto. Bills were passed and bills were withdrawn. Senator Strobridge reported that Senate Bill No. 862 had been correctly engrossed. And through it all the machine was watching for the favorable moment to force the passage of the Change of Venue bill.

The moment came just before noon. Like the snap of a trap Leavitt asked for unanimous consent to take up Assembly Bill No. 6, out of order. The anti-machine Senators are never guilty of discourteous treatment of a fellow Senator. They granted the request.

Senator Wright vouched for the bill. He stated that it was a good bill and should be made a law. Senator Wolfe spoke for it, in fact led the debate to secure its passage. On the other hand, Senator Boynton very pointedly told Senator Wright that the bill was not a good measure and should not be passed "Judges of the Supreme Court tell me," said Boynton, "that this is a bad bill."

Senator Cutten made a strong speech against the bill, which he denounced as bad in principle. Holohan stated that if the measure became a law it would give a bunco steerer a chance to disqualify every decent Judge in the State. Roseberry denounced the measure as vicious.

When the vote was taken, every Senator who supported it was in his seat, but Burnett, Estudillo and Rush were absent. This would have made the vote 18 to 18, the backers of the measure requiring three more affirmative votes for its passage. But Miller and Lewis were led to vote for the measure, which made 20 votes for the bill and 16 against it. At this point the bill lacked one vote of passage. Estudillo was, however, brought in under call of the Senate, and under what amounted to misrepresentation, voted for the measure. This passed the bill by a vote of 21 to 18. Boynton changed his vote from no to aye, to give notice that on the next legislative day he would move to reconsider the vote by which the bill had been passed. But before he could give notice the Senate took its noon recess. Boynton under the rules had all day in which to notify the Senate of his intention, but to make assurance doubly sure, he told the clerk at the desk not to send the bill to the Assembly for he would as soon as the Senate re-convened, give notice of his motion to reconsider.

Nevertheless, when the Senate reconvened, Boynton found that the bill had been rushed over to the Assembly, "to save time," according to the excuse given.

Senator Boynton insisted that the bill be returned from the Assembly. Wolfe asked Boynton "as a matter of Senatorial courtesy," to permit the vote on the bill to be taken on a motion to have it returned from the Assembly. This request was so ludicrous, in view of the treatment that had been accorded Boynton, that it provoked a smile. Boynton refused to be "courteous," the bill was returned from the Assembly and regularly reconsidered the next day.

With 21 votes against the measure, there seemed little doubt that it would be reconsidered and defeated. Twenty-one votes were necessary for reconsideration. Lewis and Miller had thought better of their vote of Friday and were prepared to vote against the bill. Estudillo, understanding the measure thoroughly, was anxious to set himself right in the record by voting against it. These, with Burnett and Rush, gave twenty-one votes, enough to force reconsideration and to defeat the bill.

But there was a weak link in the combination,Kennedy. Senator Kennedy voted throughout the session consistently with the Wolfe-Leavitt element, but he voted against the Change of Venue bill. When Saturday morning came, however, Kennedy could not be found. When reconsideration of the bill came up, Burnett and Rush were out in the hallway. Miller and Lewis voted to reconsider, which made the vote eighteen to eighteen. Twenty-one votes were necessary for reconsideration. With Kennedy, Burnett and Rush, reconsideration could be forced and the bill defeated. The only way the absent Senators could be reached was through a call of the Senate, which required a majority vote of those present. A motion for a call of the Senate was defeated by a vote of eighteen to eighteen[78].

This was the real test vote on the Change of Venue bill. It will be seen that Miller and Lewis and Estudillo, who had voted for the bill the day before, voted for a call of the Senate. They would, on reconsideration, have voted against the bill, and its passage on reconsideration would have been impossible. Had Kennedy or Rush or Burnett been present, the motion for a call of the Senate would have prevailed, the vote on the Change of Venue bill been reconsidered, and the measure defeated.

Half an hour later, when Kennedy's vote was necessary to enable the machine to continue the deadlock on the Direct Primary bill, Kennedy turned up to do his part in that not very creditable performance.

In this way did the machine element secure the passage of the Change of Venue bill. It was a question of good generalship, or, if you like, trickery. Perhaps trickery is the better name for it.

[74] Black's Senate bill, 1,144, came very near being defeated in the Assembly by similar "good generalship." The measure in effect prohibits the sale of intoxicating liquors within a mile and a half of Stanford University. Assemblyman Bohnett was in charge of the bill.

Bohnett, the day that the bill was to come up, was called from the room to attend a committee meeting. Immediately did the Assembly show astonishing activity in consideration of the file. So fast did they go that the Stanford bill seemed destined to be reached while Bohnett was out of the room. Had it been reached with Bohnett away it could have been dropped to the bottom of the file, where it would have been lost, so far as the session of the Legislature of 1909 was concerned.

Charles R. Detrick, of Palo Alto, happened to go to the Assembly chamber at this critical moment and took in the situation at a glance. He accordingly hunted up Bohnett, who got back to the Assembly chamber before the bill could be reached on file. For once "good generalship" had failed at the legislative session of 1909.

[74a] In 1907, the Change of Venue bill was slipped through the Assembly, but in a form not to affect the San Francisco graft cases. In the Senate, however, it was amended to apply to Ruef, Schmitz and their associates. The exposure of this turn raised such a storm that the bill was not brought to vote. However, on the night before adjournment, the measure was slipped through the Senate as an amendment tacked on another bill. But the trick was discovered in the Assembly and defeated.

[75] Governor Gillett's reasons for vetoing the bill are set forth in footnote 1, Chapter 1.

[76] The Assembly vote on the change of venue bill was as follows:

For the Change of Venue bill - Barndollar, Beatty, Black, Cattell, Coghlan, Collier, Collum, Cronin, Drew, Feeley, Flint, Gibbons, Griffiths, Hammon, Hans, Hawk, Hayes, Hewitt, Hinkle, Holmquist, Johnson
of Sacramento, Johnson of San Diego, Juilliard, Lightner, Macauley, Maher, McClellan, McManus, Melrose, Mendenhall, Moore, Mott, Pugh, Rech,
Schmitt, Silver, Stuckenbruck, Telfer, Transue, Wagner, Wheelan, and Wilson - 42.

Against the Change of Venue bill - Baxter, Bohnett, Butler, Callan, Cogswell, Dean, Gerdes, Gillis, Kehoe, Otis, Polsley, Preston, Sackett, Whitney, and Young - 15.

[77] The Senate Judiciary Committee for example.

[76a] The Senators whose names are printed in italics became involved in the confusion which led to the passage of the measure.

[78] The vote was as follows:

For the call of the Senate - Bell, Birdsall, Boynton, Caminetti, Campbell, Cartwright, Curtin, Cutten, Estudillo, Holohan, Lewis, Miller, Roseberry, Sanford, Stetson, Strobridge, Thompson, Walker - 18.

Against the call of the Senate - Anthony, Bates, Bills, Finn, Hare, Hartman, Hurd, Leavitt, Martinelli, McCartney, Price, Reily, Savage, Weed, Welch, Willis, Wolfe, Wright - 18.

CHAPTER XVII.

Passage of the Wheelan Bills.

Measures Extended Abuses Which the Commonwealth Club Bills Had Been
Drawn to Prevent - Went Through Both Houses Without the Members Thoroughly Understanding Their Significance.

The so-called Wheelan bills were passed in much the same way as was the Change of Venue bill. These measures will perhaps be better understood in comparison with certain of the Commonwealth Club bills which were considered in a previous chapter.

Among the Commonwealth bills was one which denied a defendant under indictment a copy of the testimony taken in the Grand Jury room. The measure was drawn on the theory that Grand Juries deal principally with secret offenses, and that the testimony had better be brought out before the trial Court. One object of the proposed law was to prevent the defendant giving out testimony with the deliberate object of prejudicing the entire community against him, and thus increasing the difficulty of getting petty juries to try him.

Furthermore, there are instances, as when Abe Ruef was before the Grand Jury at San Francisco, when the ends of justice require that the testimony given shall be kept secret. But, in spite of these and other considerations, the measure in question was allowed to die in Committee.

On the other hand two bills requiring that transcript of such testimony be given the defendant passed both Senate and Assembly. They were introduced by Wheelan of San Francisco.

Section 925 of the Penal Code, as it stood up to the time of the opening of the session, provided that "the Grand Jury whenever criminal causes are being investigated before them, on demand of the District Attorney must appoint a competent stenographic reporter to be sworn and to report the testimony that may be given in such causes in shorthand, and reduce the same upon request of the District Attorney to long hand or typewriting." It was thus left with the District Attorney to say whether the stenographic reporter should be present, and whether his notes should be transcribed.

The first of the Wheelan bills, Assembly bill 221[79], amended the law by cutting out the words in italics "on demand of the District Attorney" and "upon request of the District Attorney," making it mandatory upon the Grand Jury to have the reporter in attendance.

Further on in the section and in Assembly bill 222[79], it was provided that a true copy of the testimony thus taken should be given the defendant at the time of his arraignment.

These two measures passed both Senate and Assembly.

Assembly bill 223[79], also introduced by Wheelan, provided another cause for the setting aside of an indictment by the Court in which the defendant is arraigned, upon such defendant's motion. The Commonwealth bills aimed to prevent technical attacks upon indictments. The third of the Wheelan bills - No. 223 - opened the way for further technical attacks, by providing that the Court must set aside the indictment "when it appears from the testimony taken before the Grand jury that the defendant has been indicted upon a criminal charge without reasonable or probable cause."

This measure passed both Houses. It opened the way for review before the Court of the testimony taken in the Grand jury room, and endless technical objections, all of which by clever counsel can be employed to delay the case being brought before a trial jury, and in the end perhaps wear out the prosecution, thus preventing the case being tried on its merits. With that section in the law two years ago, it is a question whether the defendants in the graft prosecution at San Francisco would ever have been brought to trial.

It will be seen that while the Commonwealth Club bills aimed to decrease the opportunities for technical defense of men charged with crime, and thus permit the cases being tried on their merits, the Wheelan bills increased opportunity for technical objection.

The history of the passage of the Wheelan bills is practically the same in each instance.

The three bills were introduced by Mr. Wheelan on January 11th, and referred to the Assembly Judiciary Committee. The Committee, which pigeon-holed sixty-three of the Commonwealth Club bills, and reported back the two remaining too late for passage, had better treatment in store for the Wheelan measures. They were reported back to the Assembly on March 6th, at a time when the Assembly was fairly swamped with pending measures. On March 17th, in the midst of a mass of legislation, they were slipped through the Assembly without many of the members apparently knowing what they were. The Assembly journal of that date shows that such men as Bohnett, Callan, Cattell, Cogswell, Flint, Gerdes, Gibbons, Gillis, Hayes, Hewitt, Hinkle, Johnson of Placer, Juilliard, Kehoe,

Mendenhall, Polsley, Stuckenbruck, Telfer, Whitney, Wilson and Wyllie, who ordinarily voted for good measures and against bad ones, voted for the Wheelan bills.

With the exception of Bill No. 223, not one vote was cast against the measures. The vote on Bill No. 223 was the last taken. Gillis, who had voted for the two others, appears to have awakened to the fact that something was wrong. At any rate, he voted against Bill 223.

His was the only vote cast against any of the three bills in the lower House, They appear to have gone through the Assembly without thorough appreciation of their significance. At any rate, there were members enough present, who were usually against bad measures, to have prevented the Wheelan bills securing the forty-one votes necessary for their passage.

A reform measure passing the Assembly on March 17th would have had no chance whatever in the Senate. The Wheelan bills were more fortunate.

The Senate Judiciary Committee, before which the Commonwealth Club bills had dragged along for weeks, received the Wheelan bills on March 17th, the day they passed the Assembly, and the same day, March 17th, reported them back to the Senate with the recommendation that they do pass. On March 18th the measures were read the second time in the Senate, and on March 20th, three days after they had passed the Assembly, the Senate passed them.

Such is the difference in action on machine-favored bills and bills which the machine does not favor. Incidentally, it may be said that at the time the Wheelan bills were before the Senate, the machine had that body tied up in the fight on the Direct Primary bill.

The reform element - at the mercy of the Senate organization - was compelled to devote its whole attention to the Direct Primary bill. The machine was thus left to run committees and Senate at its own free will. It was an admirable situation from the machine standpoint.

But by the time the Wheelan bills had been hastened to the floor of the Senate, the reform Senators apparently awoke to the fact that some sort of a job was on the way. When the bills came up for final passage, however, the anti-machine Senators were apparently as much at a loss concerning them as the anti-machine Assemblymen had been.

Bill number 221 came up first, and even Senator Bell, the staunchest opponent of bad laws of them all, voted for it. With Senator Bell voted Caminetti, Estudillo, Rush, Thompson and Walker, who were ordinarily against the passage of bad bills. As the measure received but twenty-three votes, any three of these by voting no could have defeated it.

Price, who had voted for the bill, gave notice, at the request of a fellow Senator, that on the next legislative day he would move to reconsider the vote by which the bill had been passed.

Before taking up Assembly bill 222, companion bill to 221, the Senate passed three measures and considered several others. By the time Assembly bill 222 was reached, Senator Bell had got his bearings, and voted against it. Caminetti had also found himself, and although Caminetti voted for the measure, he gave notice, that on the next legislative day he would move for its reconsideration.

The third of the bills, No. 223, followed 222, and Walker, who had voted for the two other bills, voted "no." The bill was passed by twenty-three votes, Cutten voting "aye" for the purpose of giving notice to reconsider.

The motions to reconsider were voted upon on the afternoon of Monday, March 22, the day of the final fight on the Direct Primary bill in both Senate and Assembly. Nobody was thinking of much of anything else that day. In every instance reconsideration was denied[80]. The vote by which they had passed the Senate stood.

[79] Governor Gillett signed Assembly bills Nos. 221 and 222. They are now the law of the State. Assembly bill No. 223 he did not sign. It did not, therefore, become a law.

[80] The Assembly history of March 23, fails to record that the motions to reconsider were made on the three Wheelan bills. In an article concerning these bills which the writer prepared for the Sacramento Bee, governed by the official record of the measures, the History of the House in which they originated, he stated that motions for their reconsideration were not made. The Senate Journal of March 22, however, pages 23 and 26, shows that these motions were made, and in all three cases defeated.

CHAPTER XVIII.

Defeat of the Local Option Bill.

Peculiar Arrangement by Which the Bill Was Sidetracked in the Assembly - Stanton Promised That It Should Pass the Lower House If It Passed the Senate - How It Was Smothered in the Upper House.

Because there is no particular reason why California should not have a Local Option law, in the face of popular demand for it, a large number of very worthy citizens assumed that one would be passed. The fact seems to have been lost sight of that the tenderloin element opposes such legislation, and that the management of the so-called liquor interests organized as the "Royal Arch," takes a shortsighted view of Local Option provisions. The machine was thus interested. Its representatives in Senate and Assembly did not propose that any Local Option bill should pass. So the Local Option bill was smothered. The smothering process most suggestively indicates how such things can be done.

The measure was introduced in the Assembly by Wyllie and in the Senate by Estudillo. In the face of the popular demand for the passage of such a bill, and the exasperation of a no small portion of the voters of the State, at the mistake - or trick - by which in 1907 the only measure resembling a Local Option law was rubbed off the statute books, it was not good policy to fight the bill in the open. So the machine proceeded to do covertly what would have been "poor politics" to do openly[81].

The same bill having been introduced both in Senate and Assembly, the first step was to tie up either the Assembly or the Senate measure, so that the whole crafty campaign against the bill's passage could be confined to one House. The way in which this was done was simplicity itself. The Wyllie bill, as introduced in the Assembly was, at the request of Speaker Stanton, held up in the Assembly Committee on Public Morals. Most plausible reason was given for this course. It was pointed out that since the Assembly had gone on record before the Senate on the anti-gambling bill, on women's suffrage[80a] and other "moral" issues, it was unfair to compel the lower House to go on record before the Senate on the Local Option bill. Speaker Stanton assured the proponents of the measure that if it passed the Senate, it should pass the Assembly.

Stanton accordingly recognized that the Assembly, given an opportunity, would pass the bill. Had it passed the Assembly before the middle of February, it would unquestionably have passed the Senate. But the proponents of the measure consented to the plan to make the Senate act first. The fight for the passage of the bill accordingly took place in the Senate.

Before taking up the Senate measure introduced by Estudillo, the Wyllie bill may as well be disposed of. It was introduced in the Assembly January 8th, and was sent to the Committee on Public Morals. There it lay until March 13th, two months and five days, when the proponents of the measure, realizing that they were being tricked, made their protest so loud that the measure was reported by the Committee, but without recommendation. There was no time then to pass the bill, and on March 15th it was withdrawn by its author.

The Estudillo bill, as it was known on the Senate side of the Capitol, had a more eventful history. Introduced in the Senate on January 8th, it had gone to the famous Committee on Election Laws, which had been stacked for the defeat of the Direct Primary bill. Estudillo was, to be sure, Chairman of the Committee, but a lamb herding lions never had a harder job on its hands than did Estudillo. He could not get his committee together to consider the well-backed Direct Primary bill, let alone the worthy but not politically supported local option measure.

Along about the middle of February, however, Estudillo succeeded in getting the committee to act. By a vote of four to four the committee refused to recommend the Local Option bill for passage. Senator Stetson, who favored the passage of the measure, to compel committee action and get the bill before the Senate, thereupon moved that the bill be referred back to the Senate with recommendation that it do not pass. Senator Stetson's motion prevailed.

Thus, the measure went back to the Senate with a majority committee report that it do not pass. But in spite of this adverse report, the Senate passed the measure on second reading and sent it to engrossment and third reading. It looked very much just then as though the bill would pass the Senate.

But the resourceful machine had other plans. When the measure came up for final passage on February 24th, instead of being voted upon, and passed or defeated, it was amended.

To amend a bill on third reading exasperates those who are supporting it as nothing else can. The bill must, when thus amended, be reprinted and re-engrossed before it can be passed. The delays thus caused very often result in the defeat of the measure.

But the reprinted and re-engrossed Local Option bill got back to the Senate on February 26th, and its supporters could think of no other possible excuse for delaying its passage.

But the machine could, and did. On Senator Wolfe's motion - the reader will no doubt remember that Senator Wolfe led the fight against the Direct Primary bill, against the Anti-Gambling bill and against the effective Stetson Railroad Regulation bill - on Senator Wolfe's motion the Local Option bill, instead of being put on its final passage, was sent to the Senate Judiciary Committee.

At that time, the closing days of February, the Judiciary Committee was fairly swamped with important measures. The Railroad Regulation bills, the Initiative Amendment, the measures providing for the simplification of methods of criminal procedure and other bills of scarcely less importance were pending before that committee. Prompt action on the Local Option bill was out of the question. And, although a majority of the committee favored the passage of the bill, the minority which was against it took precious good care that no undue haste should attend its consideration. Estudillo was in constant attendance upon the committee, but to little purpose. It was not until March 4th that the committee acted. The action was, of course, recommendation that the bill do pass.

The bill had been amended from time to time, but as it was finally approved by the Judiciary Committee was a reasonably effective measure. It provided that on a petition signed by 25 per cent of the electors of any city, or town, or county, the question of license or no license must be put on the regular election ballot. If a majority of the electors voted against the issuing of liquor licenses in any city or town or township, the governing body could no longer issue saloon licenses. Outside incorporated cities and towns, the basis of prohibition was made the township, although the vote was to be taken throughout the county.

After the measure had been returned from the Judiciary Committee of the Senate, Estudillo fought manfully to have it considered. He finally succeeded, on March 8th, in having the bill made a special order, that is to say, he arranged that the Senate should consider it at 8 o'clock of Thursday, March 11th.

But when Thursday came it developed that Senators Stetson and Boynton could not be present that evening, and they asked Estudillo to have the vote on the measure postponed until noon of the next day, Friday. This Estudillo attempted to do. The thing was done with other bills every day. Had Wolfe made the request, for example, or even Estudillo on any other measure than the Local Option bill, the request would have been granted without thought or comment. But on Wolfe's objection Estudillo's request was denied. The machine saw its opportunity and succeeded in having consideration of the bill postponed until the following Monday, March

15th. This meant the defeat of the bill. Even had it passed the Senate on that date, filibustering tactics would have defeated it in the Assembly.

Nevertheless, the backers of the measure - although pleaded with by weak-kneed Senators to withdraw the bill - insisted upon a vote being taken, when the measure came up on March 15th. This decision compelled Wolfe to make his famous "Fate of the Republican Party" speech, in which he predicted that if the Local Option bill became a law, utter wreck would come upon the Republican party in California. Birdsall, Caminetti, Holohan, Rush, Sanford and Strobridge, whose votes were ordinarily recorded against the machine Senators, voted against the bill, as did Anthony and Curtin. Wright voted for the measure, but otherwise those who had voted against the Walker-Otis Anti-Gambling bill, against a State-wide vote for United States Senators, against the Stetson Railroad Regulation bill, in a word, those whom for the want of a better term we call machine Senators, voted solidly against the Local Option bill[82].

The final showing for the Local Option bill was not a good one, but in spite of it, many in touch with conditions in the Senate held that had the vote been taken in the middle of February instead of the middle of March, the bill would have had a good chance for passage. After the delay of ten weeks from the time of its introduction until the final vote upon it, there was no chance at all for it to become a law.

[81] Up to the legislative session of 1907, the County Government Act provided that the Supervisors of a county could submit any question - including the matter of regulating the liquor traffic - to the voters for the purpose of ascertaining their opinion upon the issue. There was, however, no way to compel the Supervisors to take the action that might be thus decided upon by popular vote. The Supervisors could act upon the vote or ignore it, as they saw fit.

The Legislature of 1907 transferred the County Government Act to the Codes. For some reason, either by intention or oversight, the section which permitted Supervisors to submit questions to the people for an advisory vote was omitted. It has been held that this action of the Legislature repealed the section by implication. It is held, therefore, that no law is upon the Statute books by which the people may be permitted to vote even in an advisory capacity upon any question of police regulation or public policy.

[80a] A fine example of a lightning switch of plan on the part of the machine came in the fight on the Women's Suffrage Amendment. The tenderloin and liquor interests in general are opposed to the submission of this amendment to the people, which means, of course, that the machine is against it. To submit the amendment to the people, fifty-four votes are required in the Assembly and twenty-seven in the Senate. This year, the

program was to let the amendment pass the Assembly and defeat it in the Senate. Assemblymen were allowed to pledge themselves to its support until there were fifty-eight Assemblymen down to vote for it. Grove L. Johnson had introduced the measure in the Assembly, and its adoption by that body seemed assured.

But the Anti-Racetrack Gambling bill got in the way of Woman's Suffrage in a most curious manner. When the passage of this anti-gambling bill became a certainty, that branch of the group of tenderloin Senators whose interests were wrapped up in racetrack gambling, became "very sore." In their disgruntlement they decided to give reform full swing, and put the Woman's Suffrage Amendment through the Senate. This attitude seriously alarmed the safe, sane and respectable leaders of the machine, who see all sorts of trouble for the machine if women are given the ballot. So to prevent its tenderloin associates in the Senate doing anything rash, the machine decided rather late in the day to defeat the amendment in the Assembly.

When this decision was reached, and the order to carry it into effect given, the machine Assemblymen who had agreed to vote for the amendment coolly forgot their pledges. Instead of fifty-eight votes, only thirty-nine were cast for the amendment.

Grove L. Johnson, who had introduced it, and who pretended to support it, agreed to move for its reconsideration. When the hour for the motion for reconsideration came, Johnson huddled up in his seat, looking neither to right or left, let the opportunity pass.

The vote by which the amendment was defeated was as follows:

For the amendment: Barndollar, Bohnett, Butler, Callan, Cattell, Coghlan, Cogswell, Collum, Costar, Cronin, Drew, Gibbons, Gillis, Hayes, Hewitt, Hinkle, Holmquist, Hopkins, Johnson of Sacramento, Johnson of San Diego, Johnson of Placer, Juilliard, Kehoe, Maher, Melrose, Mendenhall, Otis, O'Neil, Polsley, Pulcifer, Sackett, Silver, Stuckenbruck, Telfer, Webber, Wheelan, Wilson, Wyllie, Young - 39.

Against the amendment: Baxter, Beardslee, Beatty, Beban, Collier, Cullen, Dean, Feeley, Flavelle, Fleisher, Flint, Gerdes, Greer, Griffiths, Hammon, Hanlon, Hans, Hawk, Johnston of Contra Costa, Leeds,
Lightner, Macaulay, McClellan, McManus, Moore, Mott, Nelson, Odom, Preston, Pugh, Rech, Rutherford, Schmitt, Stanton, Transue, Wagner, Whitney - 37.

[82] The vote on the local option bill was as follows:

For the bill - Bell, Black, Boynton, Campbell, Cartwright, Cutten, Estudillo, Miller, Roseberry, Thompson, Walker, Wright - 12.

Against the bill - Anthony, Bills, Birdsall, Burnett, Caminetti, Curtin, Finn, Hare, Hartman, Holohan, Hurd, Kennedy, Leavitt, Lewis, Martinelli, McCartney, Price, Reily, Rush, Sanford, Strobridge, Weed, Welch, Willis, Wolfe - 25.

CHAPTER XIX.

Defeat of the Initiative Amendment.

As in the Case of Other Reform Measures It Was Held Back Until Near the Close of the Session - Principle Adopted by Many California Municipalities - Machine Thoroughly Aroused to Its Importance.

A most estimable old lady once tried with indifferent success to hold back the incoming tide of the Atlantic with a broom. As one watches the efforts of the machine, through such agents as Gus Hartman, Eddie Wolfe and Frank Leavitt, to stem the reform movement which is sweeping the country, he is strongly reminded of the old lady's endeavor.

To be sure, the machine, at the legislative session of 1909, by trick and clever manipulation succeeded in preventing any very effective reform legislation going on the Statute books. But nevertheless the machine was compelled in response to the popular demand to permit the passage of a direct primary law, however inadequate and disappointing it may prove to be, and a railroad regulation law, however ineffective.

The machine's success was not on the whole so much in its permanent defeat of good measures as in delaying their adoption. The machine, except in the case of the race-track gamblers, could and did put off the day of the people's reckoning with machine-protected interests, but on desperately small margins at times, and under conditions which point plainly to the machine's ultimate undoing.

A bull once attempted to stop a freight train with his head. The train was brought to a standstill and the animal driven off the track. A short time later the bull tried the same experiment with an express train. The train did not stop, nor was it seriously delayed.

The aim of the reform movement is to place the government of Nation, State and city back into the hands of the people. To this end States and municipalities throughout the country are trying the direct primary system of nominating candidates for office, extending the principle of local option, establishing the Initiative, the Referendum and the Recall, and experimenting, often with admirable success, sometimes with discouraging failure, with other "wicked innovations," as Assemblyman Grove L. Johnson would call them.

Without the machine fully appreciating what has been going on, California has for a decade or more been pushing rapidly to the fore in the promotion of these reforms. In this State the reform policies have found their best expression in recently adopted municipal charters. These charters must be ratified by the Legislature, but up to the session just closed their ratification - "wicked innovations and all" - has met with no particular opposition.

Thus we find most of the modern charters of California municipalities containing provisions for really effective primary nominations by the people[83], for the initiation of laws, for the referendum, even for the recall from office of corrupt officials, which have placed in the hands of the people of the cities a club over the machine which has proved most effective.

But the machine is now fully alive to what such provisions as the initiative and the recall mean. When, for example, the machine in control of the City Council attempted to deny the Western Pacific right of way through the City of Sacramento, the people resorted to the charter provision granting them the Initiative, and by their direct vote awarded the right of way.

Even while the Legislature was in session, one of the machine's most effective workers, Walter Parker, could not be present at his post at Sacramento, because he was required at Los Angeles, where, because of the "recall," the machine was in a peck of trouble.

The people of that city were employing the recall provision of their charter against the machine Mayor trapped in corruption. Although the then Mayor is a "Democrat" and Parker a "Republican," Parker's presence was required at Los Angeles to back the machine's efforts to hold the Mayor in his job.

So Parker could not be at Sacramento, where the machine really needed him. The machine leaders did not think it possible that a real Mayor - especially a machine Mayor - could be dismissed from office through such a "fool innovation" as the recall. But that's what, in spite of machine efforts, happened at Los Angeles.

These experiences and others like them, forced it upon the understanding of machine leaders that the initiative, recall and similar "innovations," have a business end; that they put altogether too much power into the hands of the people for the machine's safety.

Up to the session of 1909 there had been practically no opposition to the ratification of charters adopted by the several municipalities. But this year the machine leader in the Senate, Wolfe, let it be known that he would henceforth oppose "freak charters," "freak charters" to Senator Wolfe being those of the initiative-referendum-recall order.

Several municipalities - Berkeley, San Diego, Palo Alto, Santa Barbara, San Bernardino, Richmond, Los Angeles, Pasadena and Oakland - had either sent new charters or important amendments to existing charters to the

Legislature for ratification. Many of the charters and amendments came decidedly under Wolfe's ideas of "freak." But there are some extremes to which the machine dare not go, and it did not dare to go on record as against popular municipal government. Wolfe and his associates could and did grumble, but they did not dare refuse the several charters and charter amendments ratification.

So they let the charters and charter amendments go by them and braced themselves against granting Statewide initiative.

That issue came up in the form of a proposed amendment to the State Constitution introduced by Senator Black, which gave the people of the State the power enjoyed by the people of Oregon and of the more advanced
California municipalities, the power to initiate laws.

Black's amendment provided that on petition of eight per cent of the electors of the State proposing a law or Constitutional amendment, such law or amendment must be submitted to a vote of the people at the next general election, precisely as Constitutional amendments are now submitted. If the proposed law or amendment received a majority vote it was to become a law of the State, independent of Legislative action. In a word, the people of California, had the amendment carried, would have been able to initiate the laws which govern them.

Naturally, the machine, always on thin ice at best, thoroughly aroused to what the initiative means, opposed any such "wicked innovation."

In its opposition, the machine was backed by that extreme conservatism, which, while sincere enough, forever hangs on the coattails of progress; the conservatism which even in New England as late as 1860 drew back its respectable skirts from abolition; the conservatism which, dragged protesting over a crisis, never fails to assume for itself all the credit for what has been accomplished. Thus the machine had some very respectable assistance in its efforts against the Initiative Amendment, the measure which more than any other before the Legislature was calculated to take the government of California out of machine hands[84].

On the other hand, the amendment had strong backing. It had been drawn up at the instance of the Direct Legislation League, which numbers among its members many of the foremost bankers, capitalists, educators and public men of the State - Rudolph Spreckels, Francis J. Heney, James D. Phelan, of San Francisco, and Dr. John R. Haynes of Los Angeles, and others fully as prominent being among the League's most active supporters.

In addition, the amendment had the endorsement of the State Grange, of, the Labor Unions, of the State, county and municipal Democratic conventions, and of many of the municipal and county Republican conventions.

But there were plenty of reasons given why the amendment should not be submitted to the people. Perhaps the most amusing came from Senator Wright, of Direct Primary and Railroad Regulation notoriety. Senator Wright held that inasmuch as the Direct Primary will result in the election of high-class legislators, the initiative will not be necessary.

But the two principal objections raised to the initiative were that:

1. It would lead to a flood of bills being submitted to the people.

2. That the people would not take sufficient interest in the proposed laws to consider them carefully.

Both these objections were readily answered by the proponents of the amendment, who gave the experience of States in which the initiative has been tried.

Oregon, for example, adopted the initiative in 1902. In 1904 but two proposed laws were introduced under it; in 1906, five; and in 1908, nineteen. Inasmuch as in 1908 California voted upon twenty-one constitutional amendments and statutes which had been submitted by the Legislature of 1907, it will be seen that Oregon was not particularly submerged by a flood of elector-initiated legislation.

In Canton Berne, Switzerland, where for half a century all the laws have been adopted by the initiative system, the average of laws proposed has been only two and a half a year.

As to the second objection, it was easily shown that in Oregon the keenest interest is taken in the measures proposed through the initiative. Some were shown to have been adopted by enormous majorities; others to have been rejected by majorities as large.

Thus the objections to the amendment were easily disposed of.

Their arguments answered, the opponents of the amendment schemed to prevent its consideration until the closing days of the session or prevent consideration entirely.

In the Assembly, the amendment had been introduced by Drew of Fresno. It was referred to the Committee on Constitutional Amendments, where it was smothered to death. Although referred to the committee on January 11, the committee took no action upon it. Coghlan of San Francisco was chairman of the committee; associated with him were Legislators of the types of Johnson of Sacramento, McClelland and Baxter. In vain those advocating the adoption of the amendment urged the committee to act.

Meetings were indeed arranged, at which the proponents of the reform would be present, but the committeemen would fail to attend.

A less exasperating, but no less effective fight was carried on in the Senate.

On the Senate side, the amendment introduced by Black went to the Judiciary Committee. This committee was made up of the nineteen lawyers in the Senate, every lawyer going on the committee. But Warren Porter named the order of their rank, and the chairman and the four ranking members of the committee voted eternally with the Wolfe-Leavitt faction. On a straight vote the majority of the committee was against the machine, as was shown in the fight for an effective railroad regulation bill. But when it came to getting results in the Senate Judiciary Committee, craft and leadership, as has been shown in previous chapters, not infrequently overcame numbers.

On February 16, the reform element of the committee insisted that action be taken on the amendment. Chairman Willis was reluctant to put the question. Few machine members of the committee were in attendance. The anti-machine members were insistent. Willis was finally forced to put the question, and the amendment, after the percentage of voters required to sign a petition for the initiation of a law had been raised from eight to twelve per cent, was favorably reported back to the Senate.

But Senator Willis was able to do on the floor of the Senate what he had been unable to do in the committee, namely, secure further delay. He protested to the Senate at the "snap judgment" of his committee, with the result that it was re-referred to that body. The committee, however, for the second time sent it back to the Senate with the recommendation that it be adopted.

Then followed a series of delays in the Senate, so that the measure was not brought to vote until March 11th.

For the adoption of a Constitutional amendment, a two-thirds vote - twenty-seven - is required in the Senate. The proponents of the amendment had good reason to believe that that number of Senators would vote for its adoption. The Senators counted upon to vote for the amendment were: Anthony, Bell, Birdsall, Black, Boynton, Caminetti, Campbell, Cutten, Estudillo, Hare, Kennedy, McCartney, Reily, Roseberry, Rush, Sanford, Stetson, Thompson, Walker, Welch - 20, who actually voted for the amendment; Finn, Strobridge, Cartwright and Holohan, who were absent when the vote was taken, but who were pledged to the reform; Lewis, Bills, Curtin and Miller, who were counted on the side of the amendment until it came to a vote. This made twenty-eight votes, one more than enough for adoption.

Kennedy, Reily, Welch, Finn and Hare, usually against reform legislation, were counted for the Initiative because of convention obligations which could not well be ignored. Lewis, McCartney and Bills were counted for it because of their alleged promise of its support; Curtin and Miller because the Democratic State Convention had endorsed the Initiative, and for the further reason that Curtin and Miller were ordinarily for reform legislation.

But on the vote, the unfortunate Hare, Kennedy, Reily, McCartney and Welch remained true to their obligations, while Curtin and Miller disappointed those who had expected their support. The negative vote of Bills and Lewis did not cause much disappointment, for little else was to have been expected, and anyway, the negative votes of Curtin and Miller were enough to defeat the amendment.

Curtin and Miller, in spite of their party's endorsement of the policy, expressed themselves as "scandalized" at such an idea as the Initiative. But as good men as Miller and Curtin were scandalized at the idea of abolition in 1860, only to become the most earnest supporters of the Emancipation Proclamation three years later.

Reform waves, like the Atlantic Ocean, are not kept back with brooms - or Gus Hartmans.

[83] For example the charters of Los Angeles and of Berkeley. The Berkeley charter is a model in this respect. It provides that any qualified citizen may become a candidate for municipal office, by petition of twenty-five electors, AND IN NO OTHER WAY. The party tag is thus done away with. At the election, if a candidate receive a majority of the votes he is declared elected. If no candidate receive a majority, then a second election is held at which the two candidates receiving the highest pluralities become candidates, the names of all other candidates who participated at the first election are dropped. The candidate at the second election who receives the majority is declared elected. A movement is on foot to have a similar provision incorporated into the San Francisco charter.

[84] "As a source of public education upon which free government must always rest, as a means of conservative progress, upon which the continued life of all nations depends, as a check upon paternalism and rich gifts calculated to lull to sleep the love of freedom, as the key that may be used to open the door to equal opportunity, the Initiative is fundamentally more important than all other proposed reforms put together. " - Arthur Twining Hadley, LL. D., in "The Constitutional Position of Property in America."

It is interesting to note, that nearly a quarter of a century ago. Bryce in his American Commonwealth, pointed out that this country could not without the initiation of laws by The People enjoy the fruits of its institutions.

CHAPTER XX.

Defeat of the Anti-Japanese Bills[86].

Stir Storm in the Assembly, But All the Bills Were Finally Defeated - Grove L. Johnson Denounces Action of Governor Gillett and President Roosevelt - Speaker Stanton Places Himself in a Very Embarrassing Position - His Effective Speech Becomes a Joke.

The Japanese problem under the bludgeoning of the big stick in the skilled hands of President Roosevelt, and free application of the organization switch in the hands of Governor Gillett, was kept fairly well under control during the entire session. That the problem is real was demonstrated by the numerous resolutions and alien-regulation bills which were introduced in both Houses. The Assembly, however, was the scene of the final defeat of the anti-Japanese element. There the legislative campaign against the Japanese was fought out, and there it was lost.

The contest in the Assembly narrowed down to three measures, Assembly Bill 78, introduced by Drew of Fresno, known as the "Alien Land Bill"; Assembly Bill 14, known as the "Anti-Japanese School Bill," and Assembly Bill 32, known as the "Municipal Segregation Bill," both introduced by Johnson of Sacramento. The final defeat of these bills settled the Japanese question so far as the legislative session of 1909 was concerned.

Drew's Alien Land bill was by far the most important of the three. It was in effect a copy of the alien land law at present in force in the State of Illinois, and generally known as the "Illinois Law." Under its provisions an alien acquiring title to lands situate in this State, was given five years in which to become a citizen of the United States; failing to become a citizen, he was required to dispose of his holdings to a citizen; failing so to do, the necessary machinery was provided for the District Attorney of the county in which the land was situated to dispose of it, and turn the proceeds of the sale over to the alien owner. Ample protection was provided for alien minors who might possess or might become possessed of California real property. Furthermore, under the provisions of the law, the leasing of land to aliens for a longer period than one year was prohibited.

Though the word, "Japanese," did not appear, the bill's introduction was a shot which if not heard round the world, at least reached Washington on the East and Tokio on the West. Finally, on January 25, Governor Gillett made the Alien bills pending before the Legislature subject of a special message to Senate and Assembly, in which he urged the Legislature to do nothing that would disrupt the pleasant relations existing between America and Japan, and recommended that an appropriation be made to enable the Labor Commissioner to take a census showing the number of Japanese now in the State, with such other information regarding them as could be used in making a proper report to the President and Congress[87a].

Governor Gillett in the paragraph of his message[87] which dealt with the Alien Land bill, stated that the measure might be amended so that its passage would not embarrass the Federal Government. Mr. Drew promptly sent the Governor a note, inquiring "how amended." The Governor replied[88], stating that, in his judgment the best possible law that could be passed on the question of alien ownership of land would be the law which had been adopted by Oklahoma. Furthermore, the Governor expressed the opinion that such a law would be satisfactory to President Roosevelt and Secretary Root.

Mr. Drew was quick to act on the suggestion. He not only yielded to the Governor's wishes[89], but in the teeth of the severest opposition from the San Francisco delegation, forced delay of the passage of his bill until the Oklahoma law could be substituted for that taken from the Illinois Statutes.

The substitute measure provided that "no alien shall acquire title or own land in the State of California," but the provisions of the act further provided that the law "shall not apply to lands now owned in this State by aliens so long as they are held by their present owners."

The substitute measure was introduced on February 1st; it came up for passage on February 3rd. In the two days which elapsed between the introduction and final action on the bill, the high State authorities decided to oppose it. Speaker Phil Stanton employed his influence against it; one by one its supports who could "be reached" were "pulled down." Drew found himself at the final with slight following. The bill was defeated by the decisive vote of 28 to 48. Mott gave notice of motion to reconsider, but the next day reconsideration was denied.

The day following the defeat of the Alien Land bill, February 4th, the "Anti-Japanese School Bill" and the "Municipal Segregation Bill" came up for final action. There was also Assembly Bill 15, classed as an anti-Japanese measure, which came up on the same day. It, as in the case of the two others, had been introduced by Johnson of Sacramento, by far the ablest parliamentarian in the Legislature. Drew had used facts and figures when arguing for his alien land bills; Johnson seasoned his statistics with a sarcasm[90] as peppery as one of Mr. Roosevelt's ingenuous opinions on "nature fakers." But while Mr. Johnson entertained with his wit and his invective, he failed to overcome the tremendous influence, State and Federal, that had been brought to bear against his bills. Assembly Bill 15, denying aliens the right to serve as directors on California corporations, was defeated by a vote of 15 for to 53 against. Assembly Bill 32, the "Municipal Segregation Bill,"[91] was defeated by the close vote of 39 for to 35 against, 41 votes being required for its passage.

And then the Assembly took another tack, and by a vote of 45 to 29, passed Assembly Bill 14, the Anti-Japanese School bill. Leeds changed his vote from no to aye to give notice that he would the next legislative day move to reconsider the vote by which the bill had been passed. The Assembly then adjourned. The day had been eventful. A more eventful was to follow.

The passage of Assembly Bill 14, after the defeat of the other so-called anti-Japanese measures, brought a characteristic telegram from President Roosevelt to Governor Gillett. "This (Assembly Bill 14) is the most offensive bill of them all," telegraphed the President, "and in my judgment is clearly unconstitutional, and we should at once have to test it in the courts. Can it not be stopped in the Legislature or by veto?"

Governor Gillett incorporated that telegram in a message which he sent to Senate and Assembly the next day. "A telegram so forcible as this," said the Governor, "from the President of the United States, is entitled to full consideration, and demands that no hasty or ill-considered action be taken by this State which may involve the whole country. It seems to me that it is time to lay sentiment and personal opinion and considerations aside and take a broad and unprejudiced view of the important question involved in the proposed legislation, and in a calm and dispassionate manner pass upon them, keeping in mind not only the interests of our State, but of the Nation as well, and the duty we owe to it in observing the treaties entered into by it with a friendly power."

"I trust," concluded the Governor, "that no action will be taken which will violate any treaty made by our country or in any manner question its good faith. I most respectfully submit this message to you with the full hope and belief that when final action shall be taken nothing will be done which can be the subject of criticism by the people of this Nation, and that no law will be enacted which will be in contravention of the Constitution or any treaty of the United States."

The Governor's message was not at all well received[92]; in fact, Governor and message were denounced by both Republican and Democratic
Assemblymen.

From the hour that the bill had been passed, the Governor had been in consultation with his lieutenants in the Assembly. Speaker Stanton made canvass of the situation. But little headway was made. That reconsideration would be denied was evident. Leeds, to save the situation, moved that reconsideration be postponed until February 10th. An amendment was made that it be re-referred to the Judiciary Committee. It was on this amended motion that the issue was fought out.

"I know what you want," declared Johnson of Sacramento in his opening speech, "and you know it. You want to bury this bill. You want time to hold another caucus on the question and decide what you will do. You want time to take another canvass of this Assembly."

Had the question been put when Johnson had concluded, reconsideration would unquestionably have been denied. In the emergency, Speaker Stanton left his desk and took the floor to plead for delay. For once in his life, at least, Phil Stanton was impressive. He did not say much, - and as the sequel showed he had little to say - but there was a suggestion of thundering guns and sacked cities and marching armies in his words, that caused the listening statesmen to follow him with unstatesmen-like uneasiness.

"It was not my intention," said Stanton, "to take the floor unless we were confronted by some grave crisis. Such a crisis is, in my opinion, upon us. I not only believe it, but I know it. But my lips are sealed."

"I would that I could tell you what I know, but I cannot for the present. But I can tell you that we are treading upon dangerous ground. I can feel it slipping from under my feet."

"In my judgment this matter should be postponed. I believe that further information will, within a few days, be given you."

The psychological moment had come in the history of Assembly Bill 14. All eyes were turned on Johnson of Sacramento. It was for him to say whether the postponement asked should be granted. Had Johnson said "no," such was the attitude of the Assembly at that moment, reconsideration of the measure would unquestionably have been denied, and Assembly Bill 14 declared passed by the House of its origin.

But Johnson did not say "no."[93] Instead, he entered upon a rambling excuse for advocating acquiescence in Stanton's request for delay. He rambled on that he believed that Governor Gillett had been indiscreet; that he (Johnson) did not propose to be dictated to by a "fanatical President eternally seeking the limelight."

"But," concluded Johnson, "I have listened to the words of our Speaker, and I see that he is profoundly moved. For this reason I am willing that the bill go over until Wednesday, but out of respect to our Speaker, and for no one else on earth."

When Johnson sat down, one could have heard a pin drop. Not a dissenting voice was heard. Further consideration of the measure was postponed until February 10.

The day preceding final action on the bill was given over to conferences and caucuses. The Democrats caucused and agreed to stand as a unit for the bill. Grove L. Johnson's immediate followers rallied to its support. On the other hand, a conference of those opposing the measure was held in Governor Gillett's office. Grove L. Johnson is alleged to have been called to the carpet. He was asked to withdraw his support of the measure. Johnson is quoted as replying:

"Show me why I should not support it. Give me the reasons, the facts and figures, why Roosevelt has any right to interfere with this measure. I want something definite. I have heard these suppositions and insinuations for years and years. Let me know, gentlemen, what information you have confided to you that should induce me to withdraw my support and bow to the telegram from Roosevelt."

The hour for reconsideration of the bill, 11 a. m. of February 10, arrived with the situation practically unchanged. Assemblyman Transue, Stanton's right hand man in the fight against the bill, presented an elaborate resolution, laboriously prepared by the opponents of the measure, setting forth why it should be defeated[94]. In it the right of the State to pass such school-regulating laws as it may see fit was affirmed, and the constitutionality of the pending measure alleged, but the Assembly was urged to do nothing to disturb the relations existing between this Government and a friendly power. The resolution did not strengthen the position of the opponents of the bill in the least. In fact, several of their number were estranged. So worked up had the Assemblymen become, that Beardslee of San Joaquin moved that Transue's resolution be considered in executive session, but the motion was lost. The resolution was later withdrawn.

The debate turned principally on demands from the supporters of the bill, that Speaker Stanton tell why he had felt "the ground slipping from under his feet" in his speech of six days before. But Stanton wouldn't or couldn't tell. He leaned on his gavel through it all looking very foolish indeed.

These speeches of denunciation pleased the supporters of the bill immensely, but the luxury of denouncing Stanton defeated the bill. Had the vote been taken at the forenoon session, reconsideration would undoubtedly have been denied. But so much time was taken in making

Stanton feel foolish, that the hour of recess arrived, and the Assembly scattered until two o'clock.

This brief respite gave the opponents of the measure a last opportunity. They improved it by bringing over to their side enough members of the San Francisco delegation to win reconsideration, and the measure's defeat. When the Assembly re-convened after the noon recess, the members by a vote of 43 to 34 granted the bill reconsideration, and by a vote of 37 ayes to 41 noes defeated it[95].

Although the Senate escaped the sensational scenes that attended the suppression of the Japanese problem in the Assembly, nevertheless Japanese bills and resolutions, with attending debates, made their appearance there. Caminetti, for example, introduced a duplicate of the Johnson anti-Japanese School bill, which was referred to the Senate Committee on Education and never heard from again.

Senate Bill No. 492, introduced by Senator Anthony, made more trouble. This measure gave the people of the State an opportunity to express themselves at the polls on the Japanese question. The Committee on Labor, Capital and Immigration recommended the measure for passage, and it was finally forced to a vote, being defeated by twelve votes for and twenty-two against[96].

A series of Senate anti-Japanese resolutions which were finally included in Senate joint Resolution No. 6[97], almost led to a riot in the Assembly. After a deal of pulling and hauling in the Senate the resolution was finally adopted and went to the Assembly. In the Assembly, Speaker Stanton, as "a select committee of one," took the resolution under his protection. The indications being that the "select committee of one" would fail to report, a storm was started by an attack on Stanton's authority to be a "select committee of one" at all. The assailants were repulsed. Nevertheless, "the select committee of one," after holding the measure a week, recommended that it be referred to the Committee on Federal Relations. The measure was finally adopted and went to the Governor.

[86] The Assembly vote on the four principal Japanese issues will be found in Table I of the Appendix.

[87a] A bill providing funds for such a census was introduced and became a law.

[87] The paragraph in Governor Gillett's message which deals with the Alien Land bill, read as follows:

"If you believe the general policy of this State and its future development demands that all aliens, that is, citizens of other countries, should be discouraged in making investments here, and that no alien should be permitted to become the owner in fee simple of any lands within this State - agricultural, grazing or mineral, or of any city property for the purposes of trade, commerce or manufacturing - then enact a law forbidding the same, but see to it that it affects the subjects of all nations alike, and that under its provisions the citizens of Japan shall have equal privileges with those of England and other favored nations; otherwise you might create a situation which may prove to be embarrassing to the Federal Government. Mr. Drew's bill might be so amended, but in its present form it clearly, as no doubt was intended, discriminates against the citizens of China and Japan. Whether any bill should pass at this time which will discourage foreign capital from seeking investments in our State is a most serious question and one not lightly to be considered. But that is a question I leave for you to solve."

[88] The Governor's letter was in full as follows:

Hon. A. M. Drew: Your little note was received.

"I am inclined to think that the best possible law that can be passed on the question of alien ownership of land would be the law adopted by Oklahoma. You will find it in the session laws of the State of Oklahoma, 1907 and 1908. The book is on file in the State Library. The Act is on page 481.

"I would strike out of the first line the words 'who is not a citizen of the United States,' because that is useless. No alien is a citizen of the United States, and cannot be.

"Then I notice the second line of Section 3, instead of having 'devise,' the word is 'device.' I suppose this must be a typographical error.

"To this bill might be added the last section of your bill, extending the time in which leases can be given - so many years on agricultural property and so many years on city property. I think one year is rather short; inasmuch as this would apply to all aliens alike, I would be reasonable as to the length of time for which leases should be granted.

"I am also of the opinion that President Roosevelt and Secretary Root would agree that this bill would be all right - in fact, I have telegrams from them which would indicate such to be the fact. Of course, the question whether or not it would be policy to pass an alien law in this State is something that the Legislature would have to consider, but if such a law is to pass, as I say, I am inclined to believe that one like the Oklahoma law would probably be the best."

[89] Assemblyman Drew's reply to the Governor's letter suggesting that the Oklahoma law be substituted for the original bill, was as follows:

"Your esteemed favor of the 26th inst., is before me, and I can assure you that I appreciate the spirit in which you have considered the Alien Land bill, presented by myself in the Assembly. I am strictly in accord with the changes you suggest. The words 'who is not a citizen of the United States' are surplusage and could easily have been left out, but they are found in both the Illinois and Oklahoma laws. I am glad the President takes the view of the matter that he does, and you may rest assured that I will work in harmony with yourself. However, I deem it advisable that some law should be enacted at this session of the Legislature. I think it will be wisdom on our part to take this step, and surely our neighbor, Japan, cannot complain so long as the bill is applicable to all aliens alike. I will submit to you a draft of the amended bill as soon as I can get it in shape."

[90] Johnson addressed himself directly to President Roosevelt and Governor Gillett. The following paragraphs are taken at random from his speech:

"I expect some member of the Assembly to introduce a bill here, the first section of which shall read: 'Before any legislation is enacted it shall bear the approval of James N. Gillett and President Roosevelt and if it is denied, the bill shall be withdrawn.' "

"Some of you think legislation is like patent medicine. It must bear on the bill, the label: 'None genuine without the note, This is a good bill, James N. Gillett.' "

"What right have we, mere Assemblymen, to have an opinion on any matter? Why should we, who were sent here by the people for the sake of convenience and formality, have any independence in our thought? What right have we to do anything but listen in awe and reverence to the words of wisdom that drop from the tongues of Governor James N. Gillett and Theodore Roosevelt?

"Of course we must surrender our individual opinion, and bow to the superior intellects of the 'Imperial Power,' which Mr. Beardslee loves so well. Since we must vote, as a matter of course, what right have we to vote otherwise than as the distinguished Governor and President say in their infinite certainty?"

Johnson complained bitterly of the interference of the President with the State and of the Governor with the Legislature.

"I have," said Johnson, "all respect for the intellect of James N. Gillett, Governor of California, and for his superior, President Roosevelt. But I am sent into this Chamber by my constituents and not by Governor James N. Gillett. I have been returned here again and again, and not because I bowed to the authority of James N. Gillett. I am here for the good of my people, the people who supported me, and who expect me to support them. I know more about the Japanese than Governor Gillett and President Roosevelt put together. I am not responsible to either of them."

"I am responsible to the mothers and fathers of Sacramento County who have their little daughters sitting side by side in the school rooms with matured Japs, with their base minds, their lascivious thoughts, multiplied by their race and strengthened by their mode of life."

"I am here to protect the children of these parents. To do all that I can to keep any Asiatic man from mingling in the same school with the daughters of our people. You know the results of such a condition; you know how far it will go, and I have seen Japanese 25 years old sitting in the seats next to the pure maids of California. I shuddered then and I shudder now, the same as any other parent will shudder to think of such a condition."

[91] The purpose of the Municipal Segregation bill, as set forth in its title, was "to confer power upon municipalities to protect the health, morals and peace of their inhabitants by restricting undesirable, improper and unhealthy persons and persons whose practices are dangerous to public morals and health and peace to certain prescribed limits, and prescribing a punishment for a violation of this Act."

The bill in full was as follows:

"Section 1. Whenever in the opinion of the governing body of any municipality the presence of undesirable, improper and unhealthy persons, or the presence of persons whose practices are dangerous to public morals and health and peace is deemed to exist in the said municipality and to be dangerous to the public morals and health and peace of said municipality and its inhabitants, the said governing body is hereby empowered to so declare by ordinance and is hereby empowered and authorized to prescribe by ordinance the district and limits within which said persons shall reside in said municipality, and thereafter it shall be unlawful for any person of the class so declared to reside in any other portion of said municipality than within the said district and limits so fixed.

"See. 2. A violation of the provisions of this Act shall be deemed a misdemeanor and shall be punished as such."

[92] "Never before have I heard of a time," said Assemblyman Cronin, "when a Governor has sent such a message to a Legislature. I am responsible to my constituents for my actions on this floor and I resent such interference. I hold the Governor's action to be indiscreet. He has no

more right to send such a message to this House than have we to dictate to the Supreme Court a policy on any action pending before it, on the ground that the best interests of the State depend upon their regarding our Instructions.

"Can we dictate to the Governor the course that is to be pursued in an executive matter? Let us stand by our guns."

"If the men change their votes on account of this fanciful talk from the President and the Governor," said Johnson of Sacramento, "I shall certainly be pained and surprised. They do not know the conditions as I know them. We have a right to protect our State, and it will not interfere with any international relations, and they know it. Their specious argument will not change my vote one bit. I know what The People want - what I want. I know influence has been brought to bear. It will be further brought to bear. Now I trust this vote will not suffer by you men changing your minds for such groundless reasons."

"Since yesterday," said Assemblyman Gibbons, "I have changed my views. I thought there were three departments in this Government, but I find I was mistaken. I recognize the error of my youthful belief. I know now that the Legislative and the Executive are one, or, rather, that the Executive is the Legislative."

[93] The question has been asked - was Johnson sincere in his advocacy of the Anti-Japanese measures? The writer does not presume to answer; the workings of Grove L. Johnson's mind and conscience are, for the writer at least, too intricate for analysis. But Grove L. Johnson voted for anti-racetrack gambling bills for years, spoke for them and fought for them as keenly as he did for the Anti-Japanese bills, always on the losing side. But when an anti-racetrack gambling bill was before the Assembly with some prospect of passage, Grove L. Johnson was found the leader of those opposed to its passage. In the case in point, to Grove L. Johnson, and not President Roosevelt or Governor Gillett, or even Phil Stanton, is due the credit for postponement of consideration of Assembly Bill 14, a postponement which meant its defeat.

[94] The Transue resolution will be found in full In the appendix.

[95] Speaker Stanton very modestly took much credit for the defeat of the bill. The following telegram was on its way to Washington almost before the vote had been announced:

"Sacramento, February 10.-Theodore Roosevelt, White House Washington, D.
C. - The Assembly just reconsidered and refused passage of the Japanese School bill. My congratulations.

P. A. STANTON."

The reply was as follows:

"Washington, February 10.-Hon. P. A. Stanton, Speaker of the Assembly, Sacramento, Cal. - Accept my heartiest thanks and congratulations for the great service you have rendered on behalf of The People of the United States. I thank the people of California and their representatives in the Legislature.

THEODORE ROOSEVELT."

A further telegram was sent to Governor Gillett:

"Washington, February 10. - To Governor J. N. Gillett, Sacramento Cal. - Accept my heartiest congratulations. All good Americans appreciate what you have done. Pray extend my congratulations individually to all who have aided you. I feel that the way in which California has done what was right for the Nation makes it more than ever obligatory on the Nation in every way to safeguard the interests of California. All that I personally can do toward this end, whether in public or private life, shall most certainly be done. THEODORE ROOSEVELT."

[96] The vote on Senate Bill 492 was as follows:

For the bill - Anthony, Black, Burnett, Caminetti, Campbell, Cartwright, Finn, Hartman, Holohan, Reily, Sanford, and Welch - 12.

Against the bill - Bates, Bell, Bills, Birdsall, Boynton, Curtin, Cutten, Hurd, Leavitt, Lewis, Martinelli, McCartney, Miller, Price, Rush, Savage, Strobridge, Thompson, Walker, Weed, Willis, and Wright - 22.

Absentees - Estudillo, Hare, Kennedy, Roseberry, Stetson, and Wolfe - 6.

[97] Senate Joint Resolution No. 6, which, as finally adopted, was a committee substitute for Senate Joint Resolution Nos. 6, 7, 11 and 17. It follows:

Whereas, The progress, happiness, and prosperity of the people of a nation depend upon a homogeneous population;

Whereas, The influx from overpopulated nations of Asia of people who are unsuited for American citizenship or for assimilation with the Caucasian race, has resulted and will result in lowering the American standard of life and the dignity and wage-earning capacity of American labor;

Whereas, The exclusion of Chinese laborers under the existing exclusion laws of the United States has tended to preserve the economic and social welfare of the people;

Whereas, We view with alarm any proposed repeal of such exclusion laws and the substituting therefor of general laws;

Whereas, The interest of California can best be safeguarded by the retention of said exclusion laws, and by extending their terms and provisions to other Asiatic people;

Whereas, The people of the Eastern states, and the United States generally, have an erroneous impression as to the real sentiment of the people of the Pacific Coast relative to the Asiatic question;

Whereas, We think it right and proper that the people of this country should be advised as to our true position on that question; therefore, be it

Resolved, by the Senate and Assembly jointly, That we respectfully urge the Congress of the United States to maintain intact the present Chinese exclusion laws and instead of taking any action looking to the repeal of said exclusion laws, to extend the terms and provisions thereof so as to apply to and include all Asiatics;

Resolved, That our Senators be instructed and Representatives in Congress requested to use all honorable means to carry out the foregoing recommendation and requests;

Resolved, That the Governor of California be, and he is, directed to transmit a certified copy of these resolutions to the President and Speaker, respectively, of the Senate and House of Representatives of the United States, and to each of our Senators and Representatives in Congress.

The resolution was adopted in the Senate by the following vote:

Ayes - Senators Anthony, Bates, Bills, Birdsall, Black, Boynton, Burnett, Caminetti, Campbell, Cartwright, Curtin, Cutten, Finn, Hare, Hartman, Holohan, Kennedy, Leavitt, Lewis, McCartney, Miller, Reily, Rush, Sanford, Savage, Walker, Welch, and Wolfe - 28.

Noes - Senators Bell, Price, Roseberry, Stetson, Thompson, Weed, and Willis - 7.

The resolution was adopted in the Assembly on March 23. There was no call for the ayes and noes, and no record was made of the vote.

CHAPTER XXI.

The Rule Against Lobbying.

Scandals of the Session of 1907 and the Dread of Pinkerton Detectives Led to a Rule Under Which Machine Lobbyists Could Work with Perfect Safety, While Advocates of Reform Measures Could Be Barred From Both Senate and Assembly.

One of the principal scandals of the Legislative session of 1907 was the openness with which machine lobbyists invaded Senate and Assembly chamber. They went so far as to move from member to member during roll-calls, giving Senator or Assemblyman, as the case might be, a proprietary tap on the shoulder, to direct his vote.

Word of the scandal got as far away from Sacramento as San Luis Obispo County, where A. E. Campbell became a candidate for the Senate against H. W. Lynch, largely on the machine issue. Campbell pledged himself ,to denounce such lobbyists as Jere Burke, the Southern Pacific attorney, if they appeared on the floor of the Senate, and to have them ejected from the chamber.

When Campbell reached Sacramento he let it be known that such would be his policy. Campbell is thickset and shaggy of eyebrow; his beard shows black on his face two hours after shaving. He has all the earmarks of a born fighter. He didn't look good to the machine, and his words didn't sound good. Incidentally, Jere Burke discreetly kept out of the Senate chamber while the Senate was in session.

Another thing which gave machine members of both Houses, as well as machine hangers-on, much concern, was the rumor started along in December that certain public-spirited citizens of Los Angeles and San Francisco would maintain at the Capital during the session a lobby to protect the interests of the people, just as the machine lobby looks after the well-being of machine-protected corporations and individuals.

This rumor caused great distress. It had all sorts of versions. One story was that a corps of Pinkertons would be employed to look for bugs in bills, boodle in sacks, and boodle-itching palms. Another account had it that the supervision was to be carried on by the San Francisco graft prosecution, and that Burns men would be in constant attendance. A report, started early in the session, that a Burns detective had secured a job as Assembly clerk almost threw that body into hysterics.

Campbell's threats and the anti-machine lobby rumors seem to have had their effect upon the Committee on Rules of each House. At any rate, both Senate and Assembly adopted rules that no person engaged in presenting any business to the Legislature or its Committees should be permitted to do business with a member while the House to which the member belonged was in session. Persons transgressing this rule were to be removed from the floor of the House in which the offense was committed, and kept out during the remainder of the session.

The rule was employed in one instance only. George Baker Anderson, of The People's Legislative Bureau, was ruled out of the Assembly, and, in effect, out of the Senate Chamber. Jere Burke kept away from both, but it was probably Campbell's threat more than the rule that influenced Burke. With these two exceptions, the lobbyists had pretty much the run of both chambers. It should be said, however, that while none of those lobbyists were threatened with expulsion from the floor of either House for advocating machine-backed measures and policies, persons advocating reform measures were threatened with the anti-lobbying rules. But Anderson was the only one to suffer because of them.

The curious feature of Anderson's case was that nobody seems to have been able to discover that he ever did any lobbying, or asked a member of either body to support or oppose any measure or policy, or that he even so much as spoke to a legislator while the House to which the legislator belonged was in session.

Anderson was in charge of a Legislative Bureau, one purpose of which was to keep the newspapers of the State which were not represented by correspondents at the Capital, informed of the votes on the various measures, and other items of importance or interest. Somebody early in the session called the bureau a "lobby," and somebody else improved the title by calling it "People's Lobby."

And then certain Senators and Assemblymen awoke to the startling discovery that in the Legislative Bureau, presided over by Anderson, was the People's Lobby that was to employ Pinkerton's or Burns' men to watch the Legislature. Anderson was a marked man from that moment.

Curiously enough this theory of Anderson's purpose didn't anger a single member of Senate or Assembly who, during the nearly three months that followed, voted against machine-advocated measures, and for measures which the machine opposed. Assemblymen of the type of Bohnett, Hinkle, Cattell, Callan and Drew, Senators like Bell, Black, Campbell and Holohan either treated the Pinkerton story as a joke or thought that a little Pinkerton watchfulness might be a pretty good proposition, all things considered.

On the other hand, many of the Senators and Assemblymen who were in constant opposition to reform policies, were very much exercised that anybody should have the audacity to have a watch kept upon the Legislature. This intense feeling found perhaps its best expression in Assemblyman McManus' denunciation of Anderson, when the question of having Anderson "investigated" was before the Assembly.

"It is a sad state of affairs," said McManus, "if a band of Pinkertons are here to follow the members up. We aren't everyday street-car conductors. We don't have to have spotters to watch us."

But perhaps the most astonishing feature of the whole astonishing Anderson incident is that nobody was ever able to connect him with a detective of any stripe whatsoever, Burns, Pinkerton, or unclassified. But this did not prevent his being ruled off the floor of the Assembly, and, in effect, of the Senate.

As the most amazing rumors about Anderson - many started as jokes[98] - multiplied, the indignation of certain Assemblymen and Senators increased. Matters came to a climax when Anderson sent a number of letters to members who had been absent from the chamber when the first vote was taken on the Walker-Otis Anti-Gambling bill, asking them if they would be willing to give the reasons for their absence.

The difference in the effect of the letters was astonishing. Assemblyman Prescott F. Cogswell, who had been favored with one of them, stated on the floor of the Assembly that he had been glad of the opportunity to make known the cause of his absence when the vote was taken. On the other hand, Assemblyman Wheelan, who had received a duplicate of the letter which Cogswell had welcomed, was very much cast down. Wheelan, arising to a question of personal privilege, read the letter, and wanted to know if he hadn't been "insulted[99]."

Assemblyman Beardslee hastened to assure Mr. Wheelan that he had been. Furthermore, Beardslee thumped his ample chest a thump, and announced:

"I, too, am insulted, for my brother has been insulted, and who insults my brother, insults me."

That seemed to settle it. The Committee on Rules was instructed to investigate the letter incident.

The Committee on Rules consisted of Johnston of Contra Costa, Transue, Grove L. Johnson, Beardslee and Stanton, the Committee, by the way, of "gag rules" notoriety. The investigation was held behind closed doors.

Anderson was asked about the letter and his purpose in writing it, to all of which he replied directly and without hesitation. And then came the burning question of the hour:

"How many Pinkertons are there in your employ in Sacramento, Mr. Anderson?" asked Johnson.

Anderson refused to answer the question. His wiser course would perhaps have been to answer truthfully, "None at all," and end the joke. But that was Anderson's business. He declined to answer.

Anderson's refusal to answer was solemnly reported by the committee back to the Assembly. Some members when the report was read laughed, others were made very serious indeed. It was finally decided that the investigation of Anderson should be turned over to the Judiciary Committee, of which Grove L. Johnson was chairman.

The Judiciary Committee was solemnly authorized to send for persons and papers, and administer oaths. While the investigation was pending, Anderson was denied admittance to the Assembly chamber. As the press badge, admitting Anderson to both Assembly and Senate chambers had been taken from him, he was unable to enter the Senate chamber either.

And the Assembly Judiciary Committee failed to investigate. Although Anderson demanded that he be given a hearing, and the matter settled, one way or the other, the Judiciary Committee would not and did not act. Under the Assembly resolution ordering the investigation, however, Anderson was for nearly two months barred from both the Assembly and Senate chambers. The session closed without the investigation being held.

It may be said in this connection that neither in the State Statutes, nor in the rules of either Senate or Assembly, is there a word which prohibits the employing of detectives at a Legislative session. Even though Johnson's committee had investigated Anderson's case, and discovered that he was really employing detectives, it is difficult to see how his punishment could have been justified. The incident is certainly one of the most extraordinary of the session - of any Legislative session ever held in this State, in fact.

The most interesting point in the Anderson case was that when pinned down for a reason for excluding him from the Assembly chamber, the offended Assemblyman would invariably reply that he was excluded under the rule which prohibited lobbying.

Curiously enough, however, lobbying, in spite of the rule, continued on the floors of both Houses even during sessions.

When the Islais Creek Harbor bill was under consideration in the Assembly, for example, Carroll Cook, and others interested in the defeat of the measure as it had passed the Senate, appeared openly on the floor and in the lobby of the Assembly, even when the debate was going on, and worked for amendment of the measure to suit their aims. All this resulted in the greatest confusion. But Speaker Stanton seemed absolutely unable to cope with the situation. The lobbying and the confusion continued in spite of Stanton's efforts to enforce something of the appearance of order.

Such scenes were often duplicated in the Senate. When the fight over the Direct Primary bill had the Senate by the ears, Johnnie Lynch, George Van Smith, even President of the Senate Warren Porter, exerted themselves to compel concurrence in the machine-backed Assembly amendments. This was done in the Senate chamber, when the Senate was in session, and Johnnie Lynch and Van Smith in particular were conspicuous in the work in behalf of the machine's policy.

But it was noticeable, that those who advocated reform policies took no such liberties on the floor of either House. They knew better. The danger involved for the lobbyist for reform measures was emphasized the night the measure prohibiting the sale of intoxicants within a mile and a half of Stanford University passed the Assembly.

Charles R. Detrick of Palo Alto, during the call of the House ordered on account of the Stanford bill, was discussing the merits of the measure with Assemblyman Bohnett, who was leading the fight for its passage. It was not a case of lobbying at all, for both men were for the bill,

Nevertheless, Assemblyman Schmitt[99a], who overheard Detrick mention the measure, warned the Stanford man, that if he (Detrick) did not cease his "lobbying" for the bill that he (Schmitt) would have him (Detrick) excluded from the chamber.

Senator Walker, although a member of the Senate, had much the same experience. Walker was discussing the Stanford bill with a friend, when one of the opponents of the measure threatened him with expulsion from the floor of the Assembly if he did not desist.

And even while these threats were being made against the proponents of the bill, opponents of the measure were working openly on the floor of the Assembly chamber against its passage. No suggestion was made that the rule prohibiting lobbying be enforced against them.

[98] A party of newspapermen were in Anderson's office one evening, when two or three machine men came in. With a wink to Anderson one of the newspapermen asked - "The head of your detective bureau is that keen looking young fellow, with reddish brown hair and brown eyes, is he not, Anderson?" Anderson joined in the Joke and nodded. One of the machine men left the room immediately. Within an hour, a hunt was being made

from one end of Sacramento to the other, for a "keen-looking young man with reddish brown hair and brown eyes."

[99] The communication which insulted Wheelan read as follows:

The Hon. Albert P. Wheelan,
    Member of Assembly.

Dear Sir: -

The People's Legislative Bureau, organized chiefly for the collection and dissemination of accurate information regarding legislation, and the attitude of members of the Legislature thereon, notes that you are recorded as having been absent when the roll was called on the motion to refer the Anti-Racetrack Gambling bill back to the committee.

As our record is intended to be permanent, and will be placed in the hands of all the newspapers and civic organizations throughout the State, we wish to ask if you have any objection to furnishing us the reason for your absence, so that we may enter it upon our record. Respectfully yours,

GEORGE B. ANDERSON,

Secretary.

[99a] This is the same Schmitt who objected so strenuously to professors of the State University being identified with reform movements.

CHAPTER XXII.

The Machine Lobbyist At Work.

How, Jere Burke Arrayed the County Officials of the State Against Two Beneficial Measures - How the Power of the Southern Pacific Was Employed
Against a California Enterprise - Danger Which Constantly Menaces Legitimate Enterprises.

The problem of drawing the line between legitimate and reprehensible lobbying has perplexed wiser men than sat in the California Legislature of 1909.

On the side of the lobbyist it may be said there seems no good reason why a citizen or representative of a corporation which is interested in pending legislation should not appear at the Capitol and in a legitimate way present his case to the members of the Legislature. In fact, the theory of committee consideration of measures introduced in Senate or Assembly, is based on the principle that it is the citizen's right to be heard on any matter that may be pending before the Legislature. The citizen cannot be heard before either the Senate or Assembly; he can, however, present his case to the committee the decision of which carries weight with that branch of the Legislature for which it acts. No one can object, for example, that Mr. P. F. Dunne appeared before the Senate Committee on Corporations, when the Railroad Regulation bill was under consideration, to present the railroad's side. Mr. Dunne appeared openly and aboveboard, and although he sought deliberately to misrepresent the situation to the Committee, nevertheless to object to his visiting Sacramento, or even to the work which he did while there, would be forced and far-fetched.

In the same way, Mr. Seth Mann, representing the shippers of California, appeared before the Committee and presented the side of the shippers. Mr. Mann spoke for the shippers precisely as Mr. Dunne spoke for the railroads. Mr. Mann, however, did not stoop to misrepresentation and deception.

But if Mr. Dunne for the railroads or Mr. Mann for the shippers had departed from openly-presented argument to buttonhole Senators or Assemblymen to tell them they must vote for or against a given measure, or look out for trouble, immediately would he be open to criticism. If either went during roll call from Legislator to Legislator to tell the members how they were to vote, again would he be justly criticized. Or had Mr. Dunne employed the influence of the great corporation which he represents to defeat or pass a measure in which his company can have no legitimate interest, again would there be good reason for complaint. Mr. Dunne could very properly - while acting as agent of the Southern Pacific Railroad Company - urge in a legitimate way the corporation's objections to the Demurrage bill, to the Full Crew bill, to the Railroad Regulation bill, or any other measure affecting common carriers. But for Mr. Dunne to have employed the influence of his position as political representative of a common carrier to force the passage of the Change of Venue bill for example, or defeat an effective Direct Primary bill, or the Party Circle bill, or the Judicial Column bill, would have been most reprehensible, for the Southern Pacific Company can have no legitimate interest in any of these measures.

So far as the writer knows, Mr. Dunne did not concern himself with any measure, except those in which his company was legitimately interested. But paid servants of the Southern Pacific Company were at Sacramento throughout the entire session, and managed to have their fingers in about all that was going on. The most conspicuous of them was Mr. J. T. Burke, more familiarly known as "Jere" Burke.

A fair sample of Burke's methods - and Burke is merely typical of the objectionable lobbyist - is found in the campaign which was carried on against Senate Bills 1229 and 1230. Had these measures become laws, it would have been possible for county assessors to discover property, owned principally by public service corporations, which at present escapes taxation. It is estimated that the total taxable value of this untaxed property is $100,000,000. It is not taxed because assessors have no means of reaching it. Mr. Burke's company could have no legitimate interest in Senate Bills 1229 and 1230. This statement is made, of course, on the assumption that the officials of the Southern Pacific Company aim to make honest returns to the tax collector. But to return to Senate Bills 1229 and 1230, and Burke's connection with them.

The two measures were intended to amend sections of the Codes relating to the assessment of property. Section 3681 of the Political Code provides that "during the session of the Board (of Supervisors sitting as a Board of Equalization) it may direct the Assessor to assess any taxable property that has escaped assessment, or to add to the amount, number and quality of property, when a false or incompetent list has been rendered."

Under this section, as it at present reads, the Supervisors may direct the Assessor to assess property that may have escaped assessment, but there is no machinery provided by which the property may be discovered. Senate Bill 1229 provided the machinery by which the unassessed property might be discovered, by adding to the section quoted above: "And the Board (the

Supervisors sitting as a Board of Equalization) may employ legal or other assistance in discovering any taxable property that has escaped assessment in the performance of their duties under this section."

Senate Bill 1230, the companion bill, provided that the Supervisors may subpena witnesses in all matters pending before them when sitting as a Board of Equalization. Under the present law, they can compel attendance of witnesses only upon the particular point under consideration.

The necessity of the amendments was generally admitted. The task of the Assessor is at best no easy one. Through his deputies he must list all the property in his county - that he can find.

The holdings of the small property owners are in sight, and, down to the last chicken, go on the assessment roll.

The property of the large corporation is not so readily discovered and $100,000,000 worth of it, according to conservative estimate, escapes assessment. The Assessors, with comparatively small force of deputies, have no way to force its assessment.

The Board of Supervisors, sitting as a Board of Equalization, may know that the unassessed property is in existence, but has no way to reach it. The Board may, under section 3681 of the Political Code quoted above, direct the Assessor to assess it, but the law stops there. There is no machinery provided for the discovery of the property. Senate Bills 1229 and 1230 provided the machinery. They were introduced by Senator Sanford of Mendocino. Before their significance was appreciated by Southern Pacific lobbyists, the Senate Judiciary Committee had recommended them for passage.

When Burke did grasp the significance of the measures, he demanded of Sanford that they be withdrawn. The argument which Burke advanced against them was in effect as follows:

"These bills are the most un-American propositions I ever heard of," said Burke. "They make of the Boards of Supervisors inquisitorial bodies. The corporations have property which they prefer to conceal. They prefer arbitrary assessments. They do not care to make returns to the Assessor. The passage of these bills would compel them to make returns."

In other words, the corporations, if Jere Burke, their legislative representative, reflects their sentiments, prefer that the Assessors continue to guess at the value of their properties. If the guess be too high, the corporations can compel reductions; if the guess be too low, they rest content. But, however the corporations may approve the guessing method of assessment, it has not proved equable, has not been fair to the farmer, the merchant and the householder, who under oath make honest returns to the Assessor.

Burke's argument, however, failed to move Sanford. The Senator from Mendocino refused to withdraw the bills. And then a curious thing happened. The members of the Senate were, within three days after Sanford had refused to withdraw the bills, fairly swamped with telegrams and letters from County Assessors and County Supervisors, protesting against the passage of the bills, on the ground that their passage would be a reflection upon the County Assessors of the State. Many who thus telegraphed or wrote, stated that they had not seen the bills but added in effect, "We understand that they are bad bills and should be defeated."

Of course, there was no evidence that Burke or his agents had instigated the telegrams. But there was a shrewd suspicion that such was the case. Sanford's answer to the Supervisors and Assessors was most effective. He mailed them copies of the Sacramento Bee which set forth the actual purpose of the bills, and copies of the bills themselves. Immediately Assessors and Supervisors who had wired their Senators to oppose the bills, sent telegrams withdrawing their opposition.

In passing it may be said that neither bill passed the Senate. Bill No. 1229 passed second reading, but was amended on third reading, March 11, and was not heard of again. Bill No. 1230 passed second reading, but was not read the third time. There are other ways to kill good bills than to bluff their authors into withdrawing them, or by stirring up State-wide antagonism to them. The incident shows, however, the State-wide ramifications of the machine. Within three days it was possible for the machine to create the impression from one end of the State to the other, that Senate Bills 1229 and 1230 were bad bills, measures casting reflection upon the County Assessors. Only the prompt action of Senator Sanford dispelled this impression. It also demonstrates the powerful backing behind the machine agents kept at Sacramento during a Legislative session.

It is bad enough when the far-reaching influence of the machine is employed to defeat measures which provide the machinery to enable public officials to enforce the law, against beneficiaries of the system, but when one of the agents employs this influence to promote his personal interests in a matter in which the particular corporation which he represents can have no interest whatever, particular emphasis is given the evils of the machine domination and reprehensible lobbying. To illustrate:

A peculiar situation which has developed at Owens Lake in Inyo County, made it necessary and proper that slight amendment be made to the law of eminent domain. The water of Owens Lake is heavily charged with soda. Some years ago, the Inyo Development Company was organized to recover this soda. The company invested $200,000 in establishing a soda-ash plant at the lakeside. This does not include the cost of building a railroad from the Lake to Mound House, Nevada, a distance of about 400 miles. The investment proved a success. The company harvests as high as 10,000 tons of soda ash a year. As the product is worth as high as $30 a ton at San Francisco, the enterprise adds an important industry to the developed resources of the State. The method of recovering the soda is simple. The water is drawn from the lake into vats, where it is left to evaporate. The soda is then recovered.

Owing to the fact that the waters of Owens Lake are constantly receding, a considerable strip of land has, during recent years, been uncovered between the company's holdings near the lake. and the water. The water from which the soda is reclaimed has to be piped over this land.

Recently former employees of the Inyo Development Company took up the land lying between the company's property and the lake, and under the name of the Natural Soda Products Company, propose to go into the business of manufacturing soda ash on their own account.

Not long since the new company began to complain of the old company's pipe, which crosses the new company's land. The old company saw that it had trouble ahead unless it could condemn a strip of the recently reclaimed land for a pipe line. It was found, however, that there is no law in California by which this could be done. Under the law of eminent domain land could be condemned for almost any other purpose than to establish a pipe line to carry water not to be used for irrigation or domestic purposes. An attempt was therefore made to have the law governing eminent domain amended so as to read that land could be condemned "for oil pipe lines and pipe lines for conducting the waters of any lake which are not fit for irrigation or domestic purposes, and which contain soda or other minerals' or chemical substances in solution, and also pumps and machinery for raising the same and forcing the same through such pipes."

This amendment was included in Senate Bill 797, and in the companion Assembly Bill 815. Senate Bill 797 passed the Senate and was referred to the Judiciary Committee of the Assembly, where the amendment providing for the soda water pipe line was added. This bill received a favorable recommendation from the Assembly Judiciary Committee and was returned to the Assembly. And then a very mysterious thing happened. Without apparent reason the bill was referred to the Assembly Committee on Corporations. Provision for soda water pipe lines, so far as the Assembly was concerned, came to a sudden ending.

At the time Senate Bill 797 was undergoing suppression in the Assembly, the companion bill, Assembly Bill 815, was pending before the Senate

Judiciary Committee. The measure was amended to make possible the condemnation of land for a soda water pipe line. Chairman Willis of the Committee expressed himself as satisfied with the amendment. And as amended, the bill was referred back to the Senate with the recommendation that it do pass as amended. Two days later, however, Senator Willis stated on the floor of the Senate that he had information from Inyo County which convinced him that the amendment was not desirable, and should be excluded from the bill. He stated that the county officials of Inyo County opposed the amendment, and for that reason suggested that the amendment be dropped. He stated that the Assembly would refuse to concur in the amendment even though the bill were passed with it. Mr. Willis' wishes were respected and the bill re-amended. Provisions for condemning land for soda water pipe lines came to as dead a stop in the Senate as in the Assembly. The next development in this comparatively unimportant incident of the session, was the discovery that Mr. J. T. Burke of Berkeley, member of the Southern Pacific law department, the Jere Burke of Southern Pacific lobbying, is one of the directors of the Natural Soda Products Company, which owns the land over which the Inyo Development Company would build a pipe line, a pipe line upon which the future prosperity of the Inyo Development Company largely rests. Burke was alleged to have opposed the amendment - and so far as the writer knows the charge was never denied - and with having brought about the defeat of the amendment. In other words, Mr. Burke is charged with throwing the full weight of the influence of the large corporation (the Southern Pacific Railroad Company, which he represents) on the side of a small corporation in which he is a director, and against a third corporation, which has large interests at stake. And the citizen who stands for fair play should not lose sight of the fact that Mr. Burke's corporation, the Southern Pacific Railroad Company, is the principal factor in the machine which works against good government, fair play, the "square deal" in business and politics which President Roosevelt insisted upon. The Inyo Development Company failed in its perfectly legitimate purpose because arrayed against it was in effect the political influence of the Southern Pacific Railroad Company, the tenderloin, and all the other elements that go to make up the political machine in California. And the fact should not be lost sight of that no other independent enterprise in California, even where it has, as has the Inyo Development Company, hundreds of thousands of dollars invested, is immune against similar experiences.

Early in the session when the lobbying question was, because of the excitement over Anderson, decidedly prominent, Sanford in the Senate and Callan in the Assembly introduced bills requiring lobbyists who appear at the Capitol during a legislative session to register their names, the names of their employers and the amount and nature of their compensation. At the close of the session they were, under the terms of the measures, required to file a detailed statement of their expenditures.

Had these measures become laws they might have proved very embarrassing to certain gentlemen who were very well received by the machine element in both Senate and Assembly chamber.

But they didn't become laws.

The Assembly bill went to the Assembly Judiciary Committee, which held it two months, finally, on March 16th, reporting it to the Assembly without recommendation. On March 19th, the measure was refused passage.

The Senate bill went to the Senate Judiciary Committee. The Committee referred it back to the Senate with the recommendation that it do not pass. On January 29th, it, too, was defeated.

The lobbying problem, like Jere Burke, continues with us.

CHAPTER XXIII.

Influence of the San Francisco Delegation.

Casts Nearly Twenty-five Per Cent of the Vote in Each House - Majority Invariably Found on the Side of the Machine - Opposed Passage of the Walker-Otis Bill - Instrumental in Amending the Direct Primary Law - Defeated Local Option Bill.

The popular idea that the State outside San Francisco is not concerned about political conditions at the metropolis is not borne out by the record of the legislative session of 1909. The San Francisco delegations in Senate and Assembly had, as they always have had and will have for many a year to come, the deciding voice in practically all important issues.

San Francisco elects within one of 25 per cent of the members of the State Senate, and within two of 25 per cent of the Assembly. In other words, nine of the forty Senators come from San Francisco, and eighteen of the eighty Assemblymen. The nine San Francisco Senators and the eighteen San Francisco Assemblymen join with the outside members in making laws not for San Francisco alone, but for the entire State. Their numbers give them decided advantage. The character of the laws passed at a legislative session almost invariably bears the stamp of the character of the San Francisco delegation. The character of the delegation depends upon political conditions at San Francisco. The whole State, then, is concerned in the efforts of the best citizenship of the metropolis to oust from power the corrupt element that has so long dominated San Francisco politics.

The record of the San Francisco delegation at the session of 1909, while better in the Assembly than in the Senate, is not one for San Francisco - or the State for that matter - to enthuse over. The votes on test questions of the eighteen members of the Assembly and of the nine members of the Senate, will be found set forth in tables in the appendix.

The table showing the votes of the nine San Francisco Senators covers sixteen roll calls, on which the San Francisco Senators cast 128 votes, ninety-nine of which were in support of machine policies and only twenty-nine against. Thus the nine Senators averaged on sixteen roll calls, eleven votes for the machine and three votes against. Had the San Francisco Senators broken even on the issues involved; that is to say, had sixty-four of the 128 votes been cast for the machine, and sixty-four against the machine, and the sixty-four anti-machine votes been evenly distributed among the several issues, the machine would have been defeated on every issue coming before the Senate.

The Assembly showing is not quite so overwhelmingly machine as that of the Senate, but it is bad enough. Eleven roll calls are considered. On these the eighteen San Francisco Assemblymen cast a total of 165 votes, of which 108 were for machine policies and fifty-seven against. Thus, even in the Assembly, the vote was approximately 2 to 1 in favor of the machine. Of the fifty-seven anti-machine votes, eleven were cast by Callan, who made an absolutely clean record, nine by Gerdes and seven by Lightner, a total of twenty-seven for the three. Deducted from the total of anti-machine votes, this leaves only thirty anti-machine votes for the remaining fifteen members of the delegation. Or to put it the other way, Callan, Gerdes and Lightner cast among them only four machine votes, which leaves 104 machine votes cast by the other fifteen San Francisco members.

On the individual issues the San Francisco Senators and Assemblymen made as bad a showing as does their vote in the aggregate. The passage of the Walker-Otis Racetrack Gambling bill for example demonstrates that the poolsellers had little hold upon the legislators of any community of the State outside of San Francisco. In the Senate but seven votes were cast against the bill. Five of the seven came from the San Francisco delegation - Finn, Hare, Hartman, Reily and Wolfe. The two remaining came from Alameda and Shasta-Siskiyou Counties. Leavitt, representing Alameda, and Weed, representing Shasta and Siskiyou, voted with the five San Francisco Senators against suppressing bookmaking and pool-selling.

The record of the San Francisco Assembly delegation on the anti-gambling measure is scarcely less suggestive. Before the Walker-Otis bill could pass the Assembly the proponents of the measure had to win six fights, as is shown by the table giving the several votes taken in the Assembly on the Walker-Otis bill. The three most important of the six were:

1. To prevent the bill being referred back to the Committee on Public Morals.

2. To pass the measure on third reading without amendment.

3. To prevent reconsideration of the vote by which the bill had been passed.

In the first fight twenty-three Assemblymen voted to refer the bill back to the Committee. Of these twelve - more than one-half - were from San Francisco.

The day of the second fight, only ten Assemblymen voted on the side of the gamblers. Every one of the ten was from San Francisco.

In the third fight, on the motion to reconsider, nineteen Assemblymen voted for reconsideration. Of these, ten, more than fifty per cent, were from San Francisco.

Or, to put it in a lump, in the three most important fights over the Walker-Otis bill in the Assembly, in the aggregate fifty-two votes were cast against the measure. Of these, thirty-two were from San Francisco Assemblymen. Only twenty were from outside San Francisco.

The universal demand throughout the State for the passage of an anti-pool selling measure offset the influence and the vote of the San Francisco delegation in both Senate and Assembly. But in the issues more involved, where the lines were more closely drawn, San Francisco practically made the laws for the whole State. This could be demonstrated by many instances. The most striking perhaps are shown by the histories of the Direct Primary measure and the Railroad Regulation bills.

When the first fight over the Direct Primary bill came up in the Senate, it will be remembered, the anti-machine forces defeated the machine by a vote of twenty-seven to thirteen. Of the thirteen Senators who voted to amend the bill to the liking of Wolfe and Leavitt, six - almost fifty per cent - were from San Francisco. They were Finn, Hare, Hartman, Kennedy, Reily, Wolfe.

When the machine element had succeeded in amending the Direct Primary measure to its liking in the Assembly and there came a new alignment on the bill in the Senate, eight of the nine San Francisco Senators voted with Wolfe and Leavitt for the amendments, which denied the people of California State-wide vote on candidates for the United States Senate. One San Francisco Senator only, Anthony, voted with the better element in the Senate, against the amendments.

Had only two of the nine Senators from San Francisco voted for the bill in its original form, the measure would have been passed by a vote of twenty-one to nineteen without the machine amendments.

The influence of the San Francisco members in shaping the Direct Primary law was even more forcibly illustrated in the Assembly. Of the eighteen San Francisco Assemblymen, fifteen voted for the Assembly amendments, two, Callan and Gerdes, voted against them, and Hopkins is not recorded as voting.

It will be remembered that the amendments were read into the bill by a vote of thirty-six to thirty-eight. Had the San Francisco delegation divided even on this vote, had nine voted for the amendments and nine against, the vote would have been forty-three against putting them in the bill, and thirty-two for, the bill would not have been amended in the Assembly; it would have become a law in the same shape that it had originally passed the Senate. It is noticeable that in an Assembly of eighty members, only twenty-three of the Assemblymen who voted for the Assembly amendments to the Direct Primary bill were from outside San Francisco. In the Senate eight of the twenty Senators who voted for the amendments were from San Francisco, only twelve were from outside that city. Thus, out of 120 members in the Legislature, ninety-three of whom were from outside San Francisco, only thirty-five from districts outside the metropolis voted for the Assembly, or machine amendments to the Direct Primary bill. But twenty-three of the twenty-seven San Francisco Senators and Assemblymen did vote for them, and only three of the San Francisco members voted against them.

It will be seen that the people of California who live outside San Francisco are decidedly interested in the character of Senators and Assemblymen whom that city sends to the Legislature.

The people of San Francisco are, of course, as much concerned over reasonable regulation of the transportation companies as Californians living outside that city. But the San Francisco Senators were a unit in their opposition to the passage of an effective railroad regulation measure.

The fight over the railroad regulation came in the Senate. The final line-up showed eighteen Senators for the effective Stetson bill and against the ineffective Wright bill; while twenty-two Senators were against the Stetson bill and for the Wright bill. The Wright bill was accordingly passed. Every one of the nine San Francisco Senators voted for the Wright bill. Only thirteen Senators who voted for the Wright bill were from outside San Francisco.

In a word, the proponents of the Stetson bill were from the start handicapped by a solid delegation of nine from San Francisco which they could not overcome. Had three of the nine San Francisco Senators been for the Stetson bill, that measure would now be the law of California.

The transportation issue was fought out in the Assembly over the Sanford Senate resolution endorsing Bristow's plan to establish a line of Government steamers between San Francisco and Panama. The fruit growers of Southern California are particularly interested in this project. The Assembly, however, amended all reference to the Bristow report and all criticism of the Pacific Mail Steamship Company and the railroads out of the resolution.

Of the eighteen San Francisco Assemblymen only one, Callan, voted against the amendments; fourteen - Beatty, Beban, Coghlan, Collum, Cullen, Hopkins, Lightner, Macauley, McManus, Nelson, O'Neil, Pugh,

Perine and Wheelan - voted for the amendments, while three - Black, Gerdes and Schmitt - did not vote at all.

The Local Option bill was also killed by San Francisco votes. This measure was strongly backed by the rural districts. The various counties, particularly those engaged in farming, dairying and fruit growing, sent representatives to the Legislature instructed to vote for Local Option. The issue in all ways concerned the country districts rather than the large cities. But the votes of the San Francisco Senators defeated the Local Option bill.

The first fight over the Local Option bill came when in the ordinary course of events it reached third reading. Instead of letting a vote be taken on the measure, Wolfe moved that it be referred to the Judiciary Committee. This was clearly a move against the passage of the bill, for it meant delay which might prove fatal. But Wolfe's motion prevailed by a vote of twenty to fifteen. The nine San Francisco Senators voted to refer the bill to the committee, only eleven Senators from outside San Francisco voted with them.

The nine members from San Francisco continued consistent in their opposition to the measure. When the Local Option bill did come to a vote their nine votes were cast against it.

The people of Del Norte county and the people of San Diego county are denied the privilege of voting "Wet or dry" because of the opposition to the Local Option bill of the solid San Francisco delegation in the Senate. It will be seen that the people of these distant counties are decidedly interested in political conditions in San Francisco, for in a large way the character of the San Francisco delegation in the Legislature is unmistakably reflected in the laws which are passed for the government of the entire State.

Taken as a whole, the San Francisco delegation in Senate and Assembly were nothing for that city to be proud of, and at a critical moment San Francisco came near paying dearly for her Hartmans, Hares, Macauleys and McManuses. But for the intervention of the country members the Islais Creek bond project would have been defeated.

The improvement calls for the purchase of sixty-three water blocks at Islais Creek to be converted into an inland harbor. The future development of San Francisco depends largely upon this improvement. But private interests demanded that nineteen of the sixty-three blocks be excluded from the plan, which would have rendered the whole project impracticable. When the fight came on, San Francisco Senators and Assemblymen opposed the purchase of the sixty-three blocks.

To begin with, Senator Wolfe, as member of the State Harbors Committee, had signed a report which recommended that forty-four blocks only be purchased. But Wolfe afterwards insisted that he had signed the report not knowing what he was doing.

When the fight for the improvement came up in the Senate, only two Senators, Hartman and Reily, both of San Francisco, opposed the project. They were in the end ignominiously defeated, every Senator present voting against them. But both Hartman and Reily did the best they knew how to defeat the purchase of the area necessary for the improvement.

The San Francisco delegation in its opposition to the Islais Creek project had better success in the Assembly. Nine San Francisco Assemblymen, Beban, Black, Cullen, Lightner, Macauley, McManus, O'Neil, Perine and Wheelan, united against the measure as it had passed the Senate. They succeeded in throwing doubt upon the necessity of the purchase of sixty-three blocks, and finally won twenty-two outside members over to their way of thinking. Had it not been for the efforts of Assemblymen Callan, Beatty and Nelson of San Francisco, backed by the Los Angeles delegation, the Islais Creek Harbor project would unquestionably have been defeated in the Assembly, solely because of the opposition of nine San Francisco Assemblymen.

But there is plenty of evidence of improved political conditions at San Francisco. An anti-machine Board of Supervisors is standing out manfully against the demands of machine-protected interests. The District Attorney's office is, indeed, pressing representatives of those interests pretty close to the doors of the penitentiary, although the District Attorney is handicapped by laws for which San Francisco is largely responsible, because of the character of the men whom session after session she has sent to the Legislature.

There is, however, enough to warrant the belief that San Francisco will improve the character of the Assembly and Senate delegation. Upon such improvement, the well-being of the whole State largely depends.

CHAPTER XXIV.

Attacks On And Defense of the Fish Commission

Fast Becoming a Powerful Political Factor - Enormous Fund Which It Expends Practically Without Check. - Legislative Investigation Blocked - Scheme to Give Commissioners Salary Fails.

Without the general public realizing just what is going on, the machine is, in the State Fish and Game Commission, building up an adjunct which seems destined to play an important part in any fight that may be carried on by the independent electors to break the machine's strangle-hold upon the State. Naturally the machine element in the Legislature was prepared always to rally to the defense of the Commission, and the defense was necessary, for the Commission is vulnerable, and was attacked at many points.

The Commission is perhaps the most extraordinary institution in the State. At its head is General George Stone, one-time chairman of the Republican State Central Committee. At its tail is Jake Steppacher, another one-time potent politician who has passed the days of his usefulness. Between Stone at the lead and Steppacher at the tail, is an astonishing array of formerly prominent politicians, as well as politicians who are decidedly in the present. In fact, the Fish and Game Commission is fast becoming one of the most potent adjuncts to the State political machine, that strictly non-partisan organization which guards the interests of the tenderloin, the Southern Pacific Railroad Company, the racetrack gamblers, their associates and allies, and which rather presumptuously assumes to be the Republican Party of California.

One of the features of the session of 1909 was the keen little fight of the anti-machine members of the Legislature to restore the Fish and Game Commission to its one-time simplicity, legitimacy and usefulness, and the efforts of the machine members to prevent this.

Up to two years ago, under the name of Fish Commission, the now Fish and Game Commission did most admirable work on an allowance of about $50,000. So far as the writer can ascertain, the Commission's income up to 1907 never exceeded $54,000 in any one year; usually it was a trifle under $50,000.

But in 1907 a tax of $1 a year was imposed upon all citizens of California who wished to go hunting. Citizens of other States, wishing to hunt in California, are under the same law taxed $10 a year, while foreigners are taxed $25. The law provides that the income thus raised be turned over to the Fish Commission.

The first year that the law was in force, the Commission received $116,579 on account of it. This, with moneys received from State appropriations, fines collected and the like, swelled the Commission's income for that year, the fiscal year ending June 30, 1908, to $184,467.70, an increase of more that $130,000 from the previous fiscal year.

For the fiscal year ending June 30, 1908, the cost of conducting the Governor's office, including the Governor's salary, the salaries of his secretaries and clerks, stationery, postage stamps, secret service, everything in a word in connection with the office, was $32,377.

In the same way the expense of conducting the State Controller's office was $23,417; of the State Treasurer's office, $16,751 ; of the Attorney General's office, $33,082; of the Surveyor General's office, $20,679; of the State Superintendent of Schools' office, $22,380.

But the General Stone captained - or perhaps generaled - Fish Commission had for that year a modest bit of $184,467. The Fish Commission then, for the fiscal year ending June 30, 1908, cost California almost six times as much as did the Governor's office, eight times as much as did the Controller's office, eleven times as much as did the State Treasurer's office, almost six times as much as did the Attorney General's office, more than nine times as much as the Surveyor General's office, and eight times as much as did the State Department of Public Instruction. And let it be borne in mind that this does not include the sums which the various counties paid for game wardens and for local protection of game, the best protection, by the way, and the most practical.

The $184,467, did not go to the counties. It went exclusively to General Stone's Commission. It will be seen that General Stone's Commission has a very good thing of it.

Another surprising feature of the Stone-Generaled Commission is that there is little check upon its expenditures. If the Governor wishes to raise the salary of his secretary or one of his stenographers he must appeal to the Legislature for permission. The State Controller, the State Treasurer, the Secretary of State, the State superintendent of Schools, and so on down the list Of State officials, are powerless to increase the salary of an assistant or of a clerk, or of an office boy, without legislative sanction.

But not so General Stone's Commission. The Commission is left to do pretty much as it pleases with its income. So, recently, without saying a word to anybody, it increased the salary of one of its deputies (Vogelsang) from $200 to $300 a month. Three hundred dollars a month is $3600 a year.

Up to this year the salary of the State Controller, of the Secretary of State, of the State Treasurer, of the Surveyor General, of the Superintendent of Public Instruction, etc., was only $3,000 a year. So it will be seen that one of General Stone's Deputies was drawing $600 a year more salary from the State than the elected State officials.

Jake Steppacher and other politicians, finding easy berths in the Commission, were also granted generous salary increases.

But in ways other than generous increase in the salaries of its deputies has the Fish Commission shown its kingly independence. The law provides that each State official and Commission shall, biennially, in the September before the Legislature convenes, file with the Governor a report of its activities and expenditures. This enables the Governor to make such recommendations as he may deem necessary in his message to the Legislature. The Controller, Attorney General, in fact all the State officials and departments, observed the law last September with but one exception. The Fish Commission, costing the State from six to eleven times more money that the State departments, did not file a report with the Governor.

The fact that the Commission had filed no report in September, the generous increase in salaries of its deputies, alleged instances of arbitrary conduct of its representatives, resulted in a resolution being introduced by Assemblyman Harry Polsley, demanding that the Commission be made the subject of legislative inquiry.

The resolution was referred to the Assembly Committee on Fish and Game, a committee notoriously in sympathy with the Commission. The Committee held a sort of preliminary hearing which resulted in a general whitewashing[100]. Polsley made out what was generally regarded as a prima facie case against the Commission, but the Committee did not choose to consider it such, and so the investigation got no further[100a].

But it was noticeable after the "preliminary hearing" that the advocates of the Fish Commission measures did not show up so sprightly confident of their passage as before. Polsley's efforts were by no means lost. Many measures intended to strengthen the already gigantically strong Commission failed of passage, or had their viciousness amended out of them, which, had it not been for Polsley's efforts, might have become laws.

The most important of these was Senate Bill 741. The measure as originally introduced by Senator Willis provided that "every person in the State of California, who hunts, pursues or kills any of the wild birds or animals, excepting predatory birds or animals, or fishes for or catches with hook and line any of the protected fish of this State, without first procuring a license therefor, as provided in this Act, is guilty of a misdemeanor."

Had the act become a law as introduced, not only those who hunt, but those who fish, would have been obliged to pay one dollar for a license. Thus, if a family of father, mother and three children wanted to go fishing, they would first have had to pay five dollars for the privilege.

The writer has it from a gentleman who has made careful study of the Fish Commission and its ways that the licensing of amateur fishers would have increased the income of the Fish and Game Commission $150,000 a year. This, with the income already enjoyed by the Commission of $184,000 a year, would have swelled its annual income to more than $330,000. This sum is $90,000 more than it cost to maintain the Stockton Hospital for the Insane for the fiscal year ending June 30, 1908; $125,000 more than the maintenance of the Agnews Asylum for that year; $122,000 more than the cost of the maintenance of the Folsom State Prison. The Fish and Game Commission was scarcely modest in its demands[101].

Naturally, the backers of the Fish and Game Commission made a hard fight for the measure's passage. But in spite of their efforts they could not edge it through the Senate until March 3d. In the Assembly, the measure met genuine opposition.

The Assembly Committee on Fish and Game of course recommended it for passage, and on March 15th, after a hot fight, it actually passed the Assembly. But Cattell gave notice of reconsideration. Incidentally, Governor Gillett let it be known that he would veto any measure that required amateur fishermen to pay license. This was a damper upon the Fish Commission crowd. When Cattell called the bill up for reconsideration it was reconsidered and defeated. However, Leeds accepted an amendment which struck out the clause which provided that amateur fishermen must pay a license tax. On Leeds' motion the next day, the amended bill was reconsidered and passed.

The three Fish and Game Commissioners serve without salary. Their compensation comes from the pleasure of disbursing upwards of $200,000 a year, what political prestige there may be in it, and rather generous expense money[102]. But a bill was introduced to give each Commissioner a salary of $3,000 a year. The measure did not become law, for which the writer believes much credit is due Assemblymen Polsley of Red Bluff. The State was thus saved $9,000 a year. General Stone and his associates are just that amount out of pocket. They have, however, given no indication of resigning their offices because the salary has been denied them.

But if the Fish and Game Commission was unsuccessful in increasing its revenue and putting through other measures from the standpoint of its members advantageous, its opponents were quite as unsuccessful in their attacks upon the Commission. Like the panther cat that guards her young, the agents of the Commission fought to retain the advantages which they had secured in 1907, and were generally successful.

The chief of the attacks was that of Assemblyman Polsley, author of Assembly Bill 433. This bill wasn't very long, contained less than five lines, in fact, and just forty-three words, but its passage would have saved the people of California more than $100,000 a year, or almost as much as it costs the State to run the Governor's office, the Controller's office, the State Treasurer's office and the office of State Superintendent of Schools combined. Assembly Bill 433 repealed the law of 1907, under which hunters are required to pay the Fish and Game Commission for the privilege of going hunting. The bill was introduced January 15th. It was referred to the notorious Assembly Committee on Fish and Game. There it was held until March 10th. It was then referred back to the Assembly with the recommendation that it "do not pass." That settled Assembly Bill 433.

Another measure which caused the agents of the Fish Commission much worry was introduced in the Assembly by Preston and in the Senate by Sanford. This bill provided that $50,000 should be paid out of the Fish and Game Commission fund each year to be used in paying bounties for exterminating coyotes. This would have left the Commission only about $130,000 a year. Naturally, the agents of the Commission resented the raid on their funds. The measure was referred to the Assembly Committee on Fish and Game. This was on January 18th. And it never was heard of after.

The companion Senate measure, introduced by Sanford, got further, but not much. The Senate Committee reported it "without recommendation." But even so, it passed second reading and went to engrossment and third reading. There it languished. On March 18th it was withdrawn by its author.

Another measure which gave the Commissioners a deal of worry was one introduced by Johnson of Placer, which provided that to each hunter who took fifty blue jay heads to the County's Clerk's office should be issued a hunter's license free. It was thought that this would encourage boys to kill blue jays for the hunter's license prize, value one dollar. But General Stone could not see it that way.

"If this bill becomes a law," said General Stone, "we shall have to retrench somewhere."

The bill didn't become a law, and the Fish and Game Commission was saved.

But the most "unkindest cut of all" came when the Assembly attempted to break into that sacred Fish and Game Commission fund by way of resolution. The Assembly actually adopted a resolution calling for a Commission to be appointed by the Governor for the purpose of ascertaining the feasibility of dividing the State into game districts, and generously providing $5,000 out of the Fish Commission fund for that purpose. Naturally the agents of the Fish Commission were scandalized at this proposed reckless expenditure of moneys from their fund by somebody else. But they were powerless. The resolution went through.

Rather late in the session the Assembly discovered that under the law it cannot "resolute" money out of any fund other than the Assembly contingent fund. The resolution was not, therefore, worth the paper it was printed on. Once again the sacred Fish Commission fund was saved.

But the Assembly could switch money out of the fund by legislative enactment, and a bill covering the same ground as the resolution was introduced without delay.

The measure passed the Assembly but did not reach the Senate until March 22d, two days before adjournment. That was very late for such a measure, but a heroic effort was made to secure its passage.

On Estudillo's motion, an attempt was made to suspend the State Constitution, declare the bill a matter of special urgency, and pass it forthwith. But the motion failed. Again did the Fish Commission escape a raid on its fund.

Senator Walker and Assemblyman Rutherford introduced measures providing for a distribution of the fund with counties, which at any rate looked pretty good to the counties, although the agents of the Fish Commission were not pleased at all.

The bills provided that one-half of the moneys collected from the sale of hunters' licenses, and on account of fines for infringement of the State game laws, should be paid to the counties in which collected, and the balance go to the Fish Commission fund.

Walker's bill was introduced on January 8th. It went to the Senate Committee on Fish and Game and was never heard of after.

Rutherford's bill was introduced on January 15th. It went to the Assembly Committee on Fish and Game. Like the Walker bill, the Rutherford bill was lost in committee oblivion.

Such, from the standpoint of the more important bills to increase and to decrease the Fish Commission fund, was the record of fish and game legislation. The Fish and Game Commission - and its overgrown fund - is still with us. But it might have been infinitely worse. Bad little boys who play hookey from Sunday-school to go fishing, for example, might have - in addition to the other frightful penalties imposed on them - been compelled to pay a license tax of $1 for the privilege.

[100] That the Fish and Game Committee would whitewash the Commission was recognized from the first. Even members of the machine who stand for genuine game protection objected to this committee making the investigation. When the motion was made to refer the resolution to this committee, Assemblyman Greer of Sacramento, took the floor to protest:

"It is useless to refer the matter to the Committee on Fish and Game," said Greer, "for we all know what that committee will do. We'll get no action there. Let it go to some committee that will give it consideration."

[100a] The Fish and Game Commission was very bitter against Polsley and all who approved his course. Because of the incident, Game Warden Welch of Santa Cruz County lost his position. Welch was a county official, paid by the county. The Commission complained that he had written a letter to Polsley commending the Assemblyman for his effort to secure a report 'from the Commission. Santa Cruz County receives a monthly stipend from the Commission toward the support of the Brookdale hatchery. The writer is reliably informed that one of the Commissioners stated that the Commission would do nothing for Santa Cruz County so long as "that man Welch" remained in office. Welch was removed by the Supervisors. Welch has a national-wide reputation as a game warden, and such papers as the "Forest and Stream," New York, and "Sports Afield," Chicago, have joined the California press in denunciation of his dismissal.

As these pages are going through the press, word comes from Santa Cruz that Welch has been reinstated by Judge Lucas F. Smith of the Superior Court of Santa Cruz County.

In summarizing his findings, Judge Smith holds that the local Board of Supervisors exceeded its legal power in declaring vacant the office of voluntary warden, which Welch held; exceeded its legal authority in removing Welch without specific charges being prepared, notice served on him and an opportunity given for a hearing.

[101] All sorts of estimates have been made of the income that would have been enjoyed by the Fish and Game Commission, had this bill become a law. The lowest that the writer knows of, made by a disinterested person, places the increase at $50,000 a year.

[102] Some of the commission's expense accounts on file with the State Controller are curiosities. For example, General Stone when he is on commission business taxes the fund $1 for breakfast, $1 for lunch, $1 for dinner. It thus costs the Commission three annual hunter's licenses to feed General Stone for a day.

CHAPTER XXV.

The Rewarding of the Faithful.

Senators and Assemblymen Whose Votes Were Cast Against Reform Measures Given State and Federal Positions in Some Instances, in Others Appointed to Holdover Committees or Sent on Trips at the Expense of the State.

The machine has many ways of rewarding the faithful who persist until the end. The faithful member of Senate or Assembly may be rewarded by a Federal appointment (Senator Bates has just been graciously recognized in this way[102a]) or he may be given a State job (witness Senator Price or Assemblyman Beardslee) ; or he may be put on a legislative hold-over committee to investigate something, or to represent the State at something, or to prepare some kind of a bill to be introduced at the next session of the Legislature.

This last is perhaps the most genteel method of reward. It entails little work, gives the beneficiary a certain distinction and pays very well.

Nine Senators were rewarded in this way in the closing hours of the session of 1909. There might have been ten, but that prince of "bandwagon" Senators, Welch, had to be rewarded twice, so but nine got holdover committeeships. They are Wolfe, Welch, Wright, Willis, Leavitt, Bills (labeled Republicans), Kennedy, Hare and Curtin (labeled Democrats). The names of the nine are not unfamiliar. With the exception of that of Curtin, their votes during the session were consistently cast on the side of the machine. For them to be rewarded came as a matter of course.

The machine will continue to reward such men until the people take the Legislature out of machine hands. But that is another story.

The Legislative Holdover Committee is about as useless a thing as can be imagined. This is very well illustrated by the State's experience with the so-called Harbors Committee, appointed by the Legislature of 1907 to inquire into harbor conditions throughout the State.

The committee consisted of three Senators and three Assemblymen. The Senators managed to incur expenses of $2,524.20. Assemblymen were more modest. Their expenses were only $1,851.80, making a total expense charge for the committee of $4,376.

But the $4,376 covers the committee's expenses only, does not provide compensation for the committeemen. A bill appropriating $6,000 for that purpose was introduced at the session of 1909. This gave the committeemen $1,000 each for their services. It made the investigation cost the State $10,376[102b].

The Harbors Committee - or somebody or something else, the writer is not sure which - prepared an elaborate report of the committee's findings. But owing to a surprising blunder that involved Senator Wolfe most curiously, the report was not filed until March 23, the day before the Legislature adjourned. The report was ordered printed in the journal, but it did not appear in the journal of the 23rd, which was circulated on the morning of the 24th. Instead, was a note to the effect that it would appear in the corrected journal. So, few knew that it had been filed at all, and it went unnoticed by the daily press.

But the details of the report[102c] were known to the general public long before it was filed with the Senate, and its provisions made Senator Wolfe appear to exceptional disadvantage. Wolfe was a member of the Harbors Committee, as was Senator Wright. Among the recommendations set forth in the report as originally prepared, was one that forty-four blocks only of land be purchased by the State for the improvement of the San Francisco Harbor at Islais Creek, instead of the sixty-three blocks necessary for practical harbor development.

Senator Wolfe was a warm advocate of the sixty-three block plan which is the only practical plan, by the way, and shows that Senator Wolfe can land on the right side of things occasionally. But it was very discouraging for Senator Wolfe to be confronted with the unfiled report of his own Harbors Committee, endorsed by his own signature as committeeman, in which the purchase of only forty-four blocks was urged.

Senator Wolfe's defense was ingenious. He stated that he had signed the report as a matter of courtesy, not really knowing what it contained. The incident illustrates the value to the State of such legislative investigations.

But in spite of the curious history of Wolfe's Harbors Committee, he was given another holdover committee in 1909. The Senate - on Wolfe's motion - adopted a resolution setting aside $5,000 to meet the expenses of a holdover committee to consist of three members to investigate the cause of recent advances in the cost of foodstuffs. Senators Wolfe, Welch and Hare are honored with the appointments. Lieutenant-Governor Porter appointed.

Senator Wolfe, from the machine standpoint, certainly earned the distinction thus thrust upon him, and his share of the money. Senator Wolfe was not in good health during the session, but in spite of his indisposition he managed to be present in the Senate Chamber, where often, pale, haggard and plainly on the verge of breakdown, he fought valiantly against the reform measures which were aimed at the prestige of the State machine, and the domination of the tenderloin, the Southern Pacific Railroad, the racetrack gamblers and allied interests in State politics.

Wolfe led the fight against the Walker-Otis Anti-Gambling bill, against the Local Option bill, against the effective Stetson Railroad Regulation bill, against the Direct Primary bill, against admitting Senator Bell of Pasadena to the Republican caucus, against the bill to prohibit the sale of intoxicants within a mile and a half of Stanford University, against the initiative amendment to the Constitution, against the amendment to the Constitution to correct ambiguities as to the powers and duties of the State Railroad Commission, and against Burnett's resolution for the investigation of the cause of the increase in freight rates and express charges. Senator Wolfe also led the fight for the passage of the Change of Venue bill.

Curiously enough, Senator Wolfe's stock argument, used in most of the opposition to reform measures, was to the effect that if such measures became laws, the Republican party in California would be undermined. Senator Wolfe's argument had great weight with Republicans like Leavitt and Weed and Democrats like Hare and Kennedy. For the "good of the Republican party," these gentlemen generally voted as Senator Wolfe dictated.

Senator Welch, the second member of the Pure Food Committee, is at least entitled to gracious consideration at the hands of the Wolfe-Leavitt element. Senator Welch was one of the twenty-seven Call-heralded heroes who defeated the Wolfe-Leavitt element in the first fight on the Direct Primary bill in the Senate. And Senator Welch was one of the seven heroes who "flopped" to the Wolfe-Leavitt side when the psychological moment came. Welch's one vote in the final struggle would have decided the Direct Primary fight for the side of the reform element. But when the reform element needed Welch he was found snugly quartered with Wolfe and Leavitt.

Welch voted for the Walker-Otis bill, but he was one of the last members of the Senate to be counted for that measure. Indeed, Welch caught the rear of the bandwagon on that issue just in time.

On railroad issues Welch's record is as good as the Southern Pacific Railroad could wish. He voted against the adoption of the practical absolute rate, and for the impracticable maximum rate; he voted for the ineffective Wright bill and against the effective Stetson bill. He voted against the Constitutional Amendment simplyfying the wording of the Constitution in those sections which prescribe the powers and duties of the Railroad Commissioners.

So Senator Welch had his appointment to the Food Investigation Committee due him. He was also made member of the Legislative Committee to represent the State at the Alaska-Yukon Exposition, of which more later. Thus Senator Welch rounded out the session very satisfactorily to Senator Welch and to the machine, if not to the State of California.

Senator Hare is down in the legislative records as a Democrat. He voted on most measures consistently under the lead of Wolfe and Leavitt. His appointment need not, therefore, cause surprise.

When the Direct Primary bill was before the Senate Committee on Election Laws, Hare's vote was with those of Wolfe and Leavitt to make the measure as ineffective as possible. Hare was among the thirteen unworthies who voted against the measure when the first fight was made for it on the floor of the Senate; he was among the twenty who finally, under Wolfe's leadership, held the measure up in the Senate until by trick it could be amended to the machine's liking. Hare was one of the seven Senators who voted against the Walker-Otis Anti-Gambling bill. He was one of those who voted for the passage of the Change of Venue bill.

On railroad measures Hare voted against the Stetson bill and for the Wright bill, against the absolute rate and for the maximum rate. He voted against the amendment to the Constitution to clear up the alleged ambiguity regarding the powers and duties of the Railroad Commissioners.

Lack of space prevents continuance of the review of Hare's votes. But enough has been said to show that this "Democrat" was entitled to the honor at the hands of the Performer, Republican Lieutenant Governor Warren Porter, of appointment to the Holdover Committee which, under the leadership of Senator Eddie Wolfe, will investigate the cause of the increase in the price of foodstuffs.

But a far more desirable appointment was to the committee which is to represent the State at the Alaska-Yukon Pacific Exposition. By concurrent resolution the Senate and Assembly decided that seven Senators, seven Assemblymen, one Lieutenant Governor (Warren Porter) and one Governor (Gillett) should attend the exposition at the State's expense. For this purpose $7,000 of the State's money has been provided.

The seven Senators appointed by Performer Porter are Wright, Willis, Welch, Leavitt, Bills, Kennedy, Curtin.

The seven Assemblymen appointed by Speaker Stanton are Transue, Beardslee, Leeds, Hewitt, McManus, McClellan and Schimtt.

The records of the Senators thus honored show them worthy the machine's consideration. Their votes on the banner measures before the Legislature last winter were as follows:

Against the Walker-Otis bill, to prohibit poolselling and bookmaking (Anti-Gambling bill) - Leavitt - 1.

For the Walker-Otis bill-Bills, Curtin, Kennedy, Willis, Welch, Wright - 6.

Only seven Senators voted against the Walker-Otis bill. Of the seven Leavitt is given the Alaska trip; Wolfe and Hare are put on the Food Investigation Committee. Thus of nine Senators who got on holdover committees three were among the seven who voted in the interest of the gambling element.

The records made by the State Senators who will attend the exposition at the State's expense in the Direct Primary fight are quite as suggestive. When the first attempt was made in the Senate to force the machine amendments into the bill, February 18, the seven Senators voted as follows:

For the machine's amendments - Bills, Kennedy, Leavitt, Willis.

Against the machine's amendments - Curtin, Welch, Wright.

Thirteen Senators on February 18 voted for the machine's amendments. Of their number Hare and Wolfe are on the Food Investigation Committee; Bills, Kennedy, Leavitt and Willis are to attend the exposition at the State's expense. Thus six of the thirteen have been rewarded.

The machine, having failed to amend the Direct Primary bill in the Senate, amended it in the Assembly. When the measure was returned to the Senate, six of the seven Senators who will attend the exposition voted to concur in the Assembly amendments. They were, Bills, Kennedy, Leavitt, Welch, Willis and Wright. Only one of the seven voted against the machine amendments, Curtin.

The records of the seven favored, trip-taking Senators on railroad regulation measures are as follows:

For the Wright bill, against the Stetson bill; for the maximum rate, against the absolute rate - Leavitt, Welch, Willis, Wright, Bills, Kennedy - 6.

Against the Wright bill, for the Stetson bill, against the maximum rate, for the absolute rate - Curtin - 1.

Against the constitutional amendment to make clear the powers and duties of Railroad Commissioners - Bills, Kennedy, Leavitt, Welch, Willis - 5.

For the amendment - Curtin, Wright - 2.

Against the Burnett resolution calling for an investigation of the cause for an increase in freight rates - Bills, Kennedy, Leavitt, Willis, Wright - 5.

For the resolution - 0.

Absent or not voting - Curtin, Welch - 2.

The records of the seven on the Local Option bill and the Change of Venue bill are:

Against Local Option - Leavitt, Welch, Willis, Bills, Curtin, Kennedy - 6.

For Local Option - Wright - 1.

For the Change of Venue bill - Bills, Leavitt, Welch, Willis, Wright - 5.

Against the Change of Venue bill - Curtin, Kennedy - 2.

Kennedy, to be sure, voted against the Change of Venue bill when that measure passed the Senate. But Senator Kennedy was unaccountably absent the next morning when the Change of Venue bill was taken up on a motion for reconsideration. Because of Kennedy's absence, the motion to reconsider the measure was lost, and its defeat prevented. Senator Kennedy is scarcely entitled to credit for being recorded on the right side of this measure.

Nine Senators are included in the two hold-over committees which are under consideration. As Wolfe and Hare invariably voted with Leavitt, it will be seen that eight of the nine voted against the Stetson bill and for the Wright bill; seven of the nine voted against the Constitutional amendment to make plain the constitutional powers and duties of the Railroad Commissioners; seven of the nine voted against investigating the cause of increase in freight and express rates to the Pacific Coast; eight of the nine voted against local option; seven voted for the Change of Venue bill, and one of the two others as good as voted for it, although on record against the measure.

As Republican Senators Bell, Birdsall, Black, Boynton, Cutten, Roseberry, Rush, Stetson, Strobridge and Thompson, who were invariably on the right side of things, look upon the records of the "Democrats" and "Republicans" included among the nine favored receivers of plums, they can scarcely be blamed for demanding with the discouraged little boy - What's the use of being good, anyhow?

And as the Democratic Senators, Caminetti, Campbell, Cartwright, Holohan, Miller and Sanford, who worked with the anti-machine Republicans for the passage of good laws and the defeat of bad ones look upon the favored Hare and Kennedy they cannot be blamed if the same question occurs to them also.

The indications are that the Senators who were thus overlooked will have "to wait for theirs," until The People of California, and not the machine, award the prizes for faithful public service.

Of the seven Assemblymen who will attend the Alaska-Yukon Exposition, one, Hewitt, voted against the machine on every important issue that came up. The other six are a spotted lot.

The six - Beardslee, Leeds, McManus, McClellan, Schmitt and Transue - voted for the famous "gag rules" which the Assembly rejected by a vote of 41 to 32. Indeed, Beardslee and Transue were on the Committee on Rules which the Assembly, when it rejected the Committee's rules, repudiated.

In the fight for the passage of the Walker-Otis Anti-Gambling bill, two of the six, Leeds and Transue, managed to keep their records straight. On the six roll-calls taken on the measure before it passed the Assembly, Beardslee voted five times against the bill and once for it; McManus voted six times against it; Schmitt voted five times against it, on one roll-call he did not vote; while McClellan voted four times for it and twice against.

Five of the six, Beardslee, Leeds, McManus, McClellan and Schmitt voted against forcing out of the Committee on Federal Relations the Sanford resolution, which called for a government line of steamers from Panama to San Francisco. The five voted for the Johnson amendments to the resolutions, which cut out all criticizing reference to the rate-boosting combinations between the great transportation companies. Transue was absent when the vote to force the resolution out of committee was taken. But he was present to vote for the Johnson amendments.

Five of the six, Leeds, McManus, McClellan, Schmitt and Transue, voted for the machine amendments to the Direct Primary bill, which were read into that measure in the Assembly, and which resulted in the Senate deadlock over the measure. Beardslee voted against the amendments.

Five of the six - Beardslee, Leeds, McManus, McClellan and Transue - voted against the Holohan bill to remove the party circle from the election ballot. Schmitt did not vote on this measure.

Assemblyman Hewitt will, at the Alaska-Yukon, find himself in distinguished company. From the Wolfe-Leavitt-Johnson standpoint, he is the only one of his associates who cannot be said to have earned the preferment thrust upon him.

[102a] As these forms are going through the press, word comes that Senator Willis has been made Assistant United States District Attorney at Los Angeles. See Willis' record, Table "A" of the appendix.

[102b] The State Constitution provides no method of compensation for such services. The providing of this compensation, therefore, becomes a matter of great delicacy. It is done, under a decision of the Supreme Court that that tribunal cannot go back of a legislative Act, but must abide by the wording of the Act. The appropriation bills to compensate the members for their services on hold-over Committees are worded to meet the opinion of the courts. The money is invariably appropriated "to pay the claim of," etc. The Legislature is, according to the courts, the sole Judge of whether the alleged claim is a claim and not a petition for a gift. The "to -pay- the-claim-of" bills never fail to pull down the money.

[102c] The report as originally drawn, and as it was signed by Senator Wolfe and his associates.

CHAPTER XXVI.

The Holdover Senators.

Eleven of Them May Be Counted Upon to Vote Against the Machine at the
Session of 1911, Two Are Doubtful, One Will Probably Vote with the Majority, While Six May Be Counted Upon to Support Machine Policies.

Twenty of the 120 members who sat in the Legislature of 1909 - half of the forty Senators - hold over and will serve in the Legislature of 1911. The twenty constitute the strength with which the machine and the anti-machine forces will enter the field in the struggle for control of the Legislature two years hence.

The machine has, long before this, taken stock of those twenty holdover Senators. Machine agents unquestionably know what the holdover members owe and to whom indebted; know their family history; know the church to which they belong, their lodges, their likes, their dislikes and their prejudices; know how they can be "reached" if vulnerable; know how they can be "kept in line" if already tarred with the machine brush.

But the plain citizen, not within the charmed circle of machine protection, is not concerning himself much about these holdovers. He scarcely knows their names. It is safe to say that not 2 per cent of the voters of California could off-hand name the twenty holdover members of the Upper House of the Legislature.

In other words, the machine is posted, and the citizen is not. And here is the secret of much of the machine's success. In its campaign for control of affairs, the machine knows to a nicety just what to expect from men in public life; the plain citizen is without such information.

In the Appendix will be found a table, "Table H," showing the votes of the twenty holdover Senators on sixteen roll calls. Representative citizens, all standing for good government, may differ as to the desirability or undesirability of several of the measures included in the list. But by and large the average normal citizen will hold that certain of the sixteen measures are desirable and others undesirable. Thus all would probably agree that the Change of Venue bill is undesirable legislation, and declare the Walker-Otis Anti-Racetrack Gambling measure to be desirable, although they might honestly differ on the Local Option bill.

On the sixteen roll calls the twenty holdover Senators cast 283 votes. Of the 283, 164 are recorded against what the normal citizen would regard as bad measures, or for what the normal citizen would regard as good measures. In other words, speaking broadly, 164 of the 283 votes were cast against machine policies. Only 119 were cast with the machine. In other words, over the whole session, on what may be fairly considered the most important roll calls taken in the Senate, the holdover Senators cast 164 votes against the machine and only 119 votes for the machine. This isn't a bad showing to start with.

The showing is strengthened by the fact that ninety-two of the 119 machine votes were cast by eight Senators, Finn, Wolfe, Bills, Martinelli, Hurd, Hare, Lewis and Welch. Senator Finn of San Francisco heads the list with fifteen of these negative votes. On one occasion Senator Finn didn't vote. After Finn comes Wolfe, also from San Francisco, with thirteen of the ninety-two negative or machine votes to his credit or his discredit; Bills of Sacramento and Martinelli of Marin follow with twelve each; Hurd of Los Angeles with eleven; Hare of San Francisco and Lewis of San Joaquin with ten each, and Welch of San Francisco with nine.

This leaves twenty-seven machine votes to be divided among twelve of the holdover Senators, about two votes on an average each.

Burnett is credited with seven of the twenty-seven, which reduces the number to twenty for eleven Senators. Of the twenty votes, seven were cast in the two ballots taken on the Local Option issue, again the bill; and eight were cast in two ballots against the Holohan bill to remove the party circle from the election ballot.

Thus, excluding the votes on local option, and on the Party Circle bill, on twelve important ballots, eleven of the holdover Senators cast only five votes for machine policies.

The eleven are Birdsall, Campbell, Cutten, Estudillo, Holohan, Roseberry, Rush, Stetson, Strobridge, Thompson and Walker.

These eleven Senators, as judged by their performances at the session just closed, may be depended upon to vote for good bills and against bad ones at the session of 1911.

To this list should be added the name of Burnett. Burnett got off wrong on the Stetson Railroad Regulation bill, and managed to land with the Wolfe element in the direct primary fight. But there is good reason to believe that Burnett was very sick of his company before the session closed. The probabilities are that Senator Burnett feels more at home with Senators Stetson, Strobridge, Thompson and Cutten than with Hare, Finn and Wolfe.

Senator Hurd is another holdover who started out very well, but went badly astray after the vote on the Railroad Regulation bills. Like Burnett, Hurd showed signs toward the end of the session of feeling himself in uncongenial company. There is reason to believe that Hurd at the next session will be found voting with the Thompson-Stetson-Strobridge element.

Senator Welch will be found voting with the majority. This reduces the number of holdover Senators who can be counted upon to accept Wolfe's leadership, machine Senators, if you like, to six. The line-up of the twenty holdovers, then, would on this basis be as follows:

Anti-machine - Birdsall, Cutten, Estudillo, Roseberry, Rush, Stetson, Strobridge, Thompson, Walker (Republicans), Campbell, Holohan (Democrats) - 11.

Doubtful - Burnett, Hurd (Republicans) - 2.

With the majority - Welch (Republican) - 1.

Machine - Bills, Finn, Lewis[103], Martinelli, Wolfe (Republicans), Hare (Democrat) - 6.

On this basis the anti-machine element will start with all the advantage in the struggle for control of the Senate in 1911. If Burnett and Hurd vote with the eleven anti-machine Senators, it will be necessary to elect only eight anti-machine Senators that the reform element may control the Senate. This will mean twenty-two votes for the reform element, for Welch, if he is to be judged by past performances, will be found with the majority.

From present indications, four important fights will be made at the Legislative session of 1911.

(1) To pass an effective railroad regulation measure and to amend those sections of the State Constitution which prescribe the duties and powers of the Railroad Commissioners.

(2) To amend the Direct Primary law passed at the session just closed to meet with the popular demand for an effective measure.

(3) To grant local option to the counties.

(4) To adopt an amendment to the State Constitution granting the initiative to the electors of the State.

Significantly enough, the line-up of the holdover Senators in the Direct Primary deadlock of the last session was nine to eleven, the eleven Senators who divide but five machine votes between them standing out against Wolfe and Leavitt for an effective provision for the selection of United

States Senators by State-wide vote, while the six machine Senators, the "bandwagon" Senator and the two doubtfuls, voted with Wolfe and Leavitt.

But the probabilities are that in the event of the anti-machine element controlling the Senate of 1911, Burnett, Hurd, Lewis, Martinelli and Welch would join with the reform forces to make necessary amendments to the measure. When the Direct Primary bill was first before the Senate, these five Senators united with the Good Government forces and assisted in defeating the machine's amendment. When the bill was amended in the Assembly, however, the five flopped to the machine side. Indeed, only four of the twenty holdover Senators voted for the machine's amendments to the Direct Primary bill when the measure was first passed upon by the Senate. They were Bills, Finn, Hare and Wolfe.

The holdover Senators made their poorest showing on the railroad measures. When the test came on the Stetson bill the twenty holdovers split even, ten being for the effective Stetson bill, ten for the ineffective Wright bill. The line-up was as follows:

For the Stetson bill - Birdsall, Campbell, Cutten, Holohan, Lewis, Roseberry, Rush, Stetson, Strobridge, Thompson - 10.

For the Wright bill - Bills, Burnett, Estudillo, Finn, Hare, Hurd, Martinelli, Walker, Welch, Wolfe - 10.

Lewis, who usually voted with the performers, voted for the Stetson bill. But the reform forces lost two votes, those of Walker and Estudillo. On another vote on the same issue, however, Burnett, Estudillo and Walker would probably be found with the anti-machine forces supporting an effective measure. This would make the vote of the holdover Senators, thirteen for effective railroad regulation, and seven for a measure of the Wright law variety.

The holdovers made a good showing on the Initiative amendment, eleven voting for it and five against it, four not voting at all. The vote was as follows:

For the Initiative - Birdsall, Campbell, Cutten, Estudillo, Hare, Roseberry, Rush, Stetson, Thompson, Walker, Welch - 11.

Against the Initiative - Bills, Hurd, Lewis, Martinelli, Wolfe - 5.

Not voting - Burnett, Finn, Holohan, Strobridge - 4.

Of the four who did not vote, three, Burnett, Holohan and Strobridge, would have voted for the amendment. Finn would probably have voted against it. This would have made the vote fourteen to six in the amendment's favor. It will be seen that those who would have the initiative granted the people, have a good start for the next session.

The outlook for local option is not so reassuring. Of the holdover Senators who ordinarily were for measures which give the people a voice in the management of public affairs, Birdsall, Holohan, Rush and Strobridge were unalterably opposed to the local option idea. The six machine Senators, of course, opposed it, which with the votes of Burnett, Welch and Hurd placed thirteen of the twenty holdover Senators against the measure.

Six of the holdovers voted for the Local Option bill - Campbell, Cutten, Estudillo, Roseberry, Thompson and Walker.

Stetson was absent and did not vote. He, however, favored the bill. His vote would have made it 13 to 7. Thus on the vote on their bill at the last session, the local option forces have seven of the holdover Senators with them, and thirteen against.

On the other hand, seventeen of the holdover Senators voted for the Walker-Otis Anti-Racetrack Gambling bill, while only three, Finn, Hare and Wolfe, voted against it. Thus on the moral issue, as well as the political and the industrial, the anti-machine element is stronger in the holdover delegation in the Senate than is the machine. It rests with the good citizenship of California to maintain its advantage by electing to the Senate in 1910, men who will stand with the majority of the holdover members for the passage of good and the defeat of vicious measures.

[103] Lewis voted with the anti-machine element in the Railroad Regulation fight, one of the most severe tests of the session. Persons who know Lewis well stated that he will, if the anti-machine forces be effectively organized at the session of 1911, be found against the machine. It is "up to Senator Lewis."

CHAPTER XXVII.

The Retiring Senators.

Of the Twenty Whose Terms of Office Will Have Expired, the Machine Loses Eleven, the Anti-Machine Element Seven - Two Who Voted With the Machine on Occasion Were Usually on the Side of Good Government.

Twenty of the forty Senators who sat in the Legislature of 1909, must, if they sit in the Legislature of 1911, be re-elected at the general elections in November 1910. They are: Senators Anthony of San Francisco, Bates of Alameda, Bell of Pasadena, Black of Santa Clara, Boynton of Yuba, Caminetti of Amador, Cartwright of Fresno, Curtin of Tuolumne, Hartman of San Francisco, Kennedy of San Francisco, Leavitt of Alameda, McCartney of Los Angeles, Miller of Kern, Price of Sonoma, Reily of San Francisco, Sanford of Mendocino, Savage of Los Angeles, Weed of Siskiyou, Willis of San Bernardino and Wright of San Diego.

By consulting Table A of the Appendix, it will be seen that on sixteen roll calls the forty members of the Senate of 1909 voted 570 times. Of the 570 votes 311 were cast against what are regarded as machine policies; 259 for such policies. Of the 311 anti-machine votes, 164 were cast by holdover Senators, and were considered in the last chapter, while 147 were cast by Senators whose successors will be elected in 1910. Thus it will be seen, that on this basis, more desirable Senators will hold over than those whose terms of office will have expired before the next Legislature convenes.

On the basis of the machine votes the result is as satisfactory. On the sixteen roll calls, 259 machine votes were cast. Of these 140 were cast by the retiring Senators, and only 119 by those who will hold over, and who will sit in the Legislature of 1911. So, on the whole, the machine loses and the people gain in the retirement of the twenty Senators.

In point of numbers the result is as satisfactory. The machine will lose eleven Senators: Bates, Hartman, Kennedy, Leavitt, McCartney, Price, Reily, Savage, Weed, Willis and Wright; while the anti-machine forces will lose only seven who can be counted constantly for reform policies: Bell, Black, Boynton, Caminetti, Cartwright, Miller and Sanford.

This leaves only Anthony and Curtin to be accounted for. Both these men stood out against the machine's amendments to the Direct Primary bill, Anthony in particular standing against the severest pressure that could be brought to compel him to vote against the interests of his constituents and of the State. But Anthony could not be moved. On the railroad measures, however, Anthony voted with the machine. But he voted for the Walker-Otis bill, and, generally speaking, for all measures which made for political reforms. With any sort of organization of the reform forces, Anthony could be counted upon as safe for reform. His record on the Direct Primary bill certainly entitles him to the highest consideration.

Curtin also was as a general thing with the reform element. He voted, however, against the bill to do away with the party circle and he voted against the Local Option bill, but in so doing he merely followed the lead of such men as Birdsall, who, while out and out against the machine, were at the same time against local option and lukewarm on ballot reform. Birdsall, however, finally voted for the bill to remove the party circle from the election ballot, although he had on the first ballot voted against the bill. Curtin did not, however, change his vote. But Curtin did vote against the Initiative Amendment. On the other hand, Curtin's record on the Direct Primary bill, on the Railroad Regulation bills, and on the Anti-Gambling bill is all that could be desired.

While the retirement of all the Senators who do not hold over would strengthen the reform element in the Senate, nevertheless the State can ill afford to lose the services of the seven who stood out so valiantly against machine policies. Senator Bell heads the list, with Caminetti, Black, Boynton and Sanford close seconds.

Senator Bell not only made the best record made in the Senate of 1909, but he made the best record of the Senate of 1907. Conscientious, fully awake to the responsibilities of his position, alive to the tricks of the machine leaders, in constant attendance, Senator Bell proved himself during the two sessions that he has served in the Senate, a power for good government. His absence from the session of 1911 would be a loss to the State.

Senators Black and Boynton at the session of 1909 made records quite as good as that made by Senator Bell. On the sixteen roll calls taken as tests of the standing of the several Senators, Black voted but once against reform policies. On the first ballot on the Party Circle bill he voted against the measure, but the day following, corrected his mistake by voting for the measure. Boynton voted to return the Local Option bill to the Judiciary Committee, but at the final test his vote was recorded for the bill[103a]. Thus neither of the two Senators can be said to have voted with the machine even on comparatively unimportant issues.

Senator Caminetti probably gave the machine more worry during the session than any other one Senator. Caminetti has, a way of saying out loud what his anti-machine associates are thinking, which is not at all popular with the machine. True to principle, he, a Democrat, voted for United States Senator Perkins because, from Caminetti's view-point, no other candidate came so near to being the popular choice of the people as Perkins, and Caminetti holds that the people and not the Legislature should select the United States Senator. The machine was glad of Caminetti's vote for Perkins, but was not at all pleased with the departure of a Democrat voting for a Republican. Caminetti's course continued in by all the members of the Legislature, and the machine would lose its monopoly of Federal Senator-making.

Caminetti's record is admirable. To be sure, he opposed Local Option, but he fought as few others fought for an effective Direct Primary law, for effective railroad regulation, in fact for practically all the reform policies which the anti-machine forces advocated and the machine opposed. Senator Sanford also voted for and worked for reform policies. Like Caminetti, however, he opposed the Local Option bill and voted against it. Senator Miller, on the other hand, supported the Local Option bill, but slipped more seriously than did either Caminetti or Sanford, by voting with the machine Senators against the Initiative amendment. Miller's work for effective railroad regulation and for an effective Direct Primary law, won him the deserved admiration and confidence of the better element of the Legislature. Senator Cartwright voted but twelve times on the sixteen roll calls, but the twelve included the votes on the Direct Primary issues, on railroad regulation, and on all the moral issues considered. And each time, Senator Cartwright's vote was cast on the side of good government.

On the other side, the machine side, Senator Bates distinguished himself but once during the session. It was Senator Bates who, to oblige a friend, had the notorious Change of Venue bill placed on the Special Urgency File, thus making the passage of the bill possible. Senator Bates' vote and influence - such as it was - were thrown in the balance against giving the people of California a State-wide vote - the only practical vote - for United States Senators. He voted against the effective Stetson bill; he voted for the ineffective Railroad Regulation bill. In fact, aside from the Walker-Otis bill, Bates was on the machine side of practically every issue[104].

Senator Hartman was during the session a mere machine vote. He was always on hand, always voted, and voted with the machine. It was Senator Hartman who named an employee of the notorious Sausalito gambling rooms for an important committee clerkship. So far as the writer can recall, Hartman made but two speeches during the session; one against the Walker-Otis Anti-Gambling bill, one against the Islais Creek Harbor bill, the passage of which meant so much for San Francisco, the city, by the way, responsible for Hartman's presence at Sacramento.

On the sixteen roll calls under consideration, Hartman voted sixteen times for machine policies. As a vote, Hartman is a valuable machine asset; otherwise a nonentity.

Those who have read the previous chapters have already formed their opinion of the advisability of returning to the Senate, Kennedy, the hero of the passage of the Change of Venue bill; McCartney, the author of the famous amendment to the Direct Primary bill; Weed, who introduced the resolution to drag Senator Black from his sick bed at Palo Alto; Reily, who with Senator Hartman, alone of all the Senate stood out against the passage of the Islais Creek Harbor bills; Willis, who as Chairman of the Judiciary Committee, backed such measures as the Change of Venue bill, and opposed such measures as the Commonwealth Club bills; Savage, who in committee and out of it, opposed the State-wide vote plan for nominating United States Senators, and Senator Price.

Price did not distinguish himself particularly. On the sixteen roll calls included in Table A, his vote was recorded against the machine as many as four times. But there were ten Senators who did even worse. However, a story of the closing days of the session is quite characteristic of Senator Price.

An important roll call was on - if the writer remembers correctly, it was on Burnett's motion to continue the investigation into the causes of the increase of freight and express rates. Price was present, but did not answer to the call of his name. The advocates of the resolution insisted that all vote, and demanded a call of the Senate. The doors were ordered closed, at which order Price made a run for the door. Caminetti saw the move, understood it and started to intercept the fleeing Senator. But if Caminetti were quick, Price was quicker. Caminetti missed his grab at Price, and so chased that gentleman to the door of the Senate chamber. The assistant Sergeant-at-Arms at the door was just swinging it closed as Price shot through. The determined Caminetti made a last grab at Price's coattails, but too late. The massive doors banged closed, with Price, coattails and all, on the outside, and the balked Caminetti on the inside. Price didn't vote on that roll call.

The failure to return Leavitt to the Senate will be a decided loss for the machine, one hard to offset. Next to Wolfe, Leavitt was by far the ablest floor leader in the Senate. The brute force of the man, his grossness, his indifference to public opinion, made him an ideal machine leader. Leavitt's return from Alameda seems extremely doubtful. His district takes in the notorious gambling community, Emeryville, which will be purged of the thug element that has dominated it, by the enforcement of the Walker-Otis law. With the loss of this portion of his constituency, Senator Leavitt's chance of re-election from Emeryville appears slim indeed.

But, according to rather persistent rumor, Senator Leavitt may be returned to the Senate, not from Alameda, but from the Siskiyou-Shasta District, the district represented by Weed. Leavitt has property up there, and the story runs that he will be a candidate from that part of the State. The voters of Shasta and Siskiyou, however, may conclude that they have something to say about it.

Senator Wright, the last of the Senators whose terms will have expired before the next session of the Legislature convenes, is being mentioned as a "reform candidate" for Governor. The idea seems to be that he will run on his record made at the session of 1909. If this be true, he may not be a candidate for re-election to the Senate. Senator Wright's record as a State Senator has already been treated at length.

[103a] Senator Boynton was a consistent supporter of the Local Option bill from the beginning to the end of the session. He held, however, that the bill as originally drawn was not in proper form, and explained that he voted to have the bill returned to the committee that amendments, which he deemed necessary, could be made.

[104] Since the Legislature adjourned Senator Bates has been given a lucrative position in the United States Mint.

CHAPTER XXVIII.

Conclusion.

Events of the Session of 1909 Show That Before Any Effective Reform Can
Be Brought About in California, Good Government Republicans and Democrats Must Unite to Organize Senate and Assembly - Appointment of Senate Committees May Be Taken Out of the Hands of the Lieutenant-Governor.

In the opening chapter it was stated that the machine element in the Legislature of 1909, although in the minority, defeated the purposes of the reform majority, because of three principal reasons:

(1) The reform element was without organization.

(2) The reform members had, except in the anti-racetrack gambling fight, no definite plan of action.

(3) The reform members of both Houses permitted the machine to name presiding officers and appoint committees.

This third reason must appeal to those who have read the foregoing pages as the most important of all. The story of every machine success, in face of opposition, is that of advantage gained through the moral support given by the presiding officers[105], or of co-operation of committees, or of both. But, unfortunately, a stupid partisanship - a partisanship which the machine finds far more potent than bribe money - makes this cause of machine success more difficult to overcome than either of the others. Already a movement is on foot, the details of which the writer is not at liberty to make public, that will unite the reform element of the next Legislature into a working body, from the day nominations are made. Steps to this end were taken before the last Legislature adjourned. In the same way, the work of bringing reform issues before the public - reform of the ballot laws, amendment of the Direct Primary law, the simplification of the mode of criminal procedure - is being taken up in the same effective, commonsense way as was the Anti-Racetrack Gambling bill. But here the progress of the commonsense element of machine opposition seems to halt. In spite of their experience of the last session, Democrats and Republicans who stand for good government hesitate at the suggestion of non-partisan organization of Senate and Assembly. The writer has shown in the foregoing chapters that the machine Republicans and the machine Democrats were for practical purposes a unit in the organization of the

Legislature of 1909. Why, then, should not the anti-machine Republicans and the anti-machine Democrats unite for purposes of organization, just as they united, at the session of 1909, to oppose vicious measures and to work for the passage of good bills? That is a question which has never been satisfactorily answered. It leads us, however, to the question of the real line of division in Senate and Assembly, and, for that matter, in State politics[106].

That the real division is no longer between political parties, or even between party factions, is apparent to the observer who has given the question any attention at all.

Not once, for example, did the California Legislature of 1909 divide on a party question; nor did it have to deal with any problem that had not at one time or another been endorsed by both parties. Both Democrats and Republicans in either State or county platforms had declared for the passage of an Anti-Racetrack Gambling law, for an effective Direct Primary law, for an effective Railroad Regulation law, for the submission to the people of a Constitutional Amendment granting the people the privilege of initiating laws. In the same way, county conventions of both parties - and county conventions are the closest to the people and most representative of them - had declared for local option, for the election of United States Senators by direct vote of the people, for amendments to the codes that should simplify proceedings in criminal cases, for effective railroad regulation. Estimating the purposes of the two parties by their county and State platforms, none of these reforms can be regarded as any more Democratic than Republican, and these were the issues with which the Legislature of 1909 was called upon to deal.

A glance at the tables of votes in the appendix will show that the Assemblymen and the Senators who voted against the Anti-Racetrack Gambling bill, generally speaking, voted against the effective Stetson Railroad Regulation bill and for the ineffective Wright bill, opposed the provision in the Direct Primary bill giving the people an effective part in the selection of United States Senators, supported the passage of the Change of Venue bill, opposed the passage of the Local Option bill, opposed the submission of the Initiative amendment to the electors of the State. This negative element, opposed to policies which the normal citizen regards as making for the State's best interests, has in these pages been called the machine[107].

As has been shown in these pages, the interests of the several beneficiaries of the system are in effect pooled; one element helps the other. The managers of the several elements, the political agents, if you like, of the tenderloin, Southern Pacific, racetrack, and public-service monopolies generally; in a word, all who seek to evade the law or to secure undue special privileges or to continue secure in the possession of such privileges already secured, recognize that they must hang together or submit to a reckoning with the public, which must necessarily result in the breaking of the particular monopoly which each enjoys, be it in transportation, nickel-in-the-slot graft, or traffic in the bodies of young women. Should the political bureau of the Southern Pacific Railroad Company, for example, lose the support of the tenderloin, or of the racetrack gamblers, or of any other powerful group of its political associates, the corporation could no longer continue its strangle-hold upon the State. But none of its associates would dare thus offend. Such is the machine, which, in the name of a protective tariff, "sound money," Abraham Lincoln, or Theodore Roosevelt, has organized the Legislature of California for sixteen years. Previous to 1895, there were California Legislatures organized in the name of Thomas Jefferson. But the machine has not taken the name of Thomas Jefferson in vain in California for many years[108].

Nevertheless, although acting under the name Republican, the machine is quite as dependent upon "Democrats" as upon "Republicans," and as dependent upon either as upon the tenderloin, the brewery trust or the racetrack gambling element. It monopolizes neither party, but it divides both parties. Or it may be described as a canker that has eaten into both, diseased both, rendered both unwholesome, until a condition exists in the dominating parties that requires that the uncorrupted element of both unite to cut the diseased portion away[109].

As the machine divides the parties, so did it divide the Republican and Democratic delegations in the Senate and the Assembly of the California Legislature of 1909. Hare and Kennedy, for example, Democratic Senators, voted constantly with Wolfe and Leavitt, Republican Senators, for machine policies. Nor was the opposition restricted to party lines. Black and Boynton and Cutten, Republican Senators, were found voting constantly with Campbell and Holohan, Democratic Senators, against the machine. Between Black and Wolfe, Republicans, there was nothing in common during the entire session; nor was there anything in common between Campbell and Kennedy, Democrats. On practically every important issue, however, Kennedy, Democrat, and Wolfe, Republican, made common cause, while Black, Republican, and Campbell, Democrat, opposed them.

The same comparisons could be made in the Assembly, where such Democrats as Wheelan and Baxter were found with Mott and Coghlan, Republicans, supporting machine policies, while opposed to them were anti-machine Republicans of the character of Bohnett and Callan, and anti-machine Democrats like Polsley and Mendenhall.

Thus, for practical purposes, the Legislature can not be divided on party lines. The only practical line of division is between the machine element, and the anti-machine element. Such, at the session of 1909, was the division on every important issue; such will it be at the legislative session of 1911. Why should not the same division govern the organization of Senate and Assembly?

As a matter of fact, the machine disregards party lines even in organizing. In making up its committees it considers fealty to machine interests above party name. For example, Hare and Kennedy were the Democratic Senators who this year affiliated with the machine. Kennedy was appointed to practically every important committee, at least to those before which important fights were to be made. Thus we find him on the Committee on Commerce and Navigation, Contingent Expenses, Elections and Election Laws, Prisons and Reformatories, and Public Morals, Hare was appointed to the Committee on Commerce and Navigation, Elections and Election Laws, Labor, Capital and Immigration, Municipal Corporations, Printing, and Public Buildings and Grounds. In committees, as well as on the floor of the Senate, Hare and Kennedy were found as a general thing casting their influence and their votes on the side of machine policies.

Had the anti-machine Democrats and the anti-machine Republicans in Senate and Assembly, who worked together for the same ends and voted together on practically every important issue, taken the same course, and united for the organization of the two Houses, reform measures which were defeated by narrow margins would have been made laws, and machine measures which became laws defeated.

Such being the case, is it not the duty of the anti-machine Republicans and the anti-machine Democrats who may sit in the Legislature of 1911, to organize both Senate and Assembly to resist machine purposes and policies?

This can be done comparatively easily in the Assembly, where a movement to elect the Speaker such as was started by Drew of Fresno this year, if carried out, would take the Assembly out of machine hands. Although the organization of the Senate looks more difficult, because the Senate has no voice in the selection of its presiding officer, nevertheless, even though a Warren Porter occupy the post of Lieutenant-Governor, at the session of 1911 the reform element can elect its President pro tem., and appoint the Senate committees. In other words, a majority of the Senate, may if it see fit, take the appointing of the committees out of the hands of the Lieutenant-Governor.

There are two important precedents for this course, one established by a Democratic Senate; the other by a Republican Senate.

The Democratic precedent was established in 1887. In that year Robert W. Waterman, a Republican, was Lieutenant-Governor and presiding officer of the Senate. The Senate was made up of twenty-six Democrats and fourteen Republicans. The Democratic majority organized the Senate under the following rule, which will be found in the Senate journal of that session:

"All Committees of the Senate, special and standing, and all joint Committees on the part thereof, shall be elected by the Senate unless otherwise ordered."

The Republican precedent was made in 1897. In that year, William T. Jeter, a Democrat, was Lieutenant-Governor, while a majority of the Senators were Republicans. Instead of leaving the appointing of the committees to the Democratic Lieutenant-Governor, the Republican Senators adopted a rule that "all standing committees of the Senate shall be named by the Senate, unless otherwise ordered, and the first named shall be chairman thereof. All other committees shall be appointed in such manner as the Senate shall determine."

In other words, the Republican majority of the Senate named the Senate committees of the session of 1897, taking their appointment out of the hands of the Lieutenant-Governor as the Democrats had done ten years before. There is no good reason why the members of the anti-machine majority in the Senate should not have taken the same course in 1909, and named the committees. Had they done so, and named the President pro tem., they would have organized the Senate in the interest of those policies in advancing which they were soon in open revolt against Lieutenant-Governor Porter, the machine Senators and the machine lobby. Failing to do so, they placed themselves under a handicap which they were unable to overcome.

The reform element of the Legislature of 1911 will have in the experience of the reform element of the session of 1909, an important lesson. And The People of California, who will elect that Legislature, have a lesson as important. The successes of the machine at the session of 1909, where a clear majority of both Houses opposed machine policies, demonstrated that the well-being of the State requires that the opponents of the machine in Senate and Assembly, regardless of party label, organize the Legislature. But back of this is the even more important requirement that there be elected to the Legislature American citizens, with the responsibility of their citizenship upon them, rather than partisans, burdened until their good purposes are made negative, by the responsibility of their partisanship.

[105] See, for example, Speaker Stanton's ruling on the Direct Primary bill when the Assembly was considering the question of receding from its amendments.

[106] The machine recognizes the real division, if the reform element does not. The machine, for example, calls itself Republican, and as such controls the patronage of the San Francisco water front. The appointments to water front jobs are, of course, partisan, but the writer is reliably informed that as many "Democrats" as "Republicans" are employed there. Senators Hare and Kennedy, we have seen, although Democrats, got appointments to holdover committees. The machine recognizes but one line in politics, that which divides those who support machine policies from those who stand for good government and the square deal. When those who stand for good government and the square deal become as clear sighted, the fight against the machine will not be quite so unequal.

[107] The term "machine" is, as a general thing, rather lightly used. It is made to stand for everything, from what might be and should be perfectly legitimate party organization, to the Southern Pacific political bureau. The Southern Pacific political bureau is, as a matter of fact, the dominating factor in machine affairs, which gives some reason for dubbing the machine Southern Pacific. But it is nor more the Southern Pacific machine than it is the Tenderloin machine or the Racetrack gamblers' machine, or the United Railroads machine, or the Electric Power Trust machine.

[108] Bryce in his American Commonwealth, more than a quarter of a century ago, showed the hollowness of the contention of the machine element for arty consideration. "The interest of a Boss in political questions," said Bryce in one of his admirable chapters on this subject, "is usually quite secondary. Here and there one may be found and who is a politician in the European sense, who, whether sincerely or not, purports and professes to be interested in some principle or measure affecting the welfare of the country. But the attachment of the ringster is usually given wholly to the concrete party, that is, to the men who compose it, regarded as office-holders or office-seekers; and there is often not even a profession of zeal for any party doctrine. As a noted politician happily observed to a friend of mine: 'You know, Mr. R., there are no politics in politics.' "

[109] One has a wider view of this condition if he look out beyond the Sacramento Capitol, into the Senate Hall at Washington. The following is from an editorial article which appeared in the Saturday Evening Post, of June 12 last:

"The Iron trade is still in a depressed state. Output is much below the capacity of the mills, and prices have not recovered from the demoralization of early spring. Yet the other day the common stock of the Steel Trust sold higher than ever before. When issued, this common stock was rather thinner than water, and it represented mostly a capitalization of the Trust's tariff graft. At the new high price the market valuation of the graft, therefore, is some three hundred million dollars. A few days before this new high price was made, eighteen Democratic Senators voted with the Aldrich Republicans to take iron ore from the free list - where the House bill had put it - and protect it by a substantial duty. This action was generally regarded as insuring a continuation of the Trust's tariff graft. Hence a record price for the common stock was logical enough, although the iron trade was not exactly flourishing at the moment.

"Similar acts by Democratic Senators were denounced by President Cleveland as party perfidy and dishonor; but the regrettable fact is there is only one party in the United States Senate - just one party, with some scattering Republicans and Democratic Insurgents. For the purpose of getting elected and making stump speeches, different labels and catchwords are employed; but when it comes down to real business in the matter of taxing eighty-odd million users of iron and steel products for the benefit of an opulent trust, we find forty-three Republican Senators and eighteen Democratic Senators staunchly voting aye, against fourteen Republicans and ten Democrats who vote nay.

"With over half of the Democratic members of the Upper House fondly recording themselves as Little Brothers to Protection, there is slight danger that the tariff will be revised otherwise than by its friends."

Appendix

Tables of Votes.

The test votes given in the several tables record in every instance the result of a contest between the machine and the anti-machine forces in Senate or Assembly. It is quite evident that a unanimous vote cannot be counted a test vote. Thus the unanimous vote by which the Reciprocal Demurrage bill passed the Senate cannot be regarded as a test, although the machine fought the demurrage principle viciously in 1907.

Nor can a vote on a measure be taken as a test vote, where the vote was taken without the members fully realizing what was before them. Thus the votes on the Wheelan bills do not appear in either Senate or Assembly tables. These measures were slipped through Senate and Assembly without the members of either House fully realizing what the bills were, their purpose, or far-reaching effects. To be sure, a member of the Legislature should know what he is voting on, but when one considers the incidents of the whirl-wind close of the session of 1909, the injustice of holding a member accountable for inadvertently voting for a measure which he had intended to oppose, becomes apparent.

Following this rule, a vote on a given measure may be a test vote in one House and not in the other. The Change of Venue bill is an example in point. The Change of Venue bill was slipped through the Assembly, without the members fully realizing its import, and hence without opposition. But in the Senate the issue was fought out. The Senate vote on the Change of Venue bill, then, is taken as a test vote, while the Assembly vote on the same measure is not so regarded. In the same way, the vote on the substitution of the Wright bill for the Stetson Railroad Regulation bill was a test vote in the Senate. But in the Assembly there was no test vote taken on the railroad regulation measures, for the Wright bill was put through practically without opposition. The test railroad vote in the Assembly came on the Sanford resolution providing for government steamships on the Pacific. There was no test vote on this in the Senate, for in the Senate it was adopted practically without opposition.

Table A - Records of Senators.

The records of the members of the Senate on sixteen test votes are shown in Table A. The names of the Senators are arranged in the order of the number of times their votes were recorded on the side of progress and reform, the name of the Senator with the most positive votes to his credit appearing at the top of the list, and the Senator with the least number at the bottom.

While few will quarrel with the fact that Senator Bell's name leads the list, while Senators Finn and Hartman divide negative honors at the bottom, nevertheless the arrangement is not, strictly speaking, fair, although it is probably as fair as it could be made.

Senator Walker, for example, has only one anti-reform vote registered against him, but it was, perhaps, the most important test vote of the session, that on the Railroad Regulation measures. Senator Cutten, on the other hand, voted on the reform side of every question with the exception of the measure intended to work political reform by removing the party circle from the election ballot. Senator Cutten is recorded twice against this bill, it being necessary, in justice to all the Senators, to give both the votes taken on this measure. But considering the relative importance of the Railroad Regulation bills and the Party Circle bill, all must admit that Senator Cutten made a better record than Senator Walker, although Cutten's name appears below that of Walker.

Unavoidable absence from the Senate Chamber cut down the records of several of the Senators. Black and Stetson, whose severe illness kept them from Sacramento toward the end of the session, furnish examples of this.

Then again, the Party Circle bill and the Local Option bill were measures on which several of the strongest of the opponents of the machine differed with the majority of their anti-machine associates. With the four votes taken on these two issues out of the reckoning, Bell, Thompson, Roseberry, Cutten, Campbell, Boynton, Sanford, Cartwright, Black, Holohan, Birdsall, Stetson, Rush and Strobridge, have not one vote for a machine-backed policy against them. Caminetti's vote to amend the Stanford bill excludes him from the list, but as this measure was of the same character and policy as the Local Option bill, Caminetti's name should in justice be included among those of the Senators who made practically clear records. Looking at the table in a broad way, the first nineteen Senators of the list made anti-machine records. Of the eleven caucus Republicans among them, only one voted against admitting Bell to the Republican caucus.

The nineteen voted for the Anti-Racetrack Gambling bill, they voted every time against the machine on the Direct Primary issue, only two of them voted for the Change of Venue bill, only two of them voted against the Railroad Regulation bill. These comparisons can be carried out indefinitely, and always to the advantage of the nineteen.

Senator Wright is twentieth on the list; Senator Anthony is twenty-first. Those who followed these two Senators through the Direct Primary bill fight will see immediately that Wright has crowded into undeserved standing. There is a very good reason for this. In the Senate, the roll of Senators is called alphabetically, and Senator Wright's name is the last on the list. A glance at the table will show that Senator Wright did not vote once against the machine when his vote would have decided the issue. He voted for the Anti-Racetrack Gambling bill, but before him thirty-two Senators had voted for the bill, and only seven against it. Wright's thirty-third affirmative vote counted for nothing. On the other hand, when Wright's name was reached on roll call on the Change of Venue bill, with the vote standing nineteen for the bill and sixteen against, and twenty-one votes necessary for its passage, Senator Wright cast the twentieth affirmative vote, thus ensuring the measure's passage. In the same way, Senator Wright's vote the following day, tied the score on the motion for a call of the Senate, thus defeating the motion, and preventing reconsideration of the Change of Venue bill which would have meant its defeat.

The query is: Had the vote on the Anti-Racetrack Gambling bill stood nineteen against the bill, and twenty for, when Wright's name was reached, with twenty-one votes necessary for its passage, would Wright's vote have been cast for or against it? Any person who has any doubt on the question, is referred to Senator Wright's part in the passage of the amended Direct Primary bill, and in the defeat of the Stetson bill.

It is most advantageous to have one's name at the bottom of a roll call. Senator Wright's position above that of Senators Anthony and Burnett, emphasizes the necessity of considering these tables in connection with the chapters dealing with the several issues involved. From the first days of the session Senators Anthony and Burnett gave indications that had the anti-machine forces been organized, they would have been found consistently against the machine. At any rate, their records are admittedly more creditable than that made by Senator Wright.

The Sixteen Test Votes.

Senator Bell did not vote in the Senate Republican caucus, nor did the nine Democratic Senators. Thus in the sixteen votes recorded, Bell and the Democratic members voted only fifteen times. An outline of each of the several issues involved follows:

Senate A - The first test vote of the Republican majority which came in the Republican caucus described in Chapter II, on motion to admit Senator Bell to caucus privileges. Lost by a vote of 16 to 14.

Senate B - Vote on proposed McCartney Amendments to Direct Primary bill.
Amendments defeated by vote of 27 to 13. See Chapter IX.

Senate C - Senate vote on Anti-Racetrack Gambling bill. See Chapter VII.

Senate D - Vote on Wolfe's motion to send the Local Option bill back to the Judiciary Committee. See Chapter XVIII.

Senate E - First vote on Senate Bill 220, abolishing the party circle on the election ballot. Measure was defeated by vote of 15 to 23.

Senate F - Vote by which the above Senate Bill 220 was passed on reconsideration. Note the Senators who changed to the side favoring the measure.

Senate G - Test vote on Senate Bill 1144, known as the "Stanford Bill," which prohibited the sale of intoxicants within a mile and a half of a University. The measure was aimed at the low groggeries maintained in the vicinity of the campus at Stanford. It was fought by the same tenderloin element that had opposed the Anti-Racetrack Gambling bill. Senator Wolfe moved to amend the measure to exclude fraternal club houses and hotels of fifty bed-rooms or more, from its provisions. The amendment would have delayed and perhaps defeated the bill. Wolfe's motion was defeated.

Senate H - Vote by which the above Senate Bill 1144 was finally passed.

Senate I - First test railroad vote in the Senate - Senator Stetson moved that Stetson bill be substituted for the Wright bill. The motion was defeated by a vote of 16 to 22. Had Rush and Roseberry been present they would have voted on the side of the Stetson measure. This would have made the vote twenty-two for the Wright bill, and eighteen for the Stetson bill. See Chapter XIII.

Senate J - Vote on the Initiative Amendment. See Chapter XIX.

Senate K - Vote on the Local Option bill. See Chapter XVIII.

Senate L - Vote on Senate Constitutional Amendment No. 4, to eliminate ambiguities from those sections of the State Constitution which prescribe the powers and duties of the Railroad Commission. See Chapter XIV.

Senate M - Vote on Assembly amendments to the Direct Primary bill. Wright moved that the Senate concur in the amendments. The motion was lost, but on Wolfe's motion to reconsider the vote, the Senate was held in deadlock for more than a week. See Chapters X and XI.

Senate N - Vote on Change of Venue bill. See Chapter XVI.

Senate O - Vote on motion to reconsider vote by which Change of Venue bill was passed. See Chapter XVI.

Senate P - Vote on Burnett's motion that the investigation into the causes for the increase of freight and express rates be continued after the Legislature adjourned. See Chapter XIV.

Tables B and C - Record of Assemblymen.

The two tables showing the votes of the members of the Assembly include eleven test votes. The names of the Assemblymen are arranged as in the case of the Senators with the names of those who made the best records at the top.

It will be seen that fourteen Assemblymen voted against the machine on every roll call, eight were absent on one roll call each, but voted the ten times they were present against the machine, while three members voted 'once each with the machine, and ten times against it. These twenty-five members, voting 267 times, cast 264 votes on the side of progress and reform, and three votes for machine policies. The record indicates what might have been done in the Assembly had the reform forces been organized. Indeed, the forty leading Assemblymen, casting 421 votes, cast only 48 votes for machine policies and 373 against.

The same considerations governed the selection of test votes in the Assembly as in the Senate. The votes are as follows:

Assembly A - The first test vote in the Assembly was on Drew's resolution to reject the report of the Committee on Rules. The resolution was adopted, and the machine's plan to force "gag rules" on the Assembly failed. See Chapter III Organization of the Assembly.

Assembly B - The test vote on the Anti-Racetrack Gambling bill. The Committee on Public Morals had recommended that the bill "do pass." Mott moved that the bill be re-referred to the committee. Motion lost by a vote of 53 to 23. See Chapter VII.

Assembly C - Vote on the Anti-Racetrack Gambling bill. See Chapter VII.

Assembly D - Vote on motion to reconsider the vote by which the Anti-Racetrack Gambling bill was passed. See Chapter VII.

Assembly E - The test railroad vote in the Assembly came on Drew's motion to recall Senate Joint Resolution No. 3 from committee. The resolution called for a line of government-owned steamships on the Pacific from San Francisco to Panama. The resolution, having been adopted by the Senate, went to the Assembly and was referred to the Committee on Federal Relations. To hasten action on the resolution, Drew moved that it be recalled from the committee. A two-thirds vote was necessary for Drew's motion to prevail. The motion failed to carry by a vote of 36 for to 29 against.

Assembly F - Vote on motion to strike out of Senate joint Resolution No. 3-considered under E - those sections which referred to Commissioner Bristow's report recommending that the Government steamship line be established, and criticizing the combinations made between the several transportation companies. The motion prevailed by a vote of 43 to 30.

Assembly G - Assembly test vote on the Direct Primary bill. Vote taken on Leed's motion that vote on United States Senators be advisory and by districts. The motion prevailed by a vote of 38 to 36. See Chapter X.

Assembly H - Vote on proposed amendments to the Islais Creek Harbor bill. Motion was made to amend by substituting 44 blocks for the 63 necessary for the improvement. Had this been done, the work would have been made impracticable. Motion lost by a vote of 30 to 45. See Chapter XXIII, "Influence of the San Francisco Delegation."

Assembly I - Leeds moved that Senate Bill 220 removing the party circle from the election ballot be denied second reading. The motion prevailed by a vote of thirty-six for, to thirty-five against.

Assembly J - Vote on Senate Bill 1144 (the Stanford bill), to prohibit the sale of intoxicants within a mile and a half of Stanford University.

Assembly K - Vote on the Judicial Column bill. This measure provided that the names of candidates for the Judiciary be placed in a separate non-partisan column on the election ballot. The bill passed the Senate, but was defeated in the Assembly.

The Other Tables.

Table D shows the six votes on the Anti-Racetrack Gambling bill. See Chapter VII.

Tables E and F - Show the records of the San Francisco delegation in the Senate and Assembly. See Chapter XXIII.

Table G - Shows the records on sixteen test votes of the twenty Senators whose terms of office will have expired before the next session convenes. See Chapter XXVII.

Table H - Shows the records on sixteen test votes of the twenty Senators who were elected in 1908, and who hold over to serve in the session of 1911. See Chapter XXVI.

Table I - Shows records of the members of the Assembly on the four principal votes arising out of the fight for the passage of the so-called Anti-Japanese bills. See Chapter XX.

Table A-Records of Senators on Sixteen Test Votes

* indicates vote on side of Progress and Reform

0 indicates vote against Progress and Reform

A B C D E F G

_____ To Test To refer To do Second admit vote Walker-Local away Vote First Bell on Otis Option Bill with party Vote to Direct Bill. to Party Circle Stanford Caucus. Primary Committee. Circle. Bill. Bill.

_____ Senator Aye No Aye No Aye No Aye No Aye No Aye No Aye No

_____ 1 Bell * * * * * * 2 Thompson * * * * 0 * * 3 Roseberry * * * * 0 * * 4 Walker * * * * * * * 5 Cutten * * * * 0 0 * 6 Campbell * * * * * 7 Boynton * * * 0 * * 8 Sanford * * 0 * * * * 9 Cartwright * * * * * 10 Caminetti * * 0 * * 0 11 Estudillo 0 * * * * * * 12 Black * * * * 0 * * 13 Holohan * * 0 * * 14 Miller * * * * * 15 Birdsall * * * 0 0 * 16 Stetson * * * * * 17 Rush * * * 0 * * 18 Curtin * * * 0 * 19 Strobridge * * * 0 0 0 * 20 Wright 0 * * * * * * 21 Anthony * * * 0 0 * 22 Burnett 0 * * 0 0 0 23 McCartney 0 0 * 0 * 24 Kennedy 0 * 0 * * 0 25 Lewis 0 * * 0 0 0 26 Willis 0 0 * * * * 0 27 Welch * * * 0 0 0 28 Bates 0 0 * * 0 0 * 29 Price 0 * * 0 0 0 * 30 Savage * 0 * 0 0 0 31 Bills 0 0 * * 0 0 * 32 Leavitt 0 0 0 * * * * 33 Hare 0 0 0 * * 0 34 Hurd 0 * * 0 0 * 35 Martinelli 0 * * 0 0 0 0 36 Wolfe 0 0 0 0 * * 0 37 Reily * 0 0 0 0 0 38 Weed 0 0 0 * 0 0 39 Finn 0 0 0 0 0 0 0 40 Hartman 0 0 0 0 0 0

Totals 14 16 13 27 33 7 20 15 16 22 23 15 8 22

H I J K L M

Second Test Vote Local Assembly Vote Railroad Initiative Option Railroad Amendment Stanford Regulation. Amendment. Bill. Amendment. to Direct Bill. Primary.

Senator Aye No Aye No Aye No Aye No Aye No Aye No

1 Bell * * * * * * 2 Thompson * * * * * * 3 Roseberry * * * * * 4 Walker * 0 * * * * 5 Cutten * * * * * * 6 Campbell * * * * * * 7 Boynton * * * * * 8 Sanford * * * 0 * * 9 Cartwright * * * * * 10 Caminetti * * * 0 * * 11 Estudillo * 0 * * 0 * 12 Black * * * * * 13 Holohan * * 0 * * 14 Miller * * 0 * * * 15 Birdsall * * 0 * * 16 Stetson * * * 17 Rush * * 0 * * 18 Curtin * * 0 0 * * 19 Strobridge * * 0 * * 20 Wright * 0 0 * * 0 21 Anthony * 0 * 0 0 * 22 Burnett * 0 0 * 0 23 McCartney * 0 * 0 * 0 24 Kennedy 0 0 * 0 0 0 25 Lewis * * 0 0 0 0 26 Willis * 0 0 0 0 27 Welch 0 * 0 0 0 28 Bates * 0 0 0 29 Price * 0 0 0 0 0 30 Savage * 0 0 0 0 31 Bills * 0 0 0 0 0 32 Leavitt 0 0 0 0 0 0 33 Hare 0 0 * 0 0 34 Hurd 0 0 0 0 0 35 Martinelli * 0 0 0 0 36 Wolfe * 0 0 0 0 0 37 Reily 0 * 0 0 0 38 Weed 0 0 0 0 0 39 Finn 0 0 0 0 0 40 Hartman 0 0 0 0 0 0

Totals 29 5 16 22 20 15 12 25 19 16 20 19

N O P

To Test Totals Change To To of reconsider investigate For Against Absent Venue Change of Freight Reform Reform Bill. Venue Bill. Rates.

Senator Aye No Aye No Aye No

1 Bell * * * 15 0 0 2 Thompson * * * 15 1 0 3 Roseberry * * * 14 1 1 4 Walker * * 14 1 1 5 Cutten * * * 14 2 0 6 Campbell * * 13 0 2 7 Boynton * * * 13 1 2 8 Sanford * * * 13 2 0 9 Cartwright * * 12 0 3 10 Caminetti * * * 12 3 0 11 Estudillo 0 * * 12 4 0 12 Black * * * 11 1 4 14 Miller 0 * 11 2 2 15 Birdsall * * * 11 3 2 16 Stetson * * 10 0 6 17 Rush * 10 2 4 18 Curtin * * 10 3 2 19 Strobridge * * 10 4 2 20 Wright 0 0 0 9 7 0 21 Anthony 0 0 7 8 1 22 Burnett * 5 7 4 23 McCartney 0 0 5 8 3 24 Kennedy * 0 5 9 1 25 Lewis 0 * 0 5 10 1 26 Willis 0 0 0 5 11 0 27 Welch 0 0 4 9 3 28 Bates 0 0 0 4 10 2 29 Price 0 0 4 11 1 30 Savage 0 0 0 4 11 1 31 Bills 0 0 0 4

12 0 32 Leavitt 0 0 0 4 12 0 33 Hare 0 0 3 10 2 34 Hurd 0 0 0 3 11 2 35 Martinelli 0 0 0 3 12 1 36 Wolfe 0 0 0 3 13 0 37 Reily 0 0 0 2 12 2 38 Weed 0 0 0 1 13 2 39 Finn 0 0 0 0 15 1 40 Hartman 0 0 0 0 16 0

_____ Totals 21 16 18 18 12 16 311 259 60

Table B-Records of Assemblymen on Eleven Test Votes

Forty Members Making Best Records

* indicates vote on side of Progress and Reform

0 indicates vote against Progress and Reform

A B C D E F

_____ Drew's To Motion to To Return Vote on To To recall amend Reject Walker-Otis Walker- reconsider S. J. R. S. J. Committee's Bill to Otis Walker-Otis No. 3 from R. No. Rules. Committee Bill. Bill. Committee. 3.

_____ Assemblymen Aye No Aye No Aye No Aye No Aye No Aye No

_____ 1 Bohnett * * * * * * 2 Callan * * * * * * 3 Cattell * * * * * * 4 Costar * * * * * * 5 Gibbons * * * * * * 6 Hewitt * * * * * * 7 Johnson, P. H. * * * * * * 8 Mendenhall * * * * * * 9 Polsley * * * * * * 10 Preston * * * * * * 11 Telfer * * * * * * 12 Whitney * * * * * * 13 Wilson * * * * * * 14 Young * * * * * * 15 Cogswell * * * * * 16 Drew * * * * * * 17 Gillis * * * * * 18 Juilliard * * * * * 19 Kehoe * * * * * 20 Maher * * * * * 21 Sackett * * * * * * 22 Wyllie * * * * * 23 Flint * * * * * * 24 Hinkle * * * * * 25 Stuckenbruck * * * * * * 26 Gerdes 0 * * * * 27 Holmquist 0 * * * * * 28 Otis * * * * * 0 29 Irwin * * * * * 30 Rutherford * * * * * 0 31 Griffiths 0 * * * * 32 Odom * 0 * * * 33 Hayes * * * * 0 * 34 Lightner * * * * 0 35 Melrose * * * * * 0 36 Silver * * * * * 0 37 Beatty * * * 0 38 Cronin * * * * 0 39 Barndollar 0 * * * * 0 40 Rech * * * * 0 0

_____ Totals 32 4 1 38 40 0 0 40 33 2 9 28

G H I J K Totals

_____

To To deny
Test Vote amend Party Vote on Vote on
on Direct Islais Circle Stanford Judicial For
Against Absent

- 205 -

Primary. Creek Bill Bill. Column Reform Reform
Harbor Second Bill.
Bill. Reading.

Assemblymen Aye No Aye No Aye No Aye No Aye No

1 Bohnett * * * * * 11 0 0
2 Callan * * * * * 11 0 0
3 Cattell * * * * * 11 0 0
4 Costar * * * * * 11 0 0
5 Gibbons * * * * * 11 0 0
6 Hewitt * * * * * 11 0 0
7 Johnson, P. H. * * * * * 11 0 0
8 Mendenhall * * * * * 11 0 0
9 Polsley * * * * * 11 0 0
10 Preston * * * * * 11 0 0
11 Telfer * * * * * 11 0 0
12 Whitney * * * * * 11 0 0
13 Wilson * * * * * 11 0 0
14 Young * * * * * 11 0 0
15 Cogswell * * * * * 10 0 1
16 Drew * * * * 10 0 1
17 Gillis * * * * * 10 0 1
18 Juilliard * * * * * 10 0 1
19 Kehoe * * * * * 10 0 1
20 Maher * * * * * 10 0 1
21 Sackett * * * * 10 0 1
22 Wyllie * * * * * 10 0 1
23 Flint * * 0 * * 10 1 0
24 Hinkle * * 0 * * 10 1 0
25 Stuckenbruck * 0 * * * 10 1 0
26 Gerdes * * * * * 9 1 1
27 Holmquist * * * * 0 9 2 0
28 Otis * * 0 * * 9 2 0
29 Irwin * 0 * 0 * 8 2 1
30 Rutherford 0 * * * 0 8 3 0
31 Griffiths * * 0 * 7 2 2
32 Odom * 0 * * 7 2 2
33 Hayes * 0 0 * 7 3 1
34 Lightner 0 0 * * * 7 3 1
35 Melrose 0 * 0 * 0 7 4 0

36 Silver * 0 0 * 0 7 4 0
37 Beatty 0 * * 0 * 6 3 2
38 Cronin 0 * 0 0 6 4 1
39 Barndollar 0 * 0 * 0 6 5 0
40 Rech 0 * 0 * 0 6 5 0

Totals 7 33 6 34 10 28 36 2 31 7 373 48 19

Table C-Records of Assemblymen on Eleven Test Votes

Forty Members Making Poorest Records

* indicates vote on side of Progress and Reform

0 indicates vote against Progress and Reform

(a) - Changed Vote from no to aye to give notice to reconsider. Was against the bill.

A B C D E

	Drew's Motion to Reject Committee's Bill to Rules.	To Return Walker-Otis Bill to Committee.	Vote on Walker- Otis Bill.	To recall S. J. R. No. 3 from Committee.
Assemblymen	Aye No	Aye No	Aye No	Aye No	Aye No
41 Hammon	* * * *
42 Hawk	0 * * * *
43 Stanton	0 * * * *
44 Transue	0 * * *
45 Hanlon	* * * * 0
46 Wagner	* 0 * 0 *
47 Webber	* 0 * * 0
48 Butler	* * * 0
49 Collum	* 0 0
50 Dean	0 * * * 0
51 Perine	0 * * *
52 Pulcifer	0 * * * 0
53 Collier	0 * * * 0

54 Moore 0 0 * 0
55 Leeds 0 * * * 0
56 Nelson 0 0 * * 0
57 Fleisher 0 * * * 0
58 Flavelle 0 * * * 0
59 McClelland 0 * * * 0
60 Beardslee 0 0 * 0 0
61 Hans 0 * * * 0
62 Johnson, G. L. 0 0 * 0 0
63 Baxter 0 0 0
64 Wheelan * * 0
65 Schmidt 0 0 0 0
66 Black * 0 0 0
67 O'Neil * 0 0 0 0
68 Coghlan 0 0 0 0
69 Hopkins * 0 0 0
70 Johnson, T. D. 0 0 * 0 0
71 Pugh 0 0 0 0 0
72 Feeley 0 * 0 0
73 Johnson, P. A. 0 0 * 0 0
74 Greer 0 0 * 0 0
75 Mott 0 0 * 0 0
76 Cullen 0 0 0 0
77 Beban 0 0 0 0
78 Macauley 0 0 0 0 0
79 McManus 0 0 0 0 0

Totals 9 28 22 15 27 10 19 17 3 27
Totals from Table B 32 4 1 38 40 0 0 40 33 2
Grand Total 41 32 23 53 67 10 19 57 36 29

F G H I J K

To To To deny
amend Test Vote amend Party Vote on Vote on
S. J. on Direct Islais Circle Stanford Judicial
R. No. Primary. Creek Bill Bill. Column
3. Harbor Second Bill.
Bill. Reading.

Assemblymen Aye No Aye No Aye No Aye No Aye No Aye No

41 Hammon 0 0 0 *
42 Hawk * 0 0 0 0
43 Stanton 0 0 * 0 0
44 Transue 0 0 * 0 * 0
45 Hanlon 0 0 0 0 * 0
46 Wagner 0 0 * 0 * 0
47 Webber *
48 Butler 0 0 * 0
49 Collum 0 0 * * 0 *
50 Dean 0 * 0 0
51 Perine 0 0 0 0 *
52 Pulcifer 0 0 0 *
53 Collier 0 0 0 0 *
54 Moore 0 * * 0 0 *
55 Leeds 0 0 * 0 0 0
56 Nelson 0 0 * * 0 0
57 Fleisher 0 0 0
58 Flavelle 0 0 0 0
59 McClelland 0 0 0 0 0
60 Beardslee 0 * 0 0 * 0
61 Hans 0 0 0 0 0 0
62 Johnson, G. L. 0 0 0 * * 0
63 Baxter 0 0 * *
64 Wheelan 0 0 0 0
65 Schmidt 0 * * (a) 0
66 Black 0 0 * 0 0
67 O'Neil 0 0 0 *
68 Coghlan 0 0 * * 0 0
69 Hopkins 0
70 Johnson, T. D. 0 0 0
71 Pugh 0 0 * 0
72 Feeley 0 0 0 0 0 0
73 Johnson, P. A. 0 0 0 0 0
74 Greer 0 0 0 0 0 0
75 Mott 0 0 0 0 0 0
76 Cullen 0 0 0 0 0
77 Beban 0 0 0 0 0 0
78 Macauley 0 0 0 0 0
79 McManus 0 0 0 0 0

Totals 34 2 31 3 24 11 26 7 9 15 4 22

Totals from Table B 9 28 7 33 6 34 10 28 36 2 31 7

Grand Total 43 30 38 36 30 45 36 35 45 17 35 29

Totals

	For Reform	Against Reform	Absent

Assemblymen

42 Hawk 5 5 1
43 Stanton 5 5 1
44 Transue 5 5 1
45 Hanlon 5 6 0
46 Wagner 5 6 0
47 Webber 4 2 5
48 Butler 4 4 3
49 Collum 4 5 2
50 Dean 4 5 2
51 Perine 4 5 2
52 Pulcifer 4 5 2
53 Collier 4 6 1
54 Moore 4 6 1
55 Leeds 4 7 0
56 Nelson 4 7 0
57 Fleisher 3 5 3
58 Flavelle 3 6 2
59 McClelland 3 7 1
60 Beardslee 3 8 0
61 Hans 3 8 0
62 Johnson, G. L. 3 8 0
63 Baxter 2 5 4
64 Wheelan 2 5 4
65 Schmidt 2 6 3
66 Black 2 7 2
67 O'Neil 2 7 2
68 Coghlan 2 8 1
69 Hopkins 1 4 6
70 Johnson, T. D. 1 7 3
71 Pugh 1 8 2
72 Feeley 1 9 1

73 Johnson, P. A. 1 9 1
74 Greer 1 10 0
75 Mott 1 10 0
76 Cullen 0 9 2
77 Beban 0 10 1
78 Macauley 0 10 1
79 McManus 0 10 1

Totals 107 258 64
Totals from Table B 373 48 19
Grand Total 480 306 83

Table D-Record of Assemblymen on Anti-Racetrack Gambling Bill
(Walker-Otis Bill)

F shows vote For the Bill

A shows vote Against the Bill

A B C D

	Assembly Vote on Walker-Otis Bill.	Motion to Return Bill to Mott's Committee.	Reconsider Defeat of Motion to Amend Bill.	Butler's Motion to Put Bill on its Passage.
Assemblymen	Aye No	Aye No	Aye No	Aye No
Barndollar	F	F	F	A
Baxter	A	A	A	A
Beardslee	A	A	A	A
Beatty	F	F	F	
Beban	A	A	A	A
Black	A	A	A	A
Bohnett	F	F	F	F
Butler	F	F	A	A
Callan	F	F	F	F
Cattell	F	F	F	F
Coghlan	A	A	A	A
Cogswell	F	F	F	
Collier	F	F	F	F
Collum	A	A	A	A
Costar	F	F	F	F
Cronin	F	F	F	F
Cullen	A	A	A	

Dean F F F F
Drew F F F F
Feeley A A A
Flavelle F F F F
Fleisher F F F F
Flint F F F F
Gerdes F F F F
Gibbons F A F
Gillis F F F F
Greer A A A A
Griffiths F F F F
Hammon F F F F
Hanlon F F F F
Hans F F F F
Hawk F A F F
Hayes F F F F
Hewitt F F F F
Hinkle F F F F
Holmquist F F F F
Hopkins A A A A
Irwin F A A A
Johnson, G. L. A A A A
Johnson, P. A. A A A A
Johnson, P. H. F
Johnston, T. D. A A A A
Juilliard F A A A
Kehoe F F F F
Leeds F F F F
Lightner F F F A
Macauley A A A A
Maher F F F A
McClellan F A F A
McManus A A A A
Melrose F F F F
Mendenhall F F F F
Moore A A F A
Mott A A F A
Nelson A A A A
Odom A A F A
Otis F F F F
O'Neil A A A A
Perine F F F A
Polsley F F F F

Preston F F F F
Pugh A A A A
Pulcifer F F F F
Rech F F F F
Rutherford F F F F
Sackett F F
Schmitt A A A A
Silver F F F F
Stanton F F F F
Stuckenbruck F F F F
Telfer F F F F
Transue F F F F
Wagner A A F F
Webber A A A A
Wheelan A A A
Whitney F F F F
Wilson F F F F
Wyatt
Wyllie F F F F
Young F F F F

Totals 23 53 30 48 23 52 44 32

E F Totals

Assembly Vote Vote Vote on For Against
on Walker-Otis on Motion to the the Absent.
Bill. Bill. Reconsider. Bill. Bill.

Assemblymen Aye No Aye No

Barndollar F F 5 1
Baxter A 5 1
Beardslee F A 1 5
Beatty F F 5 1
Beban A A 6
Black A A 6
Bohnett F F 6
Butler F F 4 2
Callan F F 6
Cattell F F 6
Coghlan A A 6
Cogswell F F 5 1
Collier F F 6

Collum A 5 1
Costar F F 6
Cronin F F 6
Cullen A A 5 1
Dean F F 6
Drew F F 6
Feeley F A 1 4 1
Flavelle F F 6
Fleisher F F 6
Flint F F 6
Gerdes F F 6
Gibbons F F 4 1 1
Gillis F F 6
Greer F A 1 5
Griffiths F F 6
Hammon F F 6
Hanlon F F 6
Hans F F 6
Hawk F F 5 1
Hayes F F 6
Hewitt F F 6
Hinkle F F 6
Holmquist F F 6
Hopkins A A 6
Irwin F F 3 3
Johnson, G. L. F A 1 5
Johnson, P. A. F A 1 5
Johnson, P. H. F F 3 3
Johnston, T. D. F A 1 5
Juilliard F F 3 3
Kehoe F F 6
Leeds F F 6
Lightner F F 5 1
Macauley A A 6
Maher F F 5 1
McClellan F F 4 2
McManus A A 6
Melrose F F 6
Mendenhall F F 6
Moore F 2 3 1
Mott F A 2 4
Nelson F F 2 4
Odom F F 3 3

Otis F F 6
O'Neil A A 6
Perine F F 5 1
Polsley F F 6
Preston F F 6
Pugh A A 6
Pulcifer F F 6
Rech F F 6
Rutherford F F 6
Sackett F F 4 2
Schmitt A 5 1
Silver F F 6
Stanton F F 6
Stuckenbruck F F 6
Telfer F F 6
Transue F F 6
Wagner F A 3 3
Webber F F 2 4
Wheelan F 1 3 2
Whitney F F 6
Wilson F F 6
Wyatt
Wyllie F F 6
Young F F 6

Totals 67 10 19 57 321 137 16

Table E-Records of the San Francisco Senate Delegation on Sixteen Test Votes

* indicates vote on side of Progress and Reform

0 indicates vote against Progress and Reform

A B C D E F G H

To Test To refer To do Second
admit vote Walker- Local away Vote First Second
Bell on Otis Option Bill with party Vote Vote
to Direct Bill. to Party Circle Stanford Stanford
Caucus. Primary Committee. Circle. Bill. Bill. Bill.

Senator Aye No Aye No Aye No Aye No Aye No Aye No Aye No Aye

No

Anthony * * * 0 0 * *
Burnett 0 * * 0 0 0 *
Finn 0 0 0 0 0 0 0 0
Hare 0 0 0 * * 0 0
Hartman 0 0 0 0 0 0 0 0
Kennedy 0 * 0 * * 0 0
Reily * 0 0 0 0 0
Welch * * * 0 0 0
Wolfe 0 0 0 0 * * 0 *

Totals 3 4 6 3 4 5 9 0 3 6 4 5 5 0 3 4						
I	J	K	L	M	N	O

Test Vote Local Assembly Change To
Railroad Initiative Option Railroad Amendment of reconsider
Regulation. Amendment. Bill. Amendment. to Direct Venue Change
of
Primary. Bill.
Venue Bill.

Senator Aye No Aye No Aye No Aye No Aye No Aye No Aye No

Anthony 0 * 0 0 * 0 0
Burnett 0 0 * 0
Finn 0 0 0 0 0 0
Hare 0 * 0 0 0 0
Hartman 0 0 0 0 0 0 0
Kennedy 0 * 0 0 0 *
Reily 0 * 0 0 0 0
Welch 0 * 0 0 0 0 0
Wolfe 0 0 0 0 0 0 0

Totals 0 9 5 2 0 9 1 7 8 1 7 1 0 7

P Totals

	To investigate Freight Rates.	For Reform	Against Reform

Senator	Aye	No

Anthony	0 7 8
Burnett * 5 7
Finn 0 0 15
Hare 3 10
Hartman 0 0 16
Kennedy 0 5 9
Reily 0 2 12
Welch 0 4 9
Wolfe 0 3 13

Totals 1 6 29 99

Table F-Records of San Francisco Assembly Delegation on Eleven Test Votes

* indicates vote on side of Progress and Reform

0 indicates vote against Progress and Reform

(a) - Changed Vote from no to aye to give notice to reconsider.
Was against the bill.

A B C D E F

	Drew's Motion to Reject Committee's Rules.	To Return Walker-Otis Bill to Rules.	To Vote on Walker-Otis Committee Bill.	To recall Walker-Otis Bill.	To reconsider S. J. R. No. 3 from Committee.	To amend S. J. R. No. 3.

Assemblymen	Aye	No	Aye	No	Aye	No	Aye	No	Aye	No	Aye	No

Beatty	*	*	*	0
Beban	0 0 0 0 0

Black * 0 0 0
Callan * * * * * *
Coghlan 0 0 0 0 0
Collum * 0 0 0
Cullen 0 0 0 0 0
Gerdes 0 * * * *
Hopkins * 0 0 0 0
Lightner * * * * 0
Macauley 0 0 0 0 0 0
McManus 0 0 0 0 0 0
Nelson 0 0 * * 0 0
O'Neil * 0 0 0 0 0
Pugh 0 0 0 0 0 0
Perine 0 * * * 0
Schmitt 0 0 0 0
Wheelan * * 0 0

Totals 7 10 12 5 7 10 10 6 2 7 14 1

G H I J K Totals

To To deny
Test Vote amend Party Vote on Vote on
on Direct Islais Circle Stanford Judicial For Against Absent
Primary. Creek Bill Bill. Column Reform Reform
Harbor Second Bill.
Bill. Reading.

Assemblymen Aye No Aye No Aye No Aye No Aye No

Beatty 0 * * 0 * 6 3 2
Beban 0 0 0 0 0 0 10 1
Black 0 0 * 0 0 2 7 2
Callan * * * * * 11 0 0
Coghlan 0 * * 0 0 2 8 1
Collum 0 * * 0 * 4 5 2
Cullen 0 0 0 0 0 9 2
Gerdes * * * * * 9 1 1
Hopkins 1 4 6
Lightner 0 0 * * * 7 3 1

Macauley 0 0 0 0 0 10 1
McManus 0 0 0 0 0 10 1
Nelson 0 * * 0 0 4 7 0
O'Neil 0 0 * 2 7 2
Pugh 0 * 0 1 8 2
Perine 0 0 0 * 4 5 2
Schmitt 0 * a* 0 2 6 3
Wheelan 0 0 0 2 5 4

Totals 15 2 9 8 5 9 5 9 5 7 57 108 33

Table G-Records of Out-Going Senators on Sixteen Test Votes

Must Be Re-Elected to Sit in Next Senate

* indicates vote on side of Progress and Reform

0 indicates vote against Progress and Reform

A B C D E F G

	A	B	C	D	E	F	G
	To admit Bell on to Direct Caucus.	Test vote Otis Primary.	To refer Walker- Local Option Bill. to Party Committee.	To do away with party Circle.	Second Vote First Bill with Party Vote Stanford Circle. Bill.		First Vote Stanford Bill.

Senator	Aye	No	Aye	No	Aye	No	Aye	No	Aye	No	Aye	No	Aye	No

Anthony * * * 0 0 *
Bates 0 0 * * 0 0 *
Bell * * * * * *
Black * * * * 0 * *
Boynton * * * 0 * *
Caminetti * * 0 * * 0
Cartwright * * * * *
Curtin * * * 0 *
Hartman 0 0 0 0 0 0 0
Kennedy 0 * 0 * * 0
Leavitt 0 0 0 * * * *
McCartney 0 0 * 0 *
Miller * * * * *

Price 0 * * 0 0 0 *
Reily * 0 0 0 0 0
Sanford * * 0 * * *
Savage * 0 * 0 0 0 *
Weed 0 0 0 * 0 0
Willis 0 0 * * * * 0
Wright 0 * * * * * *

Totals 5 8 9 11 16 4 10 8 10 9 12 6 4 12

H I J K L M

Second Test Vote Local Assembly
Vote Railroad Initiative Option Railroad Amendment
Stanford Regulation. Amendment. Bill. Amendment. to Direct
Bill. Primary.

Senator Aye No Aye No Aye No Aye No Aye No Aye No

Anthony * 0 * 0 0 *
Bates * 0 0 0
Bell * * * * * *
Black * * * * *
Boynton * * * * *
Caminetti * * * 0 * *
Cartwright * * * * *
Curtin * * 0 0 * *
Hartman 0 0 0 0 0 0
Kennedy 0 0 * 0 0 0
Leavitt 0 0 0 0 0 0
McCartney * 0 * 0 * 0
Miller * * 0 * * *
Price * 0 0 0 0 0
Reily 0 * 0 0 0
Sanford * * * 0 * *
Savage * 0 0 0 0
Weed 0 0 0 0 0
Willis * 0 0 0 0 0
Wright * 0 0 * * 0

Totals 14 3 8 12 9 10 6 12 9 9 11 9

O P Totals

	To	To		
	reconsider	investigate	For	Against
	Change of	Freight	Reform	Reform
	Venue	Bill.	Rates.	

Senator	Aye	No	Aye	No
Anthony	0	0	7	8
Bates	0	0	4	10
Bell	*	*	15	0
Black	1	1	1	
Boynton	*	*	13	1
Caminetti	*	*	12	3
Cartwright	*	12	0	
Curtin	*	10	3	
Hartman	0	0	0	16
Kennedy	0	5	9	
Leavitt	0	0	4	12
McCartney	0	5	8	
Miller	*	0	11	2
Price	0	4	11	
Reily	0	0	2	12
Sanford	*	*	13	2
Savage	0	0	4	11
Weed	0	0	1	13
Willis	0	0	5	11
Wright	0	0	9	7

Totals 7 11 4 10 147 140

Table H-Records of Holdover Senators on Sixteen Test Votes

* indicates vote on side of Progress and Reform

0 indicates vote against Progress and Reform

A B C D E F G

	To	Test	To refer	To do	Second
	admit	vote	Walker-	Local	away Vote First

Bell on Otis Option Bill with party Vote
to Direct Bill. to Party Circle Stanford
Caucus. Primary Committee. Circle. Bill. Bill.

Senator Aye No Aye No Aye No Aye No Aye No Aye No Aye No

Bills 0 0 * * 0 0 *
Birdsall * * * 0 0 *
Burnett 0 * * 0 0 0
Campbell * * * * *
Cutten * * * * 0 0 *
Estudillo 0 * * * * * *
Finn 0 0 0 0 0 0 0
Hare 0 0 0 * * 0
Holohan * * 0 * *
Hurd 0 * * 0 0 *
Lewis 0 * * 0 0 0
Martinelli 0 * * 0 0 0 0
Roseberry * * * * 0 * *
Rush * * * 0 * *
Stetson * * * * *
Strobridge * * * 0 0 0 *
Thompson * * * * 0 * *
Walker * * * * * * *
Welch * * * 0 0 0
Wolfe 0 0 0 0 * * 0

Totals 9 8 4 16 17 3 10 7 6 13 11 9 4 10

H I J K L M

Second Test Vote Local Assembly
Vote Railroad Initiative Option Railroad Amendment
Stanford Regulation. Amendment. Bill. Amendment. to Direct
Bill. Primary.

Senator Aye No Aye No Aye No Aye No Aye No Aye No

Bills * 0 0 0 0 0
Birdsall * * 0 * *
Burnett * 0 0 * 0
Campbell * * * * * *
Cutten * * * * * *
Estudillo * 0 * * 0 *
Finn 0 0 0 0 0
Hare 0 0 * 0 0
Holohan * * 0 * *
Hurd 0 0 0 0 0
Lewis * * 0 0 0 0
Martinelli * 0 0 0 0
Roseberry * * * * *
Rush * * 0 * *
Stetson * * *
Strobridge * * 0 * *
Thompson * * * * * *
Walker * 0 * * * *
Welch 0 * 0 0 0
Wolfe * 0 0 0 0 0

Totals 2 8 10 11 5 6 13 10 7 9 10 9

N O P Totals

	Change To of Venue Bill.	To reconsider Change of Venue	To investigate Freight Bill.	For Reform Rates.	Against Reform

---

Senator	Aye	No	Aye	No	Aye	No

Bills 0 0 0 4 12
Birdsall * * * 11 3
Burnett * 5 7
Campbell * * 13 0
Cutten * * * 14 2
Estudillo 0 * * 12 4
Finn 0 0 0 15
Hare 0 0 0 3 11
Holohan * * * 11 2
Hurd 0 0 0 3 11
Lewis 0 * 0 5 10

Martinelli 0 0 0 3 12
Roseberry * * * 14 1
Rush * 10 2
Stetson * * 10 0
Strobridge * * 10 4
Thompson * * * 15 1
Walker * * 14 1
Welch 0 0 0 4 9
Wolfe 0 0 0 3 13

Totals 9 9 11 7 8 6 164 119

Table I-Records of Assemblymen on Four Test Votes on Anti-Japanese Bills

F shows vote For the Bill

A shows vote Against the Bill

* Leeds changed his vote from "no" to "aye" to give notice of reconsideration.

A B C D

Assembly Vote on Assembly Assembly First Vote Second Vote Walker-Otis Bill. Bill No. Bill No. Assembly Bill Assembly Bill 78. 32. No. 14. No. 14.

Assemblymen Aye No Aye No Aye No Aye No

Barndollar A A A A
Baxter F F F F
Beardslee A A A A
Beatty F F F F
Beban A F F A
Black F F F F
Bohnett A A F A
Butler A A F F
Callan F F F F
Cattell A A A A
Coghlan A A
Cogswell A A A A
Collier A A A A

Collum F F F F
Costar A A A A
Cronin F F F F
Cullen F F F F
Dean A A A A
Drew F F
Feeley A A A A
Flavelle A
Fleisher A A A A
Flint A A A A
Gerdes F
Gibbons F F F F
Gillis F F F F
Greer A A A A
Griffiths A A A A
Hammon A A A A
Hanlon A A A A
Hans A A A A
Hawk A A A A
Hayes A F F F
Hewitt A A A A
Hinkle A A F A
Holmquist A A F A
Hopkins F F F F
Irwin F A F F
Johnson, G. L. F F F F
Johnson, P. A. A F A A
Johnson, P. H. F F F F
Johnston, T. D. A F F F
Juilliard F F F F
Kehoe A F F F
Leeds A A F* A
Lightner A F F F
Macauley F F F F
Maher F F F F
McClellan A A A A
McManus A F F F
Melrose A A A A
Mendenhall F F F F
Moore A A A A
Mott A F F F
Nelson F F F F
Odom F F F

Otis A F F F
O'Neil F F F F
Perine A F F A
Polsley F F F F
Preston F A F A
Pugh F F F F
Pulcifer A A A A
Rech A A A A
Rutherford A A
Sackett A A A A
Schmitt A F F A
Silver A F F A
Stanton A A A A
Stuckenbruck F F F F
Telfer F F F F
Transue A A A A
Wagner A A A A
Webber F F F
Wheelan F F F F
Whitney A F F F
Wilson F F F F
Wyatt
Wyllie A A F A
Young A A A A

Totals 28 48 39 35 46 28 37 41

Outline of and Arguements in Favor of the Postal Direct Primary.

By Senator L. H. Roseberry, Who Introduced the Postal Direct Primary Bill at the Session of 1909.

In order to understand the full purpose and effect of the proposed Postal Direct Primary law, it is necessary to ascertain the purpose of any system of nominations by a Direct Primary.

The sole complaint against the present system of nominations by conventions is based upon the objection that party nominations are made by a few interested parties, and that the popular choice is absolutely ignored. To remedy this evil the system of direct nominations by the voters has been suggested at primary elections. It therefore follows that that system, or primary, which will get out the largest number of votes or the greatest expression of the people on the choice of candidates is, of necessity, the best primary law. If it is true that all present direct primaries, which provide for voting at a certain time and place in person, in the form that general elections are now conducted, only draw out a little over one-half of the registered vote of all parties, it then follows beyond question, that all present direct primary laws are only half successful. Upon an examination of statistics gathered from the various States in which direct primary laws are now in operation, it is seen that only 55% to 60% of the registered vote within those States has ever been cast at any single primary election. For instance, at the primary election held in the State of Oregon in the fall of 1908, 55% of the registered Republican vote was cast, and less than 25% of the Democratic vote. In the State of Washington about 57% of the registered vote was cast in 1908, the only vote yet taken under the new Direct Primary law. In the State of Wisconsin, while 60% of the total registered vote was cast in 1906, only a little over 40% was cast at the primary election held In the year 1908. Other statistics could be offered from all the other States, having the direct primary system of nominations, from which it would appear that practically a little over 55% or even less of the registered vote has been secured at any direct primary election. Therefore, based upon these figures, it becomes patent that the present form of direct nominations, to wit: voting at a certain time and place in person only, under the same rules and regulations as at general elections, is only half successful.

It was for the purpose of bringing out at least a part of this great unvoted 45% of qualified electors, to take a part in naming the candidates who should go before the people at the general elections, that the Postal Direct Primary law was conceived.

While there is no present example of the working of a system of direct nominations through a ballot cast through the mails for public officials, there are a number of instances in which ballots are being taken by mail with wonderful success and completeness. Formerly, labor unions, fraternal societies, chambers of commerce, Granger organizations, alumni associations, and other civic, religious and benevolent associations, balloted on propositions submitted to their membership in the form that primary and general elections are now held in public elections. The vote secured from their memberships was so meager and unsatisfactory that the system of voting by mail was inaugurated, and with such splendid results, that now it is being used exclusively by a majority of the above organizations, as a method of voting upon propositions and officers coming before them for election. Where only 10% to 15% of the votes were cast under the old plan of voting in person at a particular time and place, 75%, and even 90% of the votes are now cast through the mails, and it is significant to note that the plan of voting by mail has been found by the organizations using it to be free from any objections. This fact, together with the unanimous vote cast, led to the idea of casting votes by mail at direct primaries for the nomination of public officers by political parties. The system that has been proposed is extremely simple, and it appears highly reasonable and practicable. A short outline of the provisions of the bill will assist in an understanding of the arguments offered in its favor and those advanced to refute the objections urged against this Postal Direct Primary Act.

In the first place, each elector, at the time of registering, declares his party allegiance, and this is entered upon his original affidavit of registration. At the same time, he is given a party voting number, which is written or printed upon his affidavit of registration. The Secretary of State, every four years, declares the color of ballots to be used by each party separately. For instance, all Republican ballots throughout the State, at every election must be printed upon pink colored paper and none other; the Democratic ballot upon white colored paper and none other, and so on among the other political parties.

In order for a candidate's name to be proposed to go on to the primary ballot, it must be proposed by a prescribed number of qualified electors, within the district in which that candidate is to be elected, which names must be subscribed to a verified petition. This entitles the candidate's name to be printed upon the primary ballot. Within ten days before the primary, or return day, the clerk of the board or body which is delegated by law to prepare for election matters must print, prepare and send out, primary election ballots for each separate political party through the United States mails in the following manner: To each elector within the jurisdiction is mailed a plain unmarked envelope, addressed to the business or home address of each separate elector, containing a self-addressed and stamped return envelope, returnable to the Board of Election of that precinct, together with one party primary election ballot, for the use of that elector. If the elector happens to be a Republican the color of his ballot will be pink, and only the names of the Republican candidates will be printed thereon. On the outside end of the ballot is printed the elector's party voting number, which voting number is separate and distinct from every other voting number in that precinct. On the outside end of the return envelope is a line left for the original signature of the elector to whom the ballot is mailed, whereon he must either subscribe his signature in ink, or if he be an incapable voter, and is assisted, must have his own name subscribed thereon, together with the names of two freeholders in that precinct, who assisted him in voting. Upon receipt of the envelope containing his ballot, the voter marks a cross (X) at the names of the candidates for whom he votes, and then folds his ballot so that all the names thereon are turned inside and out of sight, and his party voting number appears on the outside end of the envelope. (In the same manner that he now folds his ballot at a general election.) He then encloses this ballot in the stamped return envelope, seals the same, signs his name on the end of the envelope, and deposits it in a postoffice box. It then goes to the postoffice directed by law, addressed to the Primary or Return Board, who alone are authorized by law to receive these envelopes from the postmaster, and then only on the day and hour designated by law and in public. Upon return day, the Board receives all of these primary election envelopes from the postoffice, takes them to a public place, and after counting the number received, and comparing with the number originally sent out, compares each signature on each envelope with the same signature subscribed on the original affidavit of registration, and if it be genuine, opening the envelope, removing the ballot therefrom, without opening the same, observing that the color of the ballot corresponds to the party color to which that elector belongs, then tearing off the voting number, which appears on the end of the ballot, after comparing it with the voting number written on that elector's affidavit of registration, and then finally depositing the ballot into a general ballot box, into which all the ballots of each political party are deposited. It will thus appear that every ballot has been checked in three ways to identify it as being the original ballot sent to that elector, and as the one cast personally by him: First, it was contained in an envelope bearing his original signature; it bore his own party voting number, which was separate and distinct from every other party voting number in that precinct, and was printed under the authority of law only upon one ballot, namely, the ballot he receives; and finally it was upon the color of paper which only the political party with which that elector was affiliated was allowed by law to use. Every other political party's ballots were printed upon different colored paper.

This makes it practically impossible for any ballot to be cast or counted other than the one lawfully mailed and regularly received and voted and mailed in person by the elector to whom it was sent.

Even the most prejudiced opponents of the Postal Direct Primary bill admit that there are no practical reasons why it would not operate very successfully in the rural districts and the smaller cities and towns. Such an admission is a very far-reaching argument for the bill as a general working measure for direct nominations. It is an open confession that the plan is workable and meritorious. The only objection that has been urged with any semblance of force is the argument that the ballot could be easily corrupted in large cities, where the opportunities for fraud are great, and where the intelligence and honesty of certain classes of voters is low. It is suggested with considerable merit that among the foreign and ignorant classes in the great centers of population, corruption of suffrage is a matter easily accomplished; that there would be many of such voters willing to lend themselves to any scheme to deliver their primary ballots to certain persons to be voted as they desired under the names of the Individual electors.

At first blush, this argument appears to have some force, but upon close reading of the provisions of the bill, and its necessary effect upon the Practical operation of a primary campaign, it must be admitted that this sole objection is largely argumentative. In the first place, as pointed out above, each ballot must be cast by the person to whom it was sent, for it is contained in an envelope bearing the elector's own known signature. Therefore none other can vote the ballot. In the second place, the bill provides for extreme penal penalties for any one tampering with ballots, assisting a voter in the marking of a ballot (other than incapable voters), standing about and watching an elector mark his ballot, or in any wise influencing, or observing a voter in the marking of his ballot at the time it is voted, sealed in the envelope and dropped in the postoffice. All the penalties are for imprisonment and not for fines. This, then, will force any plan to secure ballots or corrupt the same to be done secretly and illegally. It must appear that there can be no extensive system of vote corruption carried on without discovery. It must further appear that there would be extremely few who would care to general or direct any extensive plan of corrupting or influencing primary ballots. It would be too risky a proceeding. If then votes were corrupted, it would have to be done very secretly and amongst only a trusted few. Therefore the percentage influenced in this manner could not be large.

Another bar to any tampering with ballots would be the check which each political party and each candidate would have upon the other. It would be a matter of political capital for one party to detect leaders or organizations within another party tampering with or corrupting the vote at its primary election. The various candidates for the different offices within the same party would watch one another with extreme vigilance to detect any attempt to influence or corrupt the ballots against them.

Lastly, it is suggested that because of the fact that these primary election ballots would be sent at the same time to thousands of different places throughout the precinct and city, and would be opened in offices and in homes on the same day, and in all probability fully 75% of them would be voted and remailed on the same day received; that it would be practically impossible to devise any system that would reach out and get these countless ballots in a thousand different places within a space of a few hours or a day. They would be too scattered to be gotten hold of or traced with any degree of success.

It must appear from a broad-minded consideration of the practical workings of this Postal Direct Primary law that there is no valid reason why it would not work with splendid success even in the congested and illiterate districts of our larger cities. But even admitting for the sake of argument that a certain percentage of the ignorant and vicious vote could be corrupted by the bosses, it certainly could not be large. It could not possibly exceed ten per cent of the registered vote. In light of the fact that this system would bring out at least twenty-five per cent more votes than any other primary law has ever succeeded in bringing out, it is seen at a glance that the corrupted vote would be far outweighed and overbalanced by the much larger percentage of decent vote that would be secured for the first time by means of this postal system of voting. The argument, then, is unanswerable in favor of this Postal Direct Primary law.

And it would for the first time give the intelligent and honest elements in all political parties the direct control of the power of nomination for public offices. Moreover, the mere fact that it would cause a larger number of people to vote would be of inestimable value, for it would tend to rouse and awaken public interest in civic affairs and by thus doing would educate and train the minds of the better classes in election affairs, and could not help but raise the honesty and power of popular suffrage. In other words, it would accomplish in the fullest degree, the results sought to be obtained by every direct primary law, namely, a popular choice of candidates for public office, with the power of selection for once actually in the hands of the honest electors.

In conclusion, it might be well to mention that this system of voting by mail would protect the suffrage of many of our best citizens, who, under present laws, are practically disfranchised. Such men are travelers, the sick, sailors, trainmen, and other men who, by reason of their occupation or misfortune, are forced to be absent from the place of their voting precincts on election day, but who could and would vote if an opportunity was extended to them to vote by mail. This would constitute no small class of voters.

Dr. Montgomery's Report.

55 Dr. Montgomery's report to the Senate was as follows:

Palo Alto, Cal., March 22, 1909.

Lieutenant-Governor Warren R. Porter,

President State Senate, Sacramento, Cal.

On the afternoon of March 21, 1909, about 4:30 p. m., J. L. Martin, Sergeant-at-Arms of the Senate of the State of California, called on me and informed me that I had been designated by the President of the Senate to proceed with him to Palo Alto, and to consult with the physicians of

Senator Marshall Black, to ascertain if Senator Black's health was such as to permit him to go to Sacramento. I arrived at the office of Dr. Howard Black, Senator Black's physician, at about 9:30 p. m., March 21, 1909, and there met Dr. Howard Black, Dr. H. B. Reynolds, Dr. J. C. Spencer and Dr. R. L. Wilbur. These physicians said they had held a consultation and had made an examination of Senator Marshall Black that afternoon; according to their statement, Senator Marshall Black had arrived in Palo Alto about five days previously suffering from inflammation of the eyes, commonly called "pink eye," and that this inflammation of the eyes had almost entirely cleared up, but that the inflammation traveled down the throat and bronchial tubes. According to their statement to me on the evening of March 21, 1909, Senator Marshall Black was suffering from broncho-pneumonia, and symptoms of inflammation in the lower lobe of the left lung, the temperature that afternoon was ninety-nine and the pulse ninety. The heart was in good condition. The cough was severe and the expectoration abundant. I stated to these physicians that I was delegated by the Senate of the State of California to make a thorough and complete examination of Senator Black for the purpose of ascertaining at what time it would be safe for Senator Black to proceed to Sacramento. I was informed by Dr. Howard Black that Senator Marshall Black would not permit me to see him. I then asked Senator Black's physicians, individually and collectively, if in their opinion, in Senator Black's present physical condition any serious inconvenience or injury would accrue to Senator Black from a personal examination by me. They all stated that, on their part, they were perfectly willing that such examination should be held by the Senate physician, and that such an examination in their opinion could do no injury. I asked if the patient was in sound and disposing mind. I was answered he was. At about 10 a. m., March 22, 1909, I again called on Dr. Howard Black, renewing my request of the previous evening to see Senator Marshall Black. Senator Black, through the physician, still declined to receive me. I then asked Dr. Howard Black when, in his opinion, Senator Marshall Black would be in condition to proceed to Sacramento. He said that at the consultation of the previous day it was concluded that it would be a week before Senator Black would be in such a condition as to enable him with safety to undertake the Journey. As this consultation was held on March 21st, it would, in their opinion, be March 28th before Senator Black would be in a condition to proceed to Sacramento. I asked if, in his opinion, Senator Black was convalescing. He said that in his opinion he was. He said that Senator Black's temperature this morning was 100, his pulse 90, his cough still severe, and there still was evidence of inflammation in the lower lobe of the left lung. Personally, from what I know of Senator Black's physicians, I believe these facts to be true. Taking it for granted that these facts are true, I do not find that, from them alone, I can conclude that

Senator Black is unable to proceed to Sacramento. In order to concur in this opinion of Senator Black's physicians I would have to see the patient.

Douglass W. Montgomery, M. D.

Delegated by Lieutenant-Governor Warren R. Porter to examine into the state of health of Senator Marshall Black.

The Anti-Japanese Bill's Resolution.

94 The resolution was in full as follows:

Whereas, Assembly Bill, No. 14, introduced by Mr. Johnson of Sacramento, and reading as follows:

An Act

To Amend Section 1662 of the Political Code

The people of the State of California, represented in Senate and Assembly, do enact as follows:

Section 1. Section 1662 of the Political Code is hereby amended so as to read as follows:

1662. Every school, unless otherwise provided by law, must be open for the admission of all children between six and twenty-one years of age residing in the district and the board of school trustees, or city board of education, have power to admit adults and children not residing in the district, whenever good reasons exist therefor. Trustees shall have the power to exclude children of filthy or vicious habits, or children suffering from contagious or infectious diseases, and also to establish separate schools for Indian children and for the children of Mongolian, or Japanese, or Chinese descent. When such separate schools are established, Indian, Chinese, Japanese or Mongolian children must not be admitted into any other school; provided, that in cities and towns in which the kindergarten has been adopted or may hereafter be adopted as part of the public primary schools, children may be admitted to such kindergarten classes at the age of four years; and provided further, that in cities or school districts in which separate classes have been or may hereafter be established, for the instruction of the deaf, children may be admitted to such classes at the age of three years.

Is now pending before this Assembly; and

Whereas, It has been represented by the President of the United States that the passage of this bill will, in some manner undisclosed, disturb the relations now existing between the government of the United States and the government of Japan; and

Whereas, The President of the United States has made known to this Assembly, through the Governor of this State and through the Speaker of this Assembly, his wish that said bill be not passed; and

Whereas, The President of the United States has caused it to be represented to this body that it is his judgment that said bill would conflict with the treaty now existing between the government of the United States and the government of Japan, and because of such conflict the passage of such bill would be beyond the power of the Legislature of this State, and

Whereas, The Governor of this State and the Speaker of this Assembly have conveyed to this body their desire that this bill be not passed; and

Whereas, It is the desire of this body to accede to the wishes of the Chief Executive of this State, and the Speaker of this Assembly; therefore be it

Resolved, That it is fitting and proper that a statement of the position of this Assembly upon this question be made, to the end that a mistaken impression do not result from the failure of the Assembly to pass this bill; be it further

Resolved, That such position is as follows:

1. The school system of the State of California is an institution of the State alone, maintained, supported, conducted and controlled wholly under and in accordance with the powers reserved to the State.

2. That the power to maintain, conduct and control the State school system has not been granted to the Federal Government.

3. That the Legislature of California may properly pass any law relative to the school system of this State that in its judgment may seem best.

4. That by said Assembly Bill No. 14 it is not designed to deprive children of Indian, Mongolian, Chinese, or Japanese descent of equal school privileges and opportunities, but, on the contrary, to these there shall be given, and for these there shall be provided the same privileges and opportunities as are given to and provided for all other children.

5. That Assembly Bill No. 14 contemplates the establishment and maintenance of separate schools for different races, but all schools so established and maintained shall afford equal and the same facilities for instruction.

6. That this Assembly recognize it to be a duty resting upon the State to furnish to children of Indian, Mongolian, Chinese, or Japanese descent the same facilities and opportunities as are furnished to children of other races and affirm that no more can be required and that nothing different is contemplated by said Act. That said Act gives to children of Indian,

Mongolian, Chinese, or Japanese descent who are subjects of other countries the same rights and privileges as are given to native born citizens of California, and no power has the right to demand more. That this Assembly is disposed to accede to the wishes of the Federal Government as conveyed to us by the Governor of this State and the Speaker of this Assembly, but while doing so we reaffirm and reassert that the subject matter of Assembly Bill No. 14 is purely and exclusively a matter of State concern, falling within the reserve powers of the State, and violates no provision of the Federal Constitution.

7. That it is the judgment of this Assembly that said bill does not conflict with the treaty existing between the government of the United States and the government of Japan, and that we recognize the authority to make treaties is by the Federal Constitution, vested in the President and Senate of the United States, we affirm that the right to administer our State school system can not be controlled by treaty made by the President and the Senate of the United States, nor by action of the President alone.

8. And finally, while we recognize that Assembly Bill No. 14 is drawn and could be passed by the Legislature of this State in full conformity with the powers reserved to the State and vouchsafed to it by the Federal Constitution, we are unwilling to do aught which may disturb the relations existing between this government and a friendly power, and for this reason alone, we recommend that Assembly Bill No. 14 be reconsidered and withdrawn.